I0123810

# Songs of the Empty Place

The Memorial Poetry of the Foi of the
Southern Highlands Province of Papua New Guinea

# Songs of the Empty Place

The Memorial Poetry of the Foi of the
Southern Highlands Province of Papua New Guinea

**James F. Weiner and Don Niles**

---
MONOGRAPHS IN
ANTHROPOLOGY SERIES
---

Australian
National
University

PRESS

**ANU PRESS**

Published by ANU Press
The Australian National University
Acton ACT 2601, Australia
Email: anupress@anu.edu.au
This title is also available online at http://press.anu.edu.au

National Library of Australia Cataloguing-in-Publication entry

| | |
|---|---|
| Creator: | Weiner, James F., author. |
| Title: | Songs of the empty place : the memorial poetry of the Foi of the Southern Highlands Province of Papua New Guinea / James Weiner and Don Niles. |
| ISBN: | 9781925022223 (paperback) 9781925022230 (ebook) |
| Subjects: | Foi (Papua New Guinean people)--Music. Ethnomusicology--Papua New Guinea. Folk music--Papua New Guinea. Papua New Guinea--Songs and music. |
| Other Creators/Contributors: | Niles, Don, author. |
| Dewey Number: | 781.629912 |

All rights reserved. No part of this publication may be reproduced, stored in a retrieval system or transmitted in any form or by any means, electronic, mechanical, photocopying or otherwise, without the prior permission of the publisher.

Cover design and layout by ANU Press

This edition © 2015 ANU Press

# Contents

# Acknowledgements

For this book, I undertook the original research that involved recording, transcribing, and translating the songs, as well as writing the introduction. Don Niles has contributed the other sections and edited the entire volume to bring it to its present form.

I would like to thank all of the Foi men and women, past and present, of Hegeso and Barutage villages whose compositions appear in this volume. I also thank Don Niles and the Institute of Papua New Guinea Studies for allowing me to bequeath these poetic songs to the Foi people, who have so graciously allowed me to live with and question them since 1979.

I also appreciate the efforts of Andrew McWilliam in seeing this submission through the ANU editorial committee for Anthropology in Pacific and Asian Studies, and to David Gardiner and Emily Tinker for assistance at ANU Press. Special thanks go to Nick Thieberger and others at the Pacific and Regional Archive for Digital Sources in Endangered Cultures (PARADISEC) for undertaking the digitisation of my audio recordings, thereby enabling examples to accompany this book.

James F. Weiner
Canberra, Australia

# List of Illustrations

## Figures

## Photographs

# Preface

## Singing the Earth in the Mubi Valley

### James F. Weiner

In this book are found the transcripts of every song I recorded and transcribed while I was engaged in anthropological fieldwork in Hegeso village, Mubi River Valley, Southern Highlands Province (Figure 1). I spent a total of 31 months between 1979 and 1995 in Hegeso. A complete account of the practice of composing, singing, and performing these songs in their total ethnographic context can be found in my book *The Empty Place: Poetry, Space and Being among the Foi of Papua New Guinea* (1991) and I will not here go into any detail concerning the musicological or poetic structure of the songs. All of the songs I discussed in that book are included in this complete catalogue.

Most of them are men's ceremonial songs, called *sorohabora*, and nearly all were recorded during two major pig-kill festivals held in 1985 and 1988 in Hegeso village. The women's sago melodies were gathered more continuously during my field work in Hegeso and Barutage villages between 1979 and 1988.

In recording these songs, I found that I had to take a totally different approach to that which I employed when recording and translating Foi myth (see Weiner 1988a). I found that people would recite a myth anywhere at any time, and they did not need an audience to do so. Most of the myth texts I collected were done in my own residence under ostensive interview conditions. That is, I rarely recorded them as they were spontaneously recited in the longhouse or in other communal settings.

With the song poetry, on the other hand, this was not possible. They could only be recorded as they were performed. Even the sago songs, which women sing to themselves while at work processing sago flour, could not be collected in a state divorced from the woman's bodily work of pounding and shredding sago pith, which forms a rhythmic percussive accompaniment to her singing. Likewise, the men's ceremonial *sorohabora* are meant to be sung in groups, even though each man has a distinctive song and voice within the total group performance.

In other words, while they may lack the analytical and theoretical terminology to concretise such a contrast, I think the Foi are well aware of the various degrees to which speech forms, and different specialised varieties of speech, can or cannot be detached from their communal performative context.

The three main forms of ceremonial song poetry are the women's sago songs (*obedobora*), the men's *sorohabora*, and the women's *sorohabora*. Women's sago songs are, in an important sense, work songs; they accompany the rhythmic work of sago shredding as a woman sits in front of a felled sago palm. Men too have their own work songs—I heard one man sing as he was hollowing out a new canoe—but they are not nearly as ubiquitous a part of men's work as they are of women's, because men engage in many fewer repetitive, rhythmic tasks of that sort.

As I described in *The Empty Place*, men turn the prosaic content of women's songs into their own songs, the *sorohabora*, which are performed the night following large-scale inter-community pig-kills, called *dawa* in Foi. While women sing by themselves, men sing in groups of paired men. Each pair of men sings a repertoire of between two and five songs in one evening, depending upon how many song groups there are. The pair of men is called the *soro ira*. About five or six pairs of men combine to form one *soro ga*. A large longhouse can accommodate up to twelve separate *soro ga*.

Besides the round-like, multiple-voiced structure of the men's performance, as opposed to the single voice of women's sago songs, the other major difference is that the men's version ends with what the Foi call the *dawa* or *dawabo*. This term is related to the verb *dawaye gi-*, 'to cut and give'. In this context, it refers to the end of the song, the last verse which 'cuts' the song off from the next one. The *dawabo* is the portion of the song where the names, both public and private, of the deceased are revealed, as well as the names and clan affiliations of his mother and father. Since the pig-kill and exchange ceremony, and the culminating, identifying portion of the *sorohabora* are called by the same term, *dawa*, we can take note of the importance of cutting or severing images in the most intensely public and ceremonial activities of Foi social life. Generalising, we can say that whenever the Foi perceive a flow—of pigs, pearl shells; of spatial movement over the land; the flow of words from the human voice—they see a potential for harnessing, cutting off, and redirecting that flow for human and social purposes. In my various interpretations of the Foi social world, I have made a case for the ubiquity of such imagery across a whole range of Foi social and expressive activities.

Women also told me that they have their own ceremonial version of these songs, though I never saw them performed under actual ceremonial conditions. If the men are copying the women's sago songs to make their own *sorohabora*, then it appears as if women are copying the men's copies of their original songs. Several of these songs, which were performed for me under non-ceremonial circumstances, are also included in this collection.

The subject of nearly all these songs is deceased men. The songs are memorial in intent; they are designed to commemorate the lives of men who are no longer living. Most commonly they do so by naming the places the deceased inhabited during his lifetime.

These places are chiefly those in that part of the Foi territory devoted exclusively to hunting. In Hegeso, this region was called Ayamo, and I am still unsure whether this is a generic term for 'hunting preserve' or a named part of the Hegeso territory where this activity takes place. The term appears to function as both for the Foi of Hegeso.

Men leave their traces in the forest by erecting houses and other shelters and building traps. These constitute the marks of human life in the segment of their territory where no one lives permanently and is largely seasonally visited. The traces in the land of men's presence disappear rapidly at Ayamo under such intermittent use. When a man dies, he is no longer able to renew the vivacity of these traces. They begin to be eroded and covered over by the encroaching forest. An abandoned house being given over to the forest is a poignant image of death in Foi.

In addition to the abandonment that Foi people feel when a close relative dies, they give expression to similar sentiments when their living relatives leave the area for long periods of time, a condition that, by 1995, was becoming more and more common as opportunities for mobility in Papua New Guinea were increasing for everyone. One woman thus sings of her eldest son, serving with the Papua New Guinea Defence Force in Manus Province.

However, as the texts below indicate, the songs are used to convey other messages. Reminiscent of the neighbouring Kewa (see LeRoy 1978), some of the songs convey politically competitive feelings between men of different villages; women also use the songs to complain about their mistreatment at the hands of men.

The most common prosaic property of these songs is to list the names of places in the local territory which the deceased inhabited during his lifetime. The lifespan of the individual man is thus rendered spatially as a sequence of occupied places, and these places constitute a track or trace through that territory. Theoretically, so I was told, a full longhouse of performers would recite the name of every deceased man of the longhouse and by implication the name of every place in the territory (or at least the hunting territory) inhabited by those men. The performance of the *sorohabora* thus can be seen as a poetic or narrative constitution or totalisation of the community of men as a whole, a series of lives rendered as a temporal sequence of inhabited and inhabitable places in the productive imagination. But it effects this retotalisation out of a prior act of discursive disassembly—detotalising the territory into its constituent life tracks, which each constitute the lifespan of a single man.

What is the future of this most powerful expressive form in Foi? My last trip to Hegeso for my own research purposes was in December 1994–January 1995. For the first time since I began visiting the Foi, no *sorohabora* performances occurred during the Christmas holiday season in any of the Mubi Valley villages, even though this is ordinarily a time that is reserved for pig-kills and ceremony. Since that time I have visited Hegeso regularly, if briefly, in the course of conducting social mapping, landowner identification, and other related consultancy work for various companies which have comprised the Kutubu petroleum and LNG Joint Venture Partnership between 1999 and the present.

I do not wish to be too precipitous in forecasting that the practice of Foi song composition and performance is now on the wane. Still, string instruments, and the learning and singing of string band music were more popular among young men in 1995 than they were in 1988, and I suspect that there will be more occasions for more national, 'generically' Papua New Guinean ceremonies and festivities in the Foi region, now that there has been a sharp increase in the number of non-Foi living in the area. What this will mean for the composition, learning, practising, transmission, and performance of traditional Foi memorial songs remains to be seen. I welcome current students of anthropology, linguistics, verbal art, aesthetics, cultural heritage, and ethnomusicology to give an account of the future of the Foi memorial poetic song.

# Introduction

## Foi Songs and the Performance, Publication, and Poetry of Papua New Guinea Sung Traditions

### Don Niles

I am very pleased and honoured to introduce James Weiner's book of Foi song texts. This gives me an opportunity to discuss why I think this is such a valuable publication and to highlight its importance in relation to various topics of concern to Papua New Guinea ethnomusicology.

Weiner's book *The Empty Place: Poetry, Space, and Being among the Foi of Papua New Guinea* (1991) discusses many of the song texts in this present volume and shows how they highlight or relate to certain aspects of Foi society. A number of reviews of the book appeared (e.g. Reesink 1992; Turner 1993), including a review article focusing on Weiner's approach through philosophers such as Heidegger and Merleau-Ponty (Mimica 1993; see also the reply in Weiner 1993).

Foi speakers of Southern Highlands Province today number about 6,000–8,000, living in the vicinity of Lake Kutubu (the Gurubumena) and along the Mubi River to the east (Awamena) and southeast (Foimena) (Figure 1). The Foi of Hegeso, where the majority of Weiner's research was done between 1979 and 1989, call their region *awa hao* 'the empty place', because of the absence of meat there in contrast to other regions (Weiner 1991:22). The traditional residential unit for the Foi is the longhouse community (*a hũa* 'house mother'), a central communal longhouse with smaller individual women's houses on each side. In 1980, Hegeso had a population of 266 (Weiner 1988a:23).

Linguistically, Foi is a member of the East Kutubu group of the Trans-New Guinea family. The only other member of this group is Fiwaga, spoken to the southeast.[1] The Fasu language, to the west, is the sole member of the West Kutubu group and even further to the west is the Bosavi group; to the north and east of the Foi are languages of the Engan group, all belonging to the Trans-New Guinea family (M. P. Lewis et al. 2013). Except for Fiwaga, none of these languages is closely related to Foi.

---

1    The impression shared by Weiner and many Foi speakers, however, is that Foi and Fiwaga should be regarded as one language.

In 1986, exploration near Lake Kutubu suggested oil existed in quantities large enough to warrant the development of an oilfield. Production of the Kutubu Oil Project began in June 1992 as the country's first commercial oilfield development. It is run by Oil Search Limited (Busse et al. 1993:21; Oil Search Limited 2012). Today, the Kutubu area may be featured in articles directed towards potential tourists (e.g. Brooksbank 2012) or in local television segments.

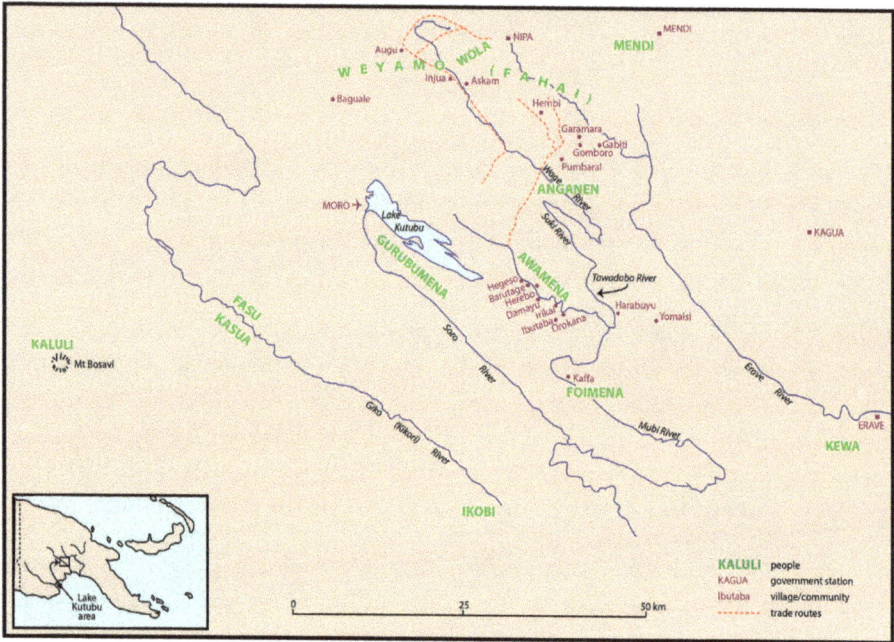

**Figure 1: The Foi and neighbouring peoples.**

Source: Based on Weiner 1988a:20 (map 1), 36 (map 2); 1991:23 (map 1-1), 24 (map 1-2).

# Foi songs in the present volume

The song texts and translations in this volume are divided into three sections, based on the genre concerned and gender of the performers involved. I follow this division here.

## Women's sago songs (*obedobora*)

A man fells a mature sago tree, 15–20 years after the sucker first appears, and then strips off the outer bark. This completes his involvement in the process. His wife and any female helper make a bench from the bark, so that she may sit at a right angle to the palm. With her knees slightly drawn up, she simultaneously hits and scrapes the exposed pith with a piece of obsidian hafted into a wooden mallet. She sings *obedobora* songs as she repeatedly lifts her arms, strikes, and scrapes the pith. Although often sung solo, a second woman may echo the sung lines a few beats later, as is the case with sago songs 6–7 in this collection (Weiner 1991:119–20, 134).[2]

The name *obedobora* '*obe* talk' comes from the vocables commonly attached to the ends of lines of such songs.[3] For example *abu biri-o, obe-u! a'a mae, obe-u* 'sago mallet, oh, *obe-u!* make sago quickly, *obe-u!*' The Foi consider *obedobora* to be their original poetic medium; men's *sorohabora* songs are derived from them (ibid. 1988a:131–32; 1991:120).

In the last few lines of her song, the woman may sing the *dawa*, in which the subject of the song is identified and the song is ended. In men's *sorohabora*, the word '*dawa*' or a variation of it is prominently sung; in sago songs, this subject-revealing section may be absent (Weiner 1991:137–38). For this reason, further information about the *dawa* is given in the discussion of men's songs below.

The turning on and off of Weiner's tape recorder made the singers provide a start and finish to their songs and an uninterrupted performance. While the result enabled easier documentation of the genre, the artificiality is also apparent; the normal soundscape is much more complicated:

> A more accurate aural image of women's singing can be obtained by walking through the swamps and pausing to listen to nearby women without actually approaching their sago camps. There, you hear snatches of a refrain, then perhaps a fragment of a wordless falsetto croon, a silence and the strong breathing of heavy exertion, the sound of a baby crying, sometimes the laughing and chatter of two women talking and gossiping as they work together, and through it all, the stop and start of the dull thud of the sago mallet and the wet *thwack!* of the pith-beating stick. (Weiner 1991:153)

*Obedobora* are work songs, sung by women to urge themselves on to complete the task quickly (Weiner 1991:119–20). But sago songs are also songs of mourning. They are primarily sung to memorialise departed kinsmen:

---

2    Information about such songs is primarily found in Weiner (1988a:131–35; 1991:116–50). By way of comparison, Kaluli women sing *heyalo* and other song genres while scraping sago (Feld 1981:A2; 1985:B7; 2001:disc 2, nos 2–3), and such songs are also performed at other times of work or relaxation. Kaluli have no specific song form for scraping sago.

3    Other frequent vocables as seen in the corpus of *obedobora* collected here are *owe, owa, oye, eye,* and *eya* (Weiner 1988a:302, n. 4). Note that such vocables are omitted when *obedobora* are made into *sorohabora*. Another name for *obedobora* is *dima* (Weiner 1991:104; Rule 1993:89). During brief fieldwork in 2013, Hahudi Farobo (from Daga village) explained to us that a generic name for such songs is *kui dima dobora* 'sago-beating song'. *Obedobora* refers more specifically to songs using *obe* vocables, typical of the area in which Weiner worked (Niles and Gende 2013).

The memory of dead kinsmen is a constant and engaging conceptualization for the Foi; the sound and sights of the forest and the innumerable creeks and rivers where one shared one's life and experience with the departed emerge as poignant evidence of a landscape now rendered empty by the loss of those who quickened it through the significant and 'concernful' acts of living.

Thus, sago melodies [*obedobora*] all begin as mourning songs; though they become thematically more varied, the 'poetics of loss and abandonment' remain a substrate of imagery throughout the entire range of song themes. (Weiner 1991:22)

At a death, mourning songs are sung by women inside the longhouse. The corpse is placed in the centre of the central corridor, surrounded by seated women who huddle over it, caress it, sway towards and away from it, while wailing and shaking rattles. This scene contrasts dramatically with the performance of men's *sorohabora*, described below (Weiner 1991:151–52).

In their sago songs, women sing of their deceased or absent husbands and male kinsmen, immortalising these men as they lived (Weiner 1991:118). Hence, these *obedobora* and the men's *sorohabora* derived from them are considered mourning songs, created to associate the memory of deceased men with the territories they used to frequent. Each song is composed by an individual woman, and she may pass her songs on to her children. These memorial songs trace the geographical and genealogical route of a person's life, the two being considered metaphorically equivalent (ibid.:118, 132, 134–35):

Women, in singing about the deaths and departures of their husbands and male relatives and the mistreatment they bear at the hands of men, contrive to represent the terms of their own feminine alienation from what must often strike them as the fatuity of men's striving. When men appropriate these songs for their own ceremonial purposes, then, they not only give expression to their own feelings of loss and abandonment, they confirm the importance of women's representation of their own male world. (Weiner 1991:146–47)

Figure 2 shows my transcription of lines 10–14 of sago song 2. D is the tonal centre, here the lowest pitch used. Note the closing melodic descent G–E–D, which is often sung on vocables and at a slower pace than the other parts of the text. Indeed, each phrase ends with a descent from C to the tonal centre and lowest pitch (D). Text before this descent is sung between pitches A and C. While the sago pounder provides a pulse at around 41 bpm,[4] it is irregular as

---

4    Comparing some of the other sago songs, the sago mallet provides a pulse of around 41–63 bpm. Note also the transcription of a sago song by Cathy O'Sullivan (Weiner 1991:xiv, 148–50).

the time between hits is variable. Because this pulse is so slow, the transcription uses a tempo derived from the rather evenly spaced quarter notes (crotchets) frequently found in the G–E–D figure.

**Figure 2: Music transcription of sago song 2, lines 10–14 (see ♫ online example 1).**

For comparison, a transcription of lines 10–15 of sago song 6, sung by two women, is given in Figure 3. Again, the tonal centre is transcribed as D. The scale used and general shape of the melody is very similar to that used in the solo sago song. In this example, though, lines and their melodic presentations are grouped in threes, and as the first woman sings a line of text, it is partially echoed by the second woman. The first line of such a group has different text each time it is sung; the second line is sung in one of two closely related forms (*na'a ibiba'ae* or *ne ibiba'ae*), and the third line is textually and musically always the same (*eye*). As the first-line text is variable, the second woman usually only sings the end of this line; she sings the second and third lines with the first woman, in a style that is very similar to the Kaluli, simultaneously in-synchrony while out-of-phase (Feld 1988:82), although it is not known to what extent the same performance aesthetics are followed here. Note also that the striking of the women's sago mallets is not in unison. These strikes are only roughly indicated in the transcription.

**Figure 3: Music transcription of sago song 6, lines 10–15 (see ♫ online example 6).**

I will now consider men's *sorohabora*, the men's transformation of women's *obedobora* for ceremonial performance.

## Men's songs (*sorohabora*)

Men hear women's sago songs (*obedobora*) when they go tap *kara'o* oil from *Campnosperma brevipetiolata* trees, and at other times when they are walking in the bush (Weiner 1991:153). The men condense and compress the images of the poetry of the women's songs, just as poetry does to discourse, and dance is the poetic rendition of everyday movement. Thus, 'poetry, song, and dance are … different facets of … the aesthetic embodiment of discourse in its most encompassing, inscriptive sense' (ibid.:154).

The men say, 'these songs belong to the women. When we perform our *sorohabora* chants, we are merely imitating the women' (ibid. 1988a:131–32). Yet, aside from context, the transformation from women's *obedobora* to men's *sorohabora* requires various modifications to structure and performance practice.[5]

Men formerly performed *sorohabora* to promote general fertility and ensure success in hunting during *bi'a'a guabora* rites for the inauguration of a new longhouse. *Sorohabora* were performed by men returning with meat to the new longhouse. Each man began to dance as he entered the longhouse. Additionally, *sorohabora* were performed during the night of the pig-kill that celebrated the completion of *bi'a'a guabora* (Weiner 1991:190–93). In the decade including Weiner's primary fieldwork in Hegeso between 1979 and 1989, *sorohabora* were commonly performed after the completion of ceremonial pig and shell wealth exchanges.

While women's sago songs are usually sung solo, men's songs are always sung by a pair of men called *soro ira* 'song tree'.[6] These men often practise and sing together; consequently, they are very familiar with each other's performance styles. If the lines of a woman's *obedobora* are *a b c d*, men in a *soro ira* perform them as $a_1 c_2 b_1 d_2$, with the subscripts showing which member of the pair sings a particular line.[7] As a result of this alteration, the first two lines $(a_1, c_2)$ produce a couplet that contrasts in content with the couplet produced by the last two lines $(b_1, d_2)$:

> The first line of the male-produced couplet describes an image of life: an animal trap in the bush, a spell or myth habitually recited, a canoe moving along the river. It identifies a previous condition of active, moving 'life-lihood'. The second line offers a contrasting assertion of what has happened to that previously vital condition: an abandoned bush track, a spell forgotten and not passed on to other men, a fallen tree. It offers a view of life's finality. The couplet form thus quite elementarily juxtaposes the most incisive Foi images of motion and the end of motion, itself the most encompassing image of the transition between vitality and mortality. (Weiner 1991:155; see also, Weiner 1998b)

---

5    Rule (1993:136) writes *sorohabora* as two words—*soro* 'song'; *soro ha-* 'sing a song'; *soro habora* 'a ceremonial song'—thereby emphasising its relation to the word for 'song' (also see Weiner 1991:154). Weiner (pers. comm., 2 Oct 2012) observes that the *-bora* participial ending to *soro ha-* makes a noun out of a verb, hence, *sorohabora* is literally the '*soro*-ing' or '*soro* making.'

6    The descriptions from here until the end of the section on men's *sorohabora* primarily derive from material presented in Weiner (1991:154–59; 1998b; 2001:39–43), supplemented where possible by additional research.

7    In Weiner (1991), compare the presentation of verses as sung on pp. 171–75 (hence, using the notation followed here: $a_1 c_2 b_1 d_2$), with those on pp. 176–81, which keep together each man's pair of lines $(a_1 b_1 c_2 d_2)$. While the former arrangement follows the style of performance, the latter allows better understanding of the poetry. The songs presented there correspond to men's songs 3, 8, and 10 in the present collection. In this collection, each singer's pairs of lines are similarly preserved, rather than following the order of those lines during performance.

Men do not sing the '*owe*' and '*eye*' vocables that frequently end lines in women's sago songs; rather, men sing '*dawa*' or a variation of this towards the end of their songs, as described below in more detail.

The men in each *soro ira* pair face each other; their skins bright from *kara'o* tree oil, face paint, and the feathers on their heads (Weiner 1988a:152). Between three and seven *soro ira* make up a *soro ga* 'song base', which sings as a group (Figure 4a).[8] *Sorohabora* songs typically consist of five verses (the songs in this collection vary between four, five, and six verses), with each verse containing four lines (= two couplets) of text. In a typical performance by the first *soro ira* of a *soro ga*, the first man sings the first line of his couplet ($a_1$), which descends to the tonal centre (the lowest pitch in the phrase) and is sustained. While this pitch is sustained, his partner then sings the first line of his text ($c_2$), descending to and sustaining the tonal centre, thereby singing the tonal centre in unison with the first singer. While the second man continues to sustain the tonal centre, the first man then sings the concluding line of his couplet ($b_1$) and sustains the tonal centre; the second singer then sings his own final line ($d_2$), descending to the tonal centre and sustaining it with his partner. An 'ululation' or 'bleating' is often sung on the pitch above the tonal centre on each sung descent, but not on the lowest pitch (the tonal centre).[9] At the end of the verse, both singers sustain the tonal centre in unison for an extended period of time. Note that the contrast of the two male-produced couplets ($a_1$, $c_2$; $b_1$, $d_2$) as described above is also maintained in their sung representation.

8    The *soro ira* is to the *soro ga* as the lineage (*ira* also means 'lineage') is to the clan. The *soro ga* is a miniature version of the clan, men's most important social identity, but not a reflection of it. *Soro ira* and *soro ga* are poetic images of Foi social identities (Weiner 1991:159).

9    In Eunice Loeweke and Jean May's 1960–64 description of Fasu *namo kesa*, they refer to this sound as a 'breathy, quavering vibrato [that] occurs on the second note of the scale' (Chenoweth 2000:187). In Loeweke's accompanying music transcription of *namo kesa*, it is notated with two dots over the note in question (ibid.:188–92). Preliminary spectrographic analysis shows that the 'bleating' in Foi songs is indeed frequency modulation, hence vibrato. In some of the examples considered, there are about 10 pulsations per second, with a variation of about 150 cents from the highest to lowest frequencies. The tonal centre in *sorohabora* songs and in the Fasu example mentioned is the lowest pitch; in both cases, bleating appears to occur only on the pitch immediately above the tonal centre. I appreciate the assistance of Julia Colleen Miller, Philip Rose, and Alan Rumsey for discussion leading towards this initial assessment.

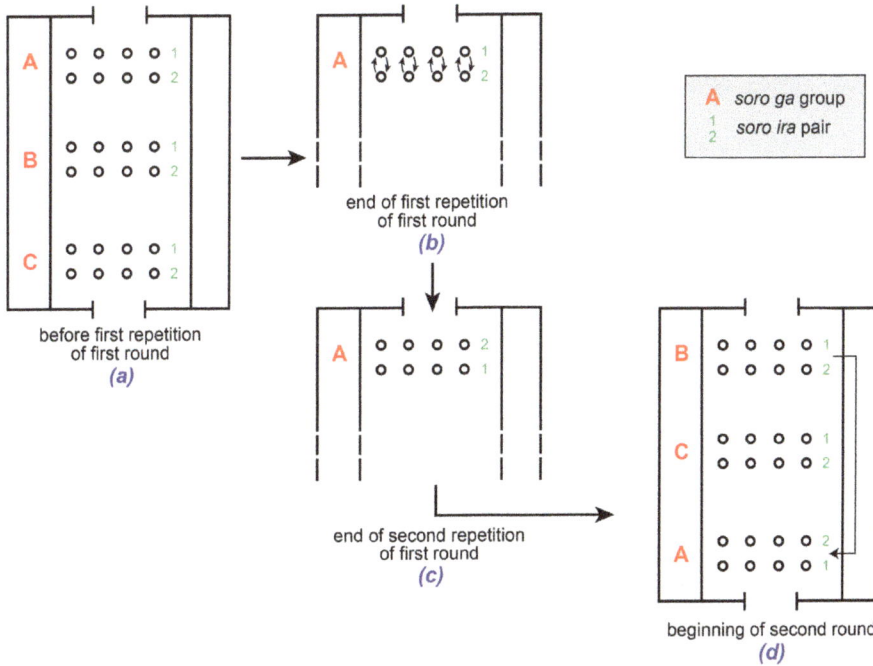

**Figure 4: The movement of male singers/dances during *sorohabora*.**

Source: Adapted from Weiner 1991:157, fig. 7-1.

At the conclusion of the first pair's first verse, the second *soro ira* performs the first verse of their song in the same manner. After the conclusion of the second pair's first verse, the third pair sings their first verse, and so on until all *soro ira* have performed their first verses. The first *soro ira* now performs their second verse in the same manner, their second verse is followed by the second *soro ira*'s second verse, and so forth. Such alternation continues for all the verses of each *soro ira*'s song. The singing of all verses of each song is one round of singing.

Men dance by bobbing up and down in a steady rhythm, bending at the knees, but keeping their backs straight, during their own singing and while they are waiting to sing.[10] In one hand a man may hold a bundle of arrows (*yaba*) plus a bow (*bi'a*), a spear (*tabu*), or a heavy stick of some kind. These are struck on the floor in time to the bobbing, thus providing a pulse. A man often begins a sung line by strongly stamping his heel down on the first syllable. One or two men in

---

10    While the characteristic position of men is standing up, opening up the chest and upper torso, with the arms providing rhythm, that for women is sitting, with an emphasis on closing up of the central body area. Women's singing and wailing takes place in such a position, with their legs bent upwards towards the body (as when making sago) or folded under their buttocks (as when sitting cross-legged next to a corpse in the longhouse) (Weiner 1991:156).

each *soro ga* shake a vessel rattle consisting of dried seeds inside cylindrical seed pods tied together (*gasore*).[11] This rattle is shaken to the rhythm of the bobbing and the instruments struck on the floor, all providing a pulse to the singing.

Comparing the pulse of the striking of a woman's mallet as she sings while preparing sago with the pulse of the rattle or other struck object in men's *sorohabora* songs, the former songs are between about 41 and 63 bpm, while the latter are between about 144 and 175 bpm; hence, the pulse of the latter is about two or three times faster than in women's sago songs. Nevertheless, the speed of the sung text in both genres appears to be similar.

Verse 2 of men's song 3 is transcribed in Figure 5. While this is the same song as more fully transcribed by Cathy O'Sullivan (Weiner 1991:176–81), my transcription attempts to show more clearly how the paired singers interact musically. The tonal centre here is transcribed as D. It is always the lowest note in performances. Note how most sung phrases descend to this D, which is then sustained while the other singer sings his next line of text. The length of these sustained final pitches is indicated in seconds in the transcription. (The first singer here neither descends to D on his first line nor sustains any phrase-final final pitch; this is another variation of performance style.) This type of multipart organisation differs considerably from the other genres of Foi music considered here.

**Figure 5: Music transcription of men's song 3, verse 2 (see ♩ online example 9).**

---

11    Rule (1993:16, 98) also calls the rattle *gasore*, while Williams (1940–42:149–50; 1977:194) writes *gasoro* and notes that it might be attached to handle—a variation I also observed in 2013. It is very likely that there is a semantic relation between the *soro ga* and the *gasore/gasoro* instrument they play (Weiner, pers. comm., 2 Oct 2012).

The 'bleated' note (indicated with a mordent above the note in question in my transcription) is on E and usually directly precedes descent to the tonal centre. The 'bleating' is always sung more loudly than other parts of the melody, sometimes significantly so. In further contrast to the accentuated frequency-modulated 'bleating' that forms a harmonic major second with the other sung and sustained part, the subsequent unison on D is often sung at a softer volume and is always sung as a stable pitch (i.e. not 'bleated'). Extended final vowels or vowel vocables are sung on these final pitches of a phrase. Finally, note the extended sustained unison at the end of this verse. While the exact length is, of course, variable, there is always an extended unison at such points.

The first three verses of each song are often about places—the names of mountains, streams, sago swamps, etc.; the last two verses reveal the identity of the man being sung about, the owner of or visitor to the places previously mentioned. Often the man's non-public name is sung, or perhaps only the clans of his parents (Weiner 1991:137–38); his everyday name is never revealed in songs. These last two verses are called the *dawa* or *dawadobora*, a word that means 'to cut up (and distribute)'. *Dawa* is the Foi name for the recently imported festival where pork is cut up and given away to mark the end of a ceremonial exchange. In men's *sorohabora*, the *dawa* of the song 'cuts off' the song from the one that follows and 'gives away' the name of the deceased man to the public. The actual singing of the word '*dawa*' or '*dawabo*' frequently occurs during these last two verses.

After the singing of one round of songs (i.e. each *soro ira* in the *soro ga* completing all the verses of their songs), each man changes position with his *soro ira* partner (Figures 4b–c). They then repeat the same songs, in the same manner as was done previously. At the end of this repetition of songs, the men stamp their feet vigorously, and the two lines of men in each *soro ga* form a single line and move to the position in the longhouse that was occupied by the *soro ga* adjacent to them. The *soro ga* at one end of the longhouse moves to the other end. In some performances, groups first move from the front to the back of the longhouse and then back again (Figure 4d).

In larger longhouses, 10–12 *soro ga* can participate simultaneously. If there are many pairs of men in a *soro ga*, the number of verses per song may be reduced from five to as few as two in order to allow all songs to be completed during the night.

As dawn approaches, one *soro ira* assumes leadership of all the performers in the longhouse, having either been selected beforehand or chosen during the night. The men now consider themselves one *soro ga*. Each pair will now sing one pair of lines as the performers leave the longhouse and descend to the plaza at sunrise.

## Women's *sorohabora*

Women told Weiner that they performed their own *sorohabora* in women's houses while the men were singing in the longhouse, but he never witnessed this during the ceremonial performances he attended. Nevertheless, one night he separately recorded the seven women's *sorohabora* included in this collection. They were all performed by pairs of women. One woman would begin a line and her partner would sing the same line, one beat later—this is quite different from the men's performances where a singer's partner sings a different text at the conclusion of a line. The women's *sorohabora*-performance technique of echoing the text of the first singer is similar to that used by two women to perform a sago song, such as occurs in sago song 6, where Kunuhuaka sings a line that is repeated three beats later by Siyame (cf. Figure 3). In women's *sorohabora* as in the men's, the *owe* and *eye* vocables of sago songs are not sung, but *dawa* verses are included (Weiner 1991:134, 146).

Figure 6 is a transcription of lines 8–11 of the women's *sorohabora* song no. 2. No *gasore* rattle or any other instrument is used to provide a pulse. Aside from the differences between men's and women's performance styles in *sorohabora* noted above, final tonal centres in unison are sustained at length in both genres. However, at the conclusion of these sustained notes, men tend to start the next verse immediately; in women's performances, however, there is a long pause before singing resumes. Lengths of these sustained tonal centres and pauses are indicated in seconds on the transcriptions. Women also do not 'bleat' pitches on the second-lowest pitch as men do.

# Relation to other studies of music in Papua New Guinea

With the above introduction to the Foi genres documented in this collection, I will now consider some particularly salient aspects of how this research, particularly on men's *sorohabora*, augments other comparable work in Papua New Guinea. This enables a reader and listener to better appreciate how the Foi relate to their neighbours, and also how this particular study adds to our knowledge of certain types of performance traditions in this country.

**Figure 6: Music transcription of women's *sorohabora* song 2, lines 8–11 (see ♫ online example 14).**

A noteworthy aspect of Foi men's *sorohabora* is its indoor performance at night; an outstanding feature of this particular publication is its presentation of Foi song texts. I will consider each of these subjects in turn and consider related work from other parts of the country.

## Indoor, nocturnal performances

Nocturnal ceremonial music/dance performances inside longhouses appear to be a key element distinguishing groups that are often felt to be part of the Highlands fringe, that is, groups that are in various ways culturally distinct from those of the main Highlands region.[12] Of course, which groups are core and which are fringe is not always easy to define, nor is it easy to list distinguishing traits (Weiner 1988b; A. Strathern 1988; Hays 1993). Yet, certainly throughout the main Highlands area—stretching from the central parts of Hela, Southern Highlands, Enga, Western Highlands, Jiwaka, Chimbu, and Eastern Highlands

---

12    In some areas, there is a mixture of different performance contexts. For example, Kirsch (1987:2) observes that Yongom (Yonggom) dances are differentiated on the basis of their performance inside or outside, during the day or night, and by men or by men and women.

provinces—most music/dance performances by groups take place outside during the day, often in a special area cleared for dancing.[13] In contrast, among the Foi and other groups, performances are usually inside and at night.[14]

There is not a total absence of indoor, nocturnal performances in the main Highlands area. Throughout much of this region from Duna in the west all the way to eastern portions of Eastern Highlands Province, courting activities, frequently involving sitting dances, also take place indoors and at night (e.g. see Stewart and Strathern 2002:29–90). However, courting dances do not have the ceremonial import of the indoor dances performed by the southern 'fringe' groups. Furthermore, decorations for courting are also often rather simple, dances are done while seated, and the singing appears to always be a cappella. In contrast, decorations for ceremonial performances inside longhouses are usually elaborate, dancers stand and move to different positions inside the house, and the singing is always accompanied by an instrument, usually a rattle, but sometimes a drum.

Groups neighbouring the Foi to the east and particularly to the west, as well as some located more distantly from them, all perform indoor ceremonial dancing at night, although the details of the performance itself, the decorations, who sings, what instrument is used, etc., may differ. In spite of these variations, however, the contrast of such a genre with the outdoor, daytime performances widely practised in the central part of the Highlands remains striking.

Researchers have written about a number of groups who claim to perform songs and dances originally from the 'Kutubu area'. While definitely including Foi speakers, the term 'Kutubu area' may also include the Fasu, immediately to the west of the Foi. The Fasu are middle men in the borrowing of traits between the Foi and Bosavi groups farther to the west (Weiner 1988a:21). The Fasu perform *namo kesa* 'essence song' inside their communal longhouse at night during the final distribution of brideprice to the bride's relatives, completion of a new longhouse, pig feast, the final moving of a deceased's bones to a cave, or when the killers of a witch responsible for a death give compensation to the witch's relatives.[15] In contrast to the Foi *sorohabora*, women do not watch.

---

13    In spite of the differences between Highlands and Highlands fringe, there can still be appreciation of contrasting traditions. Knauft (1985b:328, pers. comm. from Laurence Goldman) reports that Huli invite contingents of Dugube (their 'fringe' neighbours to the south) to stay with them for extended periods of time and perform their rituals. A dance called *hewabi bi* by the Huli 'appears to derive from the Lake Kutubu region' and involves large fronds of sago palm worn at the back of the dancers, 'very reminiscent of Papuan Plateau dancers' (Goldman 2007:159, table 9.2). Goldman does not mention if any musical instruments are part of such performances, but it would be very interesting if rattles were used as such instruments are otherwise not played in Huli performance.

14    Bruce Knauft identifies common features of rituals in the Strickland–Bosavi region: all-night dances in longhouses, dance costumes, movements, etc. (1985b:324–27), but also considers contrasts. As will be seen from the discussion below, I suggest that this region of commonalities extends over a significantly wider area.

15    A recording of *namo kesa* is found in Niles and Webb (1987:SHP-17).

Men form two rows of three men each, one row facing the other. They bob up and down in dance. Men sing in pairs, with the song being concluded by the naming of a man, his clan lands, and his son. Then the word *rauwaraka* is sung and the dance positions change. A seed rattle called *sorosore* is shaken, and axe handles are tapped on the floor (May and Loeweke 1981:227; Chenoweth 2000:180–203).[16] There are obviously many parallels with the performance of Foi men's *sorohabora*.

Outside the Foi and Fasu area, there are references to two groups who perform dances said to derive from the Kutubu area. Specific information on other groups in the region is generally lacking, rather than being negative.

In the Bosavi area, the Kaluli perform *sabio*.[17] Said to be popular in the Fasu and Foi areas, *sabio* was taught to the Kaluli by Kutubu carriers in the 1950s, particularly during the construction of the Bosavi airstrip. The Kaluli memorised the songs they were taught. As no new *sabio* are composed by the Kaluli, the repertoire is completely fixed and stable, and the texts of the songs are unintelligible to them. *Sabio* is performed in the communal longhouse in the late afternoon or early evening as a prelude to a major all-night ceremony. *Sabio* songs are sung by two or three pairs of men. The members of the pair face each other and sing alternate lines, coming together on a droned 'oooo'.[18] No 'bleating' occurs. The next pair does the same until an entire round is completed. Singers bob up and down in place, shaking the *sologa* seedpod rattle.[19] *Sabio* has apparently not been performed ceremonially since 1969 (Feld 1981:1; 1982:35; 1985:3, 6, 8; 2001:55; 2015).[20]

---

16    The most detailed descriptions of Fasu *namo kesa* and a dance called *kawari* are by Eunice Loeweke and Jean May in Chenoweth (2000:180–203); however, these descriptions are not kept separate from one another, but appear to alternate with each paragraph in their article, often making it challenging to know which performance is being described. I believe I have resolved this problem, but apologise in advance if I have erred. Tone markings on Fasu words, although included in May and Loeweke's Fasu dictionary (1981), have been omitted here.

17    Numerous commercial recordings of *sabio* have been released by Feld (1981:B2; 1985:B10; 2001:disc 3, nos 17–18).

18    The description here closely follows the Kaluli duet performance of *sabio* (Feld 2001:disc 3, no. 17). The first two lines sung by a pair consistently only descend to the second-lowest pitch; in subsequent lines, the descent is to the tonal centre (i.e. the lowest pitch). The quartet performance (Feld 2001:disc 3, no. 18) further illustrates these characteristics, but the second pair of performers more immediately echoes each other's lines, rather than singing during the sustained pitches. Such a multipart texture appears to have more similarities with other Kaluli genres.

19    Although the Kaluli *sologa* rattle (cf. Kasua *sogola*) is also used in the performance of genres deriving from outside the Kutubu region (e.g. *iwo:* and *heyalo*), note the phonetic resemblance of the word to *soro ga*, the Foi name for the group of paired men who sing *sorohabora*. See also n. 11 for the relation of this word to the Foi rattle (*gasore/gasoro*).

20    In the performance of Foi *sorohabora*, the first singer completes his line of text before the second singer begins his own. Although the Kaluli are imitating a language they do not understand in their performance of *sabio*, they maintain this distinctive relationship between voices, even though it is quite different from their performance style in all other genres of Kaluli music (Feld 2015), where the second voice more closely follows the first (resulting in a texture more similar to what is found in Foi sago songs sung by two men and female *sorohabora*). The tempo of *sabio* is also considerably faster than that of other Kaluli genres. In spite of these

In Western Province, even further to the west, the Kamula perform *sabra*, which they also claim originated in the Kutubu area. Here again, between six and 14 dancers form two lines that face each other. Singing is done by pairs of men, one after the other. Songs consist mostly of placenames. Singing may cause some of the audience members to cry (Wood 1982:3, 340, n. 8).

Although descriptions of these dances are by different authors and some information is unavailable, certain features appear to recur among the Foi *sorohabora*, Fasu *namo kesa*, Kaluli *sabio*, and Kamula *sabra*. In addition to the performance of such dances at night and in the longhouse, these elements include men standing in two parallel rows; men facing their partners as they sing in pairs, alternating lines, but singing together on a final, sustained pitch; men bobbing up and down in dance, shaking seedpod rattles.

Numerous indoor, nocturnal dances in the region also occur, but they are not described as originating from Kutubu. Not surprisingly, the more distant they are from the Kutubu area, the more they seem to deviate from the forms found there (cf. Knauft 1985b:326)—for example, difference in the details of who sings, in what kind of groups, what instruments are used, the focus of poetry, etc. And, the Foi and Fasu also perform other dances than the ones described above that fit this description as well. In the remainder of this section, I will attempt to highlight some of these relationships.

Both the Fasu and Foi perform *kawari*, which is said to have originated from the Kaluli *gisalo* and travelled to Kasua speakers and then on to the Fasu and Foi (May and Loeweke 1981:106; Weiner 1988a:22; Chenoweth 2000:180–203).[21] While the Kaluli have a number of song/dance forms, as discussed below, they claim that only *gisalo* originated with them. Certain features of *gisalo* are very similar to the Foi *sorohabora* and Fasu *namo kesa*, but differences are also apparent. Distinctively, the Kaluli *gisalo* uses a *sob* rattle of bivalve shells suspended on a string (Kasua *palo*); the rattle is bounced on the floor of the longhouse by the solo male dancer. The all-night *gisalo* ceremonies are performed by guests for their hosts. The singer attempts to move listeners to tears through the poetic images of loss and abandonment that he constructs while dancing

---

and other differences, Kaluli still describe the interaction of the paired voices and rattles as *dulugu ganalan* 'lift-up-over sounding' (ibid.). Further subtleties in the difference between the interaction of the two voices in Foi, Fasu, and Kaluli examples are also evident in the material available, but in all three areas, the sustained tonal centre is at a lower volume, often with a crescendo towards the end. The pronounced 'bleating' in Foi performance appears less pronounced in the available Fasu recordings, and totally absent in Kaluli. Scales between the three groups also appear to be mostly comparable. While these are only preliminary observations, it is obvious that many fruitful stylistic comparisons are worth pursuing.

21    Up until 2013, Kasua groups have performed at three Kundu and Digaso Festivals (2011, 2012, and 2013). In 2013, one of their groups performed *gisalo*, with other groups performing different dances. Hahudi Farobo, one of the organisers of the festival and someone intimately involved in promoting Foi culture, explained that he has discouraged the performance of such a dance by the Foi (where it is called *kawari* or *agiri*) because it is imported from another area (Niles and Gende 2013).

along the corridor of the longhouse. Initially singing and dancing in place, as he completes the *mo:* ('trunk' or refrain) section of the song, he moves to the opposite end of the longhouse where he faces the chorus and dances in place again, singing the concluding *dun* ('branches' or verses) section of the song, while the chorus echoes his singing. At the end of the song, the dancer turns around and performs the entire song again, first singing and dancing alone in place, returning back down the longhouse corridor to face the other chorus, and completing the song with their accompaniment. When overcome with sadness, members of the audience burst into tears and loud wails, grab resin torches, and jam the flames into the dancer's shoulder, resulting in mass whooping from the crowd, along with stamping feet and snapping bow strings, while the dancer continues singing (Feld 2001:58–62; also see, Feld 1982; E. L. Schieffelin 1968).

For the Fasu *kawari*, however, the *kawi aroa* rattle used consists of dried crayfish pincers, suspended from a flexible branch, which is inserted in the back of a dancer's belt. The Kaluli *degegado* (Kasua *somasuba*) is also such an instrument, but it is used in the performance of *iwo:*, *ko:luba*, and *ilib kuwo:* dances, not *gisalo*. The Foi of Lake Kutubu (Gurubumena) obtained the costume associated with Kaluli *gisalo* from the Fasu and refer to the burning of the dancers as *siri kebora* 'resin burning; scar-making burning'; however, the dance did not travel further east to other Foi (Weiner 1988a:22).

Women may watch the Fasu *kawari*; the middle partition separating the women's end of the longhouse from the men's is removed, so that the men can dance the full length. Men again sing in pairs, facing their partners. The same phrase of one singer is repeated by his partner. As the texts are borrowed from the Kasua, they are unintelligible to most listeners. Dancers are not burnt, and other participants sit at one end of the longhouse and separately sing *sia* (Chenoweth 2000:181, 185–86, 202).

The performance of Fasu *kawari* is preceded by *akiri*, the playing of *roko* drums and *kawi aroa* crayfish-claw rattles by two to four men, but without singing. They stomp up the steps of the longhouse at night, parade down the centre aisle, and sit on the men's side. One man then stands, selects his partner, and the *kawari* performance begins. The *auape keraka* drum-beating dance is also performed for healing a sick person (May and Loeweke 1981:10, 22, 106, 202; Chenoweth 2000:186).

A comparable drum dance appears to be the Foi *samoga* or *usanega*, performed during the Usane Habora ceremony to cure sickness. Here, two types of *sa'o* drum are used—with a 'fishtail' end[22] (*sa'o fare*) and with a round end (*sa'o gauwage* or *sa'o doibu/duibu*)—with a crayfish-claw rattle and without singing

---

22   Foi call this end *sa'o fare gesa*, with *gesa* referring to the fork of a tree or a support pole (Williams 1940–42:149; Rule 1993:99). Also compare the similar nomenclature among the Rumu (Petterson 1999:90).

(Rule 1993:16, 133; Weiner 1995:101, 112–13).[23] Williams (1940–42:149; 1977:193–94) suggested that this ceremony arrived from the southeast, perhaps bringing the drum along with it, where previously seedpod rattles would have been used.

Aspects of these performances appear in different combinations throughout the regions to the west and southwest.

The Kaluli *gisalo* is also reported to have been adopted by the Aemili (Aimele) as *gisala*, from whom the Kamula long ago borrowed what they call *kisama* (Crawford 1981:58–59 (Photos 31–34); Wood 1982:3, 329–38). Additionally, the Etoro (Edolo) *kɔsa* has relations with the Kaluli *gisalo* (E. L. Schieffelin 1976:193, n. 4) and the Gebusi (Gobasi) *kosaym*,[24] particularly the common usage of a shell rattle bounced on the longhouse floor and similarities between the names, suggest a close relation with the Kaluli form (Knauft 1985a:416, n. 1).[25] Moving northwards, the Samo *kosaman* involves male dancers with a rattle of black palm leaves and streamers placed in the dancers' belts. Singing is by men and women (Shaw 1975:231–32). And the Bedamini (Beami) *gosei* involves male dancers and one or more male choruses; the leader of the chorus sings about recent events, and the chorus repeats each verse. The dancers move back and forth in the middle of the longhouse, and emotional listeners may burn the dancers' backs (Sørum 1980:278; 1982:46).[26]

Drum dances also occur among the Kaluli, where they are called *ilib kuwo:*; the dance is said to originate from south of Mount Bosavi.[27] Dancers play *ilib*

---

23  Outside, diurnal dance performances with drums by Foi and Fasu performers are now features of the Kundu and Digaso Festival, held annually since 2011. The festivals are supported by Oil Search Limited and other organisations to promote local traditions. Groups from the Mount Bosavi area, Samberigi, Huli, Enga, and Goaribari have also participated (National 2012). While *kundu* is, of course, the Tok Pisin word for 'drum', *digaso* and *kara'o* are Foi words for the tree oil so valued in trade by groups to the north (Rule 1993:89); cf. Fasu *tikiaso* (May and Loeweke 1981:247).

24  Where names of languages as found in the most recent version of *Ethnologue* (M. P. Lewis et al. 2013) differ from usage in the ethnographic source being considered, the *Ethnologue* names are placed in parentheses; hence, 'Etoro' and 'Gebusi' appear in the sources cited, while 'Edolo' and 'Gobasi' are used in *Ethnologue*. Where no parenthetical additions are found, the names in both sources are the same. I have followed this practice so that the locations of the various groups mentioned can be easily located on the maps found in *Ethnologue*, a resource freely available on the Internet (http://www.ethnologue.com/).

25  Gebusi (Gobasi) may also burn their dancers, but it is not a prominent part of their performances (Knauft 1985b:335, n. 13). Although he does not name the genre but does mention the singing being performed by women, Knauft (1985b:324–25) appears to compare Kaluli *gisalo* with Gebusi *gigobra* (danced by men with drums and crayfish-claw rattles), rather than with Gebusi *kosaym* (danced by men with a rattle bounced on the floor), even though the latter seems to be more similar to *gisalo* in some aspects. This illustrates how features differentiating genres in one area may be less distinctive in another.

26  See Niles and Webb (1987:WP-10) for a recording involving the performance of *gosei* or *kosei* (two decorated singers sing face to face with *sobo* bivalve shell rattles struck on the floor; cf. Knauft 1985b:329–30), a male chorus (*gosege*) sitting to the side that responds to the text sung by the main pair, and women separately singing *lawine sagorobo hadigibi* songs.

27  An origin to the south of Mount Bosavi might lend strength to the Kamula claim for originating such a dance, as discussed later in the main text.

drums with *degegado* crayfish-claw rattles, but do not sing, as a prelude to all-night *ko:luba*, *heyalo*, or *gisalo* ceremonies (Feld 1981:1; 2001:55, 62–63).[28] Kasua *irigino* drums are played with *sogola* seedpod rattles (Niles and Gende 2013). The Kamula consider their *woiyo* 'drum' dance to be their own creation, in contrast to other dances they perform, such as *sabra* and *kisama*. It too is performed with a crayfish-claw rattle and without singing (Crawford 1981:59–61 (Photos 35, 38); Wood 1982:224, 317–29). Knauft (1985a:258, 416, n. 1; 2005:68) reports the similar Gebusi (Gobasi) *gigobra*, performed with *duɔ* drum[29] and *dias moliar* crayfish-claw rattle; women separately sing *hayay* songs to the men's drumming and dancing.[30] The Samo *hobola* is a curing dance for which the male dancer plays the *duwon* drum and inserts a crayfish-claw rattle into his belt. Women sing as the dancer moves around the sick person (Shaw 1975:226, 230–31, 296–304; National Arts School [1986?]).[31] Finally, the Bedamini (Beami) *gafoi* or *kafoi* is performed by a male dancer with an *iribu* drum. Here the dancer is surrounded by two or three female dancers with rattles (Sørum 1980:278; 1982:46, 51–52).[32]

Albert G. van Beek (pers. comm. (24 Dec 2003), as cited in Craig 2010:191–92) notes the association of *kafoi* with the final stage of the boys' initiation ceremony (*goy lèègi*), where an earlier type of drum (shorter, with a 'cubic-formed' distal end) was replaced in the late 1960s with the longer slender one used by the Samo when playing of the former did not have the desired effect following a number of earthquakes and landslides. The distal ends of both types of drums are carved to represent crocodile jaws. A properly tuned drum produces the voice of Awamuni—the cultural hero who gave the Bedamuni (Beami) their cultural identity—calling *a-ta* 'father-son'. Van Beek also notes the out-of-phase drumming of performers and the similarity of decorations to Kaluli *gisalo* dancers: 'like the Kaluli know drum performances, the Bedamuni know song performances, but the cultural importance is inverted.'

---

28 Recordings of Kaluli *ilib kuwo:* can be found on Feld (1985:B12; 2001:disc 3, no. 6) and Niles and Webb (1987:SHP-14).

29 Knauft (2005:91) reports that Gebusi (Gobasi) males conclude their initiation by dancing with drums for the first time. Kamula males must undergo a certain rite to drum, lest the noise of their playing would scare away game (Wood 1982:247). Further to the west, among Telefol speakers and other Min groups, males in their twenties learn how to drum at the fifth of seven stages of initiation, called *wotban*. While the drum (*wot*) itself is not secret, knowledge to play it is learned through ritual, where the relation of the instrument, its playing, and its sound to cultural heroes, taro, death, maggots, decay, and fertility can only be taught through initiation (Brumbaugh 1979:240–41, 368–75; 1990).

30 For a recording of women's *hayay* singing while men drum, see Knauft (2012). Other recordings from the Nomad area, including the Gebusi (Gobasi) and Kubo can be found on Huguet (1992:tr. 2–3) and a release by Oméga Studio (1981?:B1).

31 During Samo *kandila* initiation, Shaw (1975:250) reports a rattle of crayfish claws attached to vine or bark string that hits the floor when the dancer bends his knees—apparently a cross between the rattle that is bounced on the floor with one that is put in the back of dancers' belts in other areas. Here the bobbing dance is also taught to initiates as a part of their initiation (Shaw 1975:264; 1982:423).

32 For a recording of *kafoi* or *gafoi*, see Niles and Webb (1987:WP-11); a decorated male dancer with *ilibu* drum and *korokiti* crayfish-claw rattle perform *kafoi* while two young girls practise their dance and the singing of *siokoi*. The performance is to heal the headache of the man seated before them.

There are even parallels with core Highlands groups. The Huli *komia* is performed by two drumming dancers, but without singing. It is performed for drought fertility rites (*gaiya tege*)—perhaps considered another type of sickness—in which the dancers jump over the *ali damba* cult fence (Goldman 2007:159, Table 9.2). There are obviously many similarities and variations in these traditions over quite a wide area.

In the cases discussed so far, the Kutubu area has been stated as the origin for certain dances or certain dances performed by the Foi or Fasu are said to have origins elsewhere. Aside from these links, however, the inside performance of nocturnal dance ceremonies has much wider distribution.

To the southeast of the Foi, among the Polopa (Folopa), hosts sing and dance in their men's house at night prior to competitive pig-feasting, daring their guests to come and be overwhelmed by their largesse. On the day of the event itself, hosts and guests alternate in dancing in the men's house until the next morning when the bulk of the pork is cooked and given to the guests. Raiding parties also dance, drum, and sing in the men's house at night to taunt their enemies (D. J. J. Brown 1979:714–15, 721).[33]

Among South Kewa- or Erave-speaking groups to the east of the Foi, the *rupale* dance is performed inside the communal men's house (*tapanda*) at night, preceding and during pig-kills.[34] Women and children can enter the men's house at this time. Singing with rattles, men form groups of four to six,[35] enter the house through the veranda, and trample the floor of the house in unison upon their entrance. Marching along the main central corridor (*pukama*), they reach the first fireplace and form two rows of two or three abreast. A leader sings a phrase, and the others in the group join afterwards, with the final vowel being a sustained *o*. After 10 seconds of silence, there is a single repetition

---

33  Nocturnal indoor dance performances appear to be absent among the Daribi (Dadibi), to the east of the Polopa (Folopa). Dances performed during Wagner's fieldwork there were said to have origins to the east (Gimi), northeast (Gumine (Golin)), or west (Bạria (Wiru, East Kewa, or Foraba (Folopa))) reaching the Daribi in the mid-1930s (Wagner 1967:6–7; 1972:80–84, 164–65). While the Angan Baruya further to the east sing *daata* inside initiates' houses, there is no dance.

34  The following description is taken from LeRoy's work in Koiari; other descriptions of performances of *rupale* (or *tupale*) are given by Josephides (1982:45–46, 79–84) and MacDonald (1991:100–102), who worked primarily in Aka and Mararoko, respectively—all part of the Erave language area. Noteworthy differences from LeRoy's description are included here in footnotes. A recording of *rupale* is presented by Niles and Webb (1987:SHP-7), where the singing is accompanied by *sekeseke* rattles—dried seeds enclosed in a sewn, rectangular pandanus covering.

35  Josephides (1982:46) also notes men carrying axes and that there are four men in a group; MacDonald (1991:100–101) agrees and says men strike *usaane* drums as well, and observes that *rupale* may also be performed outdoors, in which case four or six men stand abreast. Note that the name of the drum here is very similar to the name of the Usane Habora ceremony the Foi perform to cure sickness, perhaps lending credence to Williams's claim that the Foi ceremony arrived with the drum from the southeast (1940–42:149; 1977:193–94).

of the same note.[36] The same song is then repeated with some variations, a second song follows, and it is also repeated. The group then marches to the second pair of fireplaces and sings the same songs there; their place at the first fireplace is taken by a second group, and then a third, etc. When a group has sung at all the fireplaces, it exits the house through the back, prepares two new songs, and enters again through the front to sing at the first fireplace again. This simultaneous singing of songs by different groups, movement between fireplaces, and the entry/exit of groups continues throughout the night (LeRoy 1978:53–54, 70, n. 2). Full decorations for such a performance are called *kewa au*, 'decorations of the southerners' (Josephides 1982:45), perhaps a reference to the similarities of such performances with fringe groups to the south.

For the West Kewa, Franklin (1978:389) notes the performance of songs in memory of the dead with a shuffling dance back and forth along the inside corridor of men's house. And LeRoy (1985:95) reports that West Kewa *yasa*, like Erave *rupale*, takes place at night so that ghosts can hear them; in both regions, songs contain messages to the dead and the living.

Now moving to the west of the Foi and Fasu, nocturnal longhouse performances are reported for the Kasua, Kaluli, and Etoro (Edolo), as noted above. In addition to the *gisalo*, *sabio*, and *ilib kuwo:* discussed above, Kaluli also perform *iwo:*, *heyalo:*, and *ko:luba*, all of which were adopted from groups ranging from the southeast to southwest of Mount Bosavi (Feld 1981:1; 1982:35; 1985:3–8; 2001:55, 63–67; B. B. Schieffelin and Feld 1998:72, 89; E. L. Schieffelin 1976:225–29).[37]

Across the border with Western Province, indoor, night-time performances are reported among the Bedamini (Beami) *gosei*; Gebusi (Gobasi) *kosaym*; and Samo *kosaman*, as reported above; Awin (Aekyom) *sia* (Depew 1983:5–10);[38] Yonggom *kibirat*, *yok*, *urumanop*, *ame'op*, *wod*, *ondan*, and *aip* (Kirsch 1987:2–3);[39] Kauwol (Faiwol) *yoron vinum*;[40] Ngalum *oksang*;[41] and the Kamula *sabra*, as described above.

---

36   The Koiari villagers with whom LeRoy worked claimed this repetition was their innovation (LeRoy 1978:54).

37   For recordings of Kaluli ceremonial genres, see Feld (1981:B1–3; 1985:B8, 10; 2001:disc 3) and Niles and Webb (1987:SHP-13–14, 16).

38   See Niles and Webb (1987:WP-8) for a recording involving men in two groups, with *kosiai* rattles of seeds suspended from a cane frame in the back of their bark belts, their group singing and dancing punctuated with solo dancing and drumming. Women sit at the side.

39   See Niles and Webb (1987:WP-12) for a recording of a *kibirat* performance to determine the identity of the person who has caused an illness.

40   See Niles and Webb (1987:WP-13) for a recording involving dancing in a twisting line inside the house, with men singing in alternation with the snapping of bowstrings and *fotfot* whistling, made on inhalation.

41   Abmisibil, Bonai (both Ngalum), and Okbap (Ketengban) dance houses have springy floors and belong to several village communities (Simon 1993:170–71, CD 6, It. 1–3). See Niles and Webb (1987:WP-18) for a recording of *amsang*, performed by men singing and dancing while holding at their backs *yaso* rattles made of fronds from the *bot* tree. This recording was made of a visiting group. While they appear to have been Ngalum speakers, this identification is not definite.

Further south in Western Province, ceremonial nocturnal performances still occur in some longhouses, but they seem to be increasingly concerned with initiation, the presentation of secret knowledge, etc. This appears to be true for dances such as those presently or formerly found among the Gogodala (Crawford 1981:176, 253–56, 274–83)[42] and Kiwai (Southern Kiwai), such as, *wete*, *madia*, *maure moguru*, *ganu*, *baiduo*, *mado*, *gama mutu*, *barari*, *upipoo*, *asasi*, etc., performed in the *darimo* 'men's house' or *moto* 'communal houses', often involving drumming men in two rows, with women, boys, and girls singing, but some of these dances may also be performed outside and during the day (Beaver 1920:180; Riley 1925:40–44, 47; Landtman 1927:351, 408–20).

This trend seems to continue eastwards into Gulf Province. For example, among Morigi speakers on the western banks of the Turama River, dances were associated with headhunting and the display of skulls on *agibe* boards in the longhouse. *Mipa* and *barari* are performed nocturnally, but there are also indoor *diurnal* performances. Paired dancers are led by warriors with drums, their wives, then bachelors who can carry drums but have not passed a certain stage of initiation, then bachelors who have not killed a bush pig and consequently cannot play drums, with the lines ending with warriors and their wives again (Austen 1936). Among Kerewo speakers to the east, similar indoor dances called *gibumamu* are performed with drums (Austen 1934).

From at least the Koriki (Purari) and further eastwards, communal longhouses were absent, but men's longhouses existed. However, most performances did not appear to take place inside these longhouses; instead, masked dancers dramatically emerged from them during the day. For the Koriki (Purari), masked *gopi* dancers were accompanied by singing and drumming from men seated at the front of the *ravi* longhouse (Williams 1924:171, 173). Among the Orokolo, the masked *hevehe* dancers themselves played drums. While women were not allowed into the longhouses, upon emergence from the longhouse, each masked dancer was met by its own group of adoring females who danced with it in the village plaza and down to the beach over a period of a month. Such ceremonial cycles took between one and three decades to complete. Similar forms appeared among groups further to the east as well (Williams 1939:145, 152–55; 1940:357–58; Welsch 2006:11–12, 23).

Such similarities with groups to the south, but also involving significant contrasts, are perhaps to be expected as groups such as the Foi are 'culturally coastal peoples who have moved north and have settled in the southern fringe of the New Guinea Central Highlands' (Weiner 1988b:3). Andrew Strathern also writes of 'longhouse culture' moving from the south to the north (1988:196).

---

42    See Niles and Webb (1987:WP-6) for a recording in which the singing and dancing is accompanied by striking the distal end of the *sololo* split-bamboo rattle against the longhouse floor during *aida* initiation.

While the affinities with groups to the south are clear, indoor dances, sometimes at night, are also reported for some groups on the northern fringe of the Highlands, such as the Kalam *smiy* where men sing inside and reveal esoteric knowledge to initiates, while women beat drums and dance around the house (Bulmer 1967:13; Grove 1978:17), Hewa *yap mofau* performed in a new house before the inhabitants move in (Steadman 1971:55, 76, 108–10), and Awiakay *kaunjambi* all-night performances of spirits singing through male performers (Hoenigman in prep.).[43] While performances take place inside some Sepik spirit houses, these often represent or create the voice of spirits, frequently using instruments; such performances can be heard, but not seen, by the uninitiated, and are associated with the presentation of secret knowledge, initiation, and aspects of male ceremonial life—see, for example, descriptions for the Iatmul (Wassmann 1991; Spearritt and Wassmann 1996), Ambonwari (Tabriak) (Telban 1998; 2008), and Waxei (Watakataui) (Yamada 1997).

Across the border and into the Indonesian province of Papua, the Eipomek appear to only perform outside, but the Kapauku (Ekagi) construct an *ema* dance house during pig festivals when nocturnal dancing takes place (Pospisil 1963:72–76). Among the Konda Valley Dani (Western Dani), courting parties take place that somewhat resemble the nocturnal indoor activities in parts of the Papua New Guinea Highlands, but it seems that song and dance are absent (O'Brien 1969a:212, 349–50, 383–85; 1969b:212). Hence, while indoor performances may be found, many aspects of their performance are quite different from my concern here.

After this consideration of some of the distinctive aspects of the performance of Foi ceremonial dance and song and its relation to other groups in the region, I turn now to a focus on the collection itself and the texts it contains.

A collection of song texts in the original language and in translation is significant in itself. While spoken stories are often published in translation and rarely in the original language (except in specialised linguistic studies), vernacular song texts and their translations are frequent components of many ethnographic studies. This suggests that there is something special about these texts. Songs are sung poetry, that is, their texts are in a language that is somehow different from normal speech. For a knowledgeable listener, these texts also tend to encapsulate important aspects of culture. Here I am interested in what makes sung language different from normal speech.

---

43   Awiakay speakers number about 300 and live in Kanjimei village, East Sepik Province. Although presently not included in *Ethnologue* (M. P. Lewis et al. 2013), their language belongs to the Arafundi group (Hoenigman in prep.).

In the following sections I consider two features of this volume that are of relevance to more general studies of Papua New Guinea song.[44]

## Collections of song texts for sociocultural revelations

Researchers frequently discuss song texts as part of more general ethnographic accounts. Indeed, it would seem that most Papua New Guinea ethnographies contain at least a few song texts. While publications focused on music would naturally be assumed to make use of such texts—such as Stella's monograph on the Banoni (Bannoni) (1990) and Feld's on the Kaluli (1982)—songs are actually cited in a much wider range of works.

Song texts often encapsulate or provide insights into various sociocultural concerns, such as Fortune's frequent use of Dobu songs throughout the main text of his book and in an appendix (1932). Or the publications may consider

---

44    For the following discussion of poetry, I consulted about 150 articles, theses, and books in the Music Archive of the Institute of Papua New Guinea Studies. While not exhaustive, and generally omitting sources consisting solely of texts and translations without significant commentary (e.g. Brash and Krauth 1973; Helfert and Holdsworth 1974), the sources below cover a good range of materials and serve as an introduction to this subject. In order to keep the main text here as uncluttered as possible, I have avoided detailed referencing except where discussing specific issues in more detail. Apart from a few initial sources of general discussion, the groups and the references I have consulted are listed here under the conventional four geo-political regions of Papua New Guinea: *General discussion* (Niles 2011b; Niles and Rumsey 2011; Webb and Niles 1990); *Highlands region:* Baruya (Niles and Webb 1987:EHP-8); Benabena (Young 1968); Daribi (Dadibi) (Wagner 1972); Duna (Gillespie 2010; Gillespie and San Roque 2011; Kendoli 2011; Niles and Rumsey 2011; Sollis 2010; 2011; A. Strathern and Stewart 2011); Enga (Talyaga 1973; 1974; 1975; Gibbs 2001; 2011; Niles and Rumsey 2011); Erave (LeRoy 1978; Josephides 1982); Golin (Donohoe 1987); Huli (Pugh-Kitingan 1981; Lomas 2011); Ialibu (Imbongu) (Kerema 1976?); Ipili (Ingemann 1968; 2011; Borchard and Gibbs 2011); Kalam (Pawley and Bulmer 2011); Kaluli (E. L. Schieffelin 1976; Feld 1978; 1982; 1985; 1990; 2001); Karinj (Angal Heneng) (Reithofer 2011); Ku Waru (Bo-Ung) (Rumsey 2001; 2007; 2011; Niles 2007; 2011a; Niles and Rumsey 2011); Kuman (Whiteman 1965; Bergmann 1971; Gende 1998); Kyaka (Koyati 1979); Melpa (A. Strathern 1974; G. Strathern and Strathern 1985; A. Strathern and Stewart 2005; 2011; Niles 2007; 2011a; 2011b; Niles and Rumsey 2011); North Wahgi (Luzbetak 1954); Usarufa (Chenoweth 1979); Wahgi (Jimben 1984); West Kewa (Franklin 1970; 1978); Wiru (Paia and Strathern 1977); *Momase region:* Alamblak (Coulter 2007); Awiakay (Hoenigman in prep.); Boiken (Boikin) (Niles 2000); Central Buang (Mapos Buang) (Hooley 1987; Chenoweth and Hooley 2010); Gnau (G. Lewis 1980); Iatmul (Bateson 1932; Wassmann 1982; 1988; 1991); Irumu (Tuma-Irumu) (Kelsey 1993); Jabêm or Yabim (Yabem) (Pöch 1905; Zahn 1996); Kairiru (Niles 2000); Karesau (Kairiru) (Schmidt 1909); Karawari (Tabriak) (Telban 2008); Manambu (Harrison 1982; 1986; Aikhenvald 2014); Mapos Buang (Sankoff 1977); Maring (Rappaport 1968); Monumbo (Pöch 1905; Vormann 1911; Graf 1950; Niles 2000); Nekgini (Reigle 1995; 2001); Sissano (Niles 2000); Tifal (Roberts 1996; 2014); Tumleo (Niles 2000); various parts of Morobe province (Neuhauss 1911); Waxei (Watakataui) (Yamada 1997); Wovan (Haruai) (Flanagan 1983); *Southern region:* Binandere (Waiko 1984; 1991; 1995; 1982); Bwaidoga (Bwaidoka) (Jenness and Ballantyne 1926–29; 1928); Dobu (Fortune 1932); Gebusi (Gobasi) (Knauft 1985a; 1985b); Gizra (Gizrra) (Laba et al. 1980); Keraki (Nambo) (Williams 1936); Kilivila (Baldwin 1945; 1950; Kasaipwalova 1978; Kasaipwalova and Beier 1978a; 1978b; 1979; Senft 1999; 2011); Kiwai (Southern Kiwai) (Landtman 1913; 1927); Koita (Koitabu) (Niles 2000); Korafe (Korafe-Yegha) (James 1978); Koriki (Purari) (Williams 1924); Motu (Barton 1910); Okena (Korafe-Yegha or Ewage-Notu) (Niles 2000); Orokolo (Williams 1940); Suau (Cooper 1975); Toaripi (H. A. Brown 1968); Wagawaga (Seligman 1910); *Islands region:* Akara (Lele) (Laba et al. 1980); Baining (Qaqet) (Aerts and Hesse 1979; Fajans 1985); Banoni (Bannoni) (Stella 1990); Buin (Terei) (Thurnwald 1912; 1936; 1941; Laycock 1969a; 1969b; 1969c; 1970; 1972; Oliver-Berg 1979); Kaulong (Goodale 1995; Drüppel 2009; Niles 2009); Lak (Siar-Lak) (Wolffram 2007); Mandak (Madak) (Clay 1986); Takū (Takuu) (Moyle 2007); Tolai (Kuanua) (Laba et al. 1980); *Western New Guinea:* Central Asmat (Voorhoeve 1977); Eipomek (Simon 1978; Heeschen 1990; Simon 1993).

some aspect particularly well presented through song texts. Publications in which song texts are a major focus include studies by Baldwin (1945; 1950) and Senft (2011) on the language and interpretation of Kilivila songs; Ingemann (1968) on the structure of Ipili courting songs; Franklin (1970) and LeRoy (1978) on the metaphors used in West Kewa and Erave song, respectively; Hooley (1987) on the poetic transformations of Central Buang (Mapos Buang) song texts; Wassmann's detailed consideration of Iatmul mythopoetic ceremonial songs (1982; 1988; 1991); and Rumsey's explorations of Ku Waru (Bo-Ung) sung tales, *tom yaya kange* (2001; 2005; 2007; 2010; 2011), a form having characteristics of both songs and storytelling.

Weiner's exploration of the texts presented in this volume was published separately as *The Empty Place* (1991). As such, it straddles the category mentioned above along with publications that appear to be primarily meant as simply collections of song texts, usually appearing in the original language and in translation. Notes in such collections comment on various aspects of the songs presented, such as performance contexts, dance movements, origins, poetry, performance style, etc.[45] Such collections, often consisting of dozens of songs, are well represented for the following languages, moving out from the Foi area (collections containing more than 100 songs are noted): Enga (Talyaga 1973; 1975; Gibbs 2001); Ialibu (Imbongu) (Kerema 1976?); Kyaka (Koyati 1979), containing 123 songs; Kewa (Erave) (Josephides 1982); Wiru (Paia and Strathern 1977); Melpa (A. Strathern 1974; G. Strathern and Strathern 1985); Tifal (Roberts 1996; 2014), with 200 songs and music transcriptions; Kilivila (Kasaipwalova 1978; Kasaipwalova and Beier 1978a; 1978b; 1979); Bwaidoga (Bwaidoka) (Jenness and Ballantyne 1926–29; 1928), containing 144 songs and incantations; and Buin (Terei) (Thurnwald 1912), with 130 songs. Perhaps most similar to Weiner's volumes is the consideration of Manambu love songs by Harrison (1982; 1986): 21 song texts, translations, and summaries are preceded by a lengthy consideration of the genre, its structure, and the circumstances of its performance.

As such, Weiner's work on Foi songs well complements the work of others in exploring the importance of sung texts to ethnography in Papua New Guinea.

---

45    Michael Webb and I have published a collection of traditional song texts and translations, accompanied by cassettes of the songs, which is meant to be used in schools, *Ol Singsing bilong Ples* (Webb and Niles 1990). Although not the focus of my introduction, a comparable collection of stringband songs, meant to be used by people wanting to learn to play guitar, is *Riwain! Papua New Guinea Pop Songs* (Webb and Niles 1986). A collection of transcriptions and translations of Akara (Lele), Tolai (Kuanua), and Gizra (Gizrra) texts from Institute of Papua New Guinea Studies recordings is found in Laba et al. (1980).

# Poetic devices of song

Weiner's discussion of the poetic language used in Foi songs is scattered throughout *The Empty Place*. He considers various devices that are used in Foi sung performances that distinguish those texts from everyday language; hence, he is concerned with the poetic expression found in Foi songs. These devices include parallelism, metaphor, poetic vocabulary, the construction of a map based upon the places mentioned in a song, phonological features reflecting motion and space, and 'hidden' names used to identify the subject of a song.

While a detailed consideration of Papua New Guinea song poetry is not appropriate here, the following overview of some of the poetic devices used is meant to assist readers interested in understanding how the Foi examples relate to other groups in the country. For what is probably the most detailed consideration of the song poetry of any one group, see Feld's writings on the Kaluli (especially, Feld 1982:130–62).

## Poetic language

In almost every source that discusses Papua New Guinea song texts, mention is made of the use of poetic language, either in reference to individual words or longer parts of the text. These might be words from specialised or less familiar vocabulary;[46] an archaic version of the present language; another dialect or language (perhaps, thereby, suggesting origin, trade, purchase, or prestige); the language of spirits or ghosts; or newly created words as the result of word taboos. Sometimes such poetic usage can be readily understood, but more often it appears to challenge and entice listeners.

This usage differs from that described in the following section for vocables in that the latter are not suggested to be from another language, but simply to fill out a line, hence they often fulfil a formal, musical function; there is no consideration of them having meaning aside from a functional one. Certain vocables might be associated with specific genres, but they are generally regarded as filler, necessary to complete a song, but not endowed with any other meaning.

Foi use poetic designations to reference villages (Weiner 1991:162), and the use of the 'hidden name' used to identify the subject in the *dawa* of *sorohabora* could also be considered poetic language.[47] Additionally, Duna poetry makes

---

46    Metaphorical meanings of everyday words are not considered here, but in the following section concerning modifications.

47    Weiner (1991:19–20) contrasts spells and songs. A spell's efficacy is related to its rote memorisation and recital, with the words often in esoteric language; whereas a song is always an individual composition in generally accessible language, attempting to rend an emotion or interior state in terms of a concrete object or sensual experience. Furthermore, the song evokes, but the spell does not. While the song produces direct emotional response, the spell seeks pragmatic transformation.

extensive use of *kẽiyaka*, glossed by researchers as 'praise names', special poetic terms that are used in *pikono* sung tales, often resulting in parallelism (see below) (Gillespie and San Roque 2011), and the Central Asmat use *arcer* (everyday speech) and *ta-poman* (poetic word or metaphor) in songs, with some of the latter terms coming from inland areas, but the origins of most are unknown (Voorhoeve 1977). What may be untranslatable to one researcher at one moment in time, may prove decipherable by someone else later, such as the Iatmul texts Bateson thought were in a shaman's language subsequently being clarified through the diligent, meticulous research of Wassmann (Bateson 1932:403–4, 407; Wassmann 1991:63–64, 230). While there are many statements by researchers that an archaic form of language is being used, it does not appear that historical linguists have attempted to validate such claims. In their songs, Trobriand Islanders use a variety of Kilivila language they call *biga baloma* 'speech of the spirits of the dead' or *biga tommwaya* 'old peoples' speech'. They are convinced that it is language of the spirits of the dead in the Tuma underworld and that it is an archaic variety of Kilivila; only a few elders still know the meanings of such songs (Senft 2011:43–48).

Modifications to sung texts in the learning process also bring about changes to song texts, particularly when the learners are not fluent in the original language of the song. Gunnar Landtman relates how Southern Kiwai speakers imitated a song they heard at Budji, an Agob-speaking village, eventually quite distorting the original text:

> they simply copy the dances and words, but, in spite of their natural cleverness in mimicry, both tunes and words must get more or less changed, still more so the interpretation which they may give to the songs. (Landtman 1927:423)

Neuhauss (1911:388) makes a similar observation about how the words of a song change when performers do not know the language they are singing in. Although specifically mentioning the Ka-iwa (Iwal) of Morobe province, he intends his remarks to be relevant over a much wider area. Indeed, writers had been noting the unintelligibility of song texts to their singers in the Morobe and Madang area for over two decades (e.g. Schmidt-Ernsthausen 1890:232; Pöch 1905).

Manambu *namai* love songs consist of two nearly identical stanzas (*apǝk*), the first in Manambu, the second in the western dialect of Iatmul, a language the singers are fluent in (Harrison 1982:18).[48] Kaluli *gisalo* makes extensive use of words,

---

48    According to Aikhenvald (2014), Manambu women refer to the second verse of their *namay* as using wording considered the 'shadowy' register or 'the other side' (*agǝkem* 'on the (other) side of two'). While many of these words in the 'shadowy' register derive from Iatmul, others may derive from Manambu itself as antonyms or more generalised terms being used for specific ones.

lines, or whole texts from the Sonia language to their west (E. L. Schieffelin 1976:178; Feld 1982:139–42, 152). In all areas, while the use of such language appears to make the texts more poetic, listeners differ in their ability to understand them. Even though the words of a song may not be completely understood, listeners are often adept at trying to interpret them anyway.

For the Gnau, song words are thought to be from ancestors, and the general sense of each verse is known, but words often differ from what is used now. For example, the word *simarei* in song is translated as 'it flares', but in everyday language the word *mərərə'a* has such a meaning. While the words are said to be archaic, song verses can be interpreted because words resemble those in neighbouring languages or even in Tok Pisin, and the names of places and persons are recognisable, but often distorted through much syllable repetition and drawing out (G. Lewis 1980:41, n. 1, 59). A fascinating discussion of such meanings and how they relate to the important question of the order of performance of around 150 songs in a Gnau song cycle is also presented by Gilbert Lewis (ibid.:60–61).

As songs are sung in unison by a group of performers in many regions, songs must be learned by the group, regardless of their intelligibility. Yet even if the meaning of the text remains generally unknown to performers, the numerous rehearsals and performances of such songs generate other meanings among the individuals who perform and who observe. Among the Lak (Siar-Lak) of southern New Ireland, this feeling is intensified as a result of the long periods of fasting and isolation necessary for performance, hence the 'opening lines of [such] a song are responded to by a barrage of weeping from the audience as they recall poignant associations generated by narratively "meaningless" lyrics' (Wolffram 2007:185).

Awiakay *kaunjambi* texts contain parts identifiable as everyday Awiakay, an untranslatable 'spirit language', neighbouring languages (some related to Awiakay, others not), and archaic language (Hoenigman in prep.).

The Gebusi (Gobasi) like the songs of their Bedamini (Beami) neighbours, although few Gebusi are fluent enough in that language to understand the poetry of songs. Rather, Gebusi react to the 'visual and raw auditory sensation of Bedamini performance, rather than to its discursive meaning' (Knauft 1985b:329).

## Vocables

A distinction was made in the preceding discussion between a song entirely of or containing words in a poetic or unknown language, on the one hand, and the use of vocables or 'nonsense syllables', on the other. The former might be described by performers as being in an archaic or different language, but the latter is often described as syllables added to fill out a melody. These vocables typically appear at the end of lines of sung text as lengthened or added vowels. More lengthy sequences of vocables may be used to fill in a text that does not fully accommodate a melody or as an entire section of the song, and may often be called a 'chorus' or 'refrain' by the author writing about them. Such vocables are particularly important where a repetitive metric system is important, such as in the Mount Hagen area. Vocables may also completely replace the 'meaningful' text in statements of the melody. In many of these uses, they are an essential structural component of song.

Lengthened or added vowels at the end of a line of text are found in many different parts of the country. Although frequently associated with the Highlands area, entire lines or verses of vocables are also found in areas as diverse as Jabêm (Yabem), Irumu (Tuma-Irumu), Gnau, Alamblak, Central Buang (Mapos Buang), Kaulong, and Akara (Lele). For example, Drüppel notes how in Kaulong songs, 'strings of lexically-meaningful words are interrupted by strings of vocables. These too are learned and are an integral, non-interchangeable part of the song' (2009:124). Chenoweth observes that Usarufa vocables 'beautify the words of a song' (1979:90). Baruya *daata*[49] consist of three sections: *daimaata* (vocables sung to establish the melody, repeated an indefinite number of times), *daluya* (addition of text to melody, repeated an indefinite number of times), and *daimaata* (as before, but sung only once to conclude the song).

What is then striking about the Foi texts presented here is the relative absence of such non-lexical syllables—Foi song texts appear to be predominantly in the language of everyday discourse. Other comparable examples are not so commonly reported, although Fortune stresses the absence of 'meaningless word[s]' in Dobu songs (1932:255). And, as in the Iatmul case cited above, but also true for Central Asmat songs (Voorhoeve 1977:27, n. 26), seemingly incomprehensible songs might actually be translatable.

Yet the contrast between texts of vocables and of other languages is not quite so easily maintained as it can sometimes be difficult to differentiate the two. Generally, melodies sung to vowels with few consonants unequivocally tend to be vocables, but it is also possible to imagine words sung in a language not understood by the performers gradually becoming distorted (as in the Landtman story above), so that a text in a different language finally becomes vocables. And certainly 'nonsense' syllables sung during the sixth and final stage of Wovan (Haruai) initiation (*aime*) are loaded with meaning for participants and onlookers alike (Flanagan 1983:217).

---

49    See Niles and Webb (1987:EHP-8) for a recording performed by males sitting in the initiate's house.

## Repetition

Although not often identified, songs frequently involve strict repetition of words, phrases, or lines. Additionally, of course, whole songs are often repeated in the course of the same or different performances. As this deviates from normal speech, I also consider it a poetic device. Repetition has been reported from such widely separated groups as Enga, Wiru, Benabena, Southern Kiwai, Central Buang (Mapos Bunag), and Baining (Qaqet).

## Parallelism

In my usage here, parallelism is related to repetition, but instead of being a strict repetition, it involves change. Rumsey (1995:108; 2007:261) describes parallelism as 'the ordered interplay of repetition and variation'; it is a very common poetic feature found in all regions of Papua New Guinea (Niles 2011b:70–72, 413–14, 496–97; Niles and Rumsey 2011:13, n. 9) and throughout the world (Jakobson 1960; Fox 1977). For Papua New Guinea song texts, parallelism (also called substitution), most frequently involves the change of one or more words in the repetition of a line or lines. For example, in the opening of a Iatmul song where pairs of totemic names are sung:

> —m kan wana nyan-a –i–e
> kumbui Kumbuindemineli- a-la –i–e, –e–e
> kan wuna mbaandi-a –i–e
> kumbui Kwalimbangimeli- –i–e, –e–e

> You my child,
> you flying fox Kumbuindemineli;
> you my novice,
> you flying fox Kwalimbangimeli. (Wassmann 1991:3–4)

Comparable mythic references are also found among Manambu *namai* in what purport to be the more mundane songs of failed relationships (Harrison 1982; 1986).

Foi songs use parallelism extensively, as can be seen in looking at the song texts in this volume.[50] For example, in this excerpt of lexical and semantic parallelism from men's song 38:

> nomo ira fiwa dera
> forabi'ae
> nomo ira furabo dera
> foramaibi'ae

---

50  Also note the semantic parallelism of Foi magic spells (Weiner 1991:16–17) and Ambonwari (Tabriak) songs (Telban 2008:227).

*nomo kosa'a buru ga merabe*
*kigiboba'a*
*nomo ira furubu ga merabe*
*aodoboba'a*

My *fiwa* tree there
Has fallen by itself
My *furabo* tree there
Has fallen down

My harbour near the base of the *kosa'a buru* tree
The forest has reclaimed it
My harbour near the base of the *furubu* tree
The bush has obliterated it

Some of the most extensive uses of parallelism are found in Kaulong songs of West New Britain where the initial 'chorus listing' of a song enumerates names or objects having the lowest level of appreciation; each repeat of a line substitutes a different name or object, ending with that most highly regarded (Drüppel 2009:126; also see, Niles 2009:xvii–xviii). As described above, the Duna use of *kẽiyaka* also results in parallelism, as does Central Asmat use of *arcer* and *ta-poman*.

Grammatical parallelism has also been described by Rumsey for Ku Waru (Bo-Ung) *tom yaya kange* performances. Here, distinctive grammatical structures, not words, are repeated in subsequent lines (Rumsey 2007:263–64).

## Modification

Song texts may also be modified versions of normal spoken language. Such modifications can be phonological, grammatical, or semantic.

At a phonological level, vowels or consonants may be altered from their everyday values. As noted by Telban (2008:219) for the Ambonwari (Tabriak), but certainly very widely applicable, the words of a song may be 'merely indicated and not fully articulated', thereby setting them apart from everyday language and adding to their esoteric nature. That is, sounds are altered simply through singing. Chenoweth (1979:97) notes the 'broader phonetic range in singing than in speaking' for Usarufa. In Takū (Takuu) songs, an *a* often changes to *o*, so that *vaka* 'canoe' becomes *voko*, and *ava* 'channel' becomes *ovo* (Moyle 2007:174). In Central Asmat songs, voiceless consonants become voiced, and some stops become fricatives (p > β; k > ɣ) (Voorhoeve 1977:35, n. 7). Laycock (1969c) notes the use of archaic morphology in Buin (Terei) songs.

Vowels are often lengthened or added to the final word, thereby overlapping with the vocables discussed above. But syllables may also be added mid-word, such as in Central Buang (Mapos Buang) modifications *verup* > *veröörup* 'come up' (Hooley 1987:76).

Some of the most elaborate word transformations have been described for Buin (Terei) songs (Laycock 1969c:6–13), where two syllables are added to the first or last two syllables of a normal word, creating a form suitable for songs; or the two syllables from a normal word might be reduplicated. For example: *kugunia* > *niakoto* 'Venus'; *maikuna* > *kunapiŋ* 'dog'; *kamuai* > *kamukamu* 'man's name'. Other transformations are also possible. Brown (1968:iii) remarks how words can be divided between musical phrases, and Roberts (1996; 2014) notes the alteration of words to fit melodies.

Phonemes, syllables, or words can also be deleted, all contributing to the 'telegraphic brevity' of Daribi (Dadibi) *bạria* dance songs and laments (Wagner 1972:80), an apt description also applicable to many other traditions.

The deletion of words, of course, overlaps with modifications at the grammatical level. The texts of West Kewa songs, for example, have shortened verbs, with many tenses and aspects deleted, thereby making the actor obscure and possibly obliterating subject, location, and goal markers (Franklin 1978:392). Rumsey (2007:261) observes the use of shorter syntactic units in Ku Waru (Bo-Ung) sung tales. Often, however, written descriptions of grammatical modifications are less precise, with authors noting an unspecific type of poetic grammar or grammatical changes.

Semantic modification concerns words taking on new meanings or interpretations. Such use of metaphors in song texts is used by the Foi (e.g. Weiner 1988a:126; 1991:19, 28; 1998a) and is widely reported for Papua New Guinea. As LeRoy (1978:71, n. 6) stresses, a metaphorical language is not a different one, but is constructed from everyday language. Understanding such meanings is often challenging to listeners who lack special knowledge about poetic usage.[51] Furthermore, in those areas requiring initiation to different types of knowledge, secret subjects may also be sung about publicly, hidden by metaphors that make their meaning inaccessible to those without the requisite knowledge.

## Sound-play

By 'sound-play' I refer to various ways the sounds of words are combined in song texts. Examples of the general similarity between the vowels of words

---

51    Weiner (1991:28) contrasts the images in poetry with those in dream interpretation. While the latter are standardised, poetic images are individually created, so their interpretation is dependent upon the knowledge of the creating poet.

(assonance) or consonants of words (consonance; with alliteration being a subtype) are occasionally noted, but not frequently. For example, the pairing of words such as *eklka / maklka, röngim / röngan, rarla / marla, nginouö / minouö*, and *ekita / ronggeta* in Melpa songs (A. Strathern and Stewart 2005:208–9). The Foi use of phonological features reflecting motion and space might also be included here (Weiner 1991:80–87).

Rhyme—similar sounds at the end of words or lines—while used occasionally in *obedobora* and *sorohabora*, is generally rare in Foi song (Weiner 1991:134, 170). This also seems to be true for most other groups in Papua New Guinea, with few exceptions.

What can be considered another type of sound-play, onomatopoeia or phonaesthesia, is an important aspect of Kaluli song composition, as reported by Feld (1978:15–16; 1982:144–50).

## Mapping

Finally, the mapping of places mentioned in a song is of great importance for the Foi (Weiner 1998a:105–6) and the Kaluli (Feld 1978:15–16; 1982:150–56), but also for groups such as the Gnau (G. Lewis 1980:59–67). Weiner observes that 'Mountain Papuan' peoples, such as the Kaluli and Foi, poetically depict genealogical relationships as spatial ones between place names (1988b:23). Ayamo place names figure prominently in Foi songs as they evoke pleasant memories of hunting during the wet season. Yet as they are removed from the Mubi Valley, they are also associated with death (Weiner 1991:114). Kaluli songs map out lands, waters, and trees of significance to their hosts. These images of loss and abandonment move them to tears and they burn with a torch the dancer responsible for evoking their grief (Feld 1985:3).

In contrast, the place names in Gebusi (Gobasi) songs are rarely of the hosts' lands, rather they are of distant places felt to be ideal for secret encounters and sexual trysts. Gebusi respond to these songs sung by women not with weeping and burning, but with

> an enthusiastic and bawdy expression of sexual vitality. Hosts and visitors joke hilariously, fantasizing how they will bring to fruition the sexual scenario evoked by the beautiful dancer and the women's seductive songs. (Knauft 1985b:325)

While this overview of poetic devices has been very brief and deserves to be fleshed out elsewhere, it describes some of the ways in which texts become sung poetry for the Foi and other groups in Papua New Guinea.

# Closing and acknowledgements

I hope that these introductory remarks will be of assistance to someone wanting to understand more about the Foi songs presented in this volume. In particular, I have tried to bring together some details about the contexts of their performance, their relation to other genres in the region, the importance of song texts to anthropological studies, and the poetry of song in the Papua New Guinea area.

I also hope that this book, in combination with other writings by Weiner, will help reveal the importance of understanding Foi traditional modes of expression. As contemporary Papua New Guinea faces many challenges and some people feel that traditional beliefs hinder the nation on the path towards development, this study strongly reconfirms the importance of understanding such creativity. This book celebrates Foi traditional knowledge and the wonderful, full, and complex world that is revealed in song.

James Weiner sent me an initial draft of his manuscript in 1995. I was initially enthusiastic about its possible publication, but suggested he expand the introduction to more widely consider song traditions in the country. In retrospect, I realise that that was probably a rather scary, off-putting response, no doubt contributing to the manuscript lying dormant for a long stretch of time. Early in 2012, his manuscript and the insights it contained still haunted me. I felt that it must be made more widely available, so I contacted James to see if he was still interested in pursuing its publication. Happily, it was also something that remained important to him, so we began to work together to bring it to its present form, with me taking on the task of expansion I originally suggested he do: considering other song traditions, song collections, and the sung poetry of songs as part of an introduction to the songs. I very much appreciate James's continuing enthusiasm for these songs and his desire to publish them, even after two decades. It has been a pleasure to collaborate with him.

Other individuals and organisations have enabled this project to proceed. In addition to providing the research environment necessary to work on this book, the Institute of Papua New Guinea Studies enabled Edward Gende and me to observe and document the Kundu and Digaso Festival and to experience some aspects of Foi music and dance first-hand, especially with Hahudi Farobo as our gracious and expert guide and teacher.

In my position as Research Associate in the Department of Anthropology, School of Culture, History, and Language, College of Asia and the Pacific at The Australian National University, I have had access to the wonderful electronic resources available through their libraries. I also appreciate comments by Steven

Feld in reconfirming and expanding my understanding about how Bosavi *sabio* relates to other Kaluli genres stylistically. David Gardiner and Emily Tinker at ANU Press have greatly assisted in the production of this book.

Weiner's research materials are deposited in The Australian National University Archives (Series 432: http://archivescollection.anu.edu.au/index.php/james-f-weiners-cassettes). Nick Thieberger at the Pacific and Regional Archive for Digital Sources in Endangered Cultures (PARADISEC) kindly arranged the digitisation of Weiner's recordings, so that a representative sample could be made available for this publication. Weiner's full collection of digitised recordings can be found at: http://catalog.paradisec.org.au/repository/JW1.

I am most grateful for the support from all concerned.

# Women's Sago Songs (*Obedobora*)

## Sago Song 1[1]

### Singer: Mu'ubiaka. Recorded 18 October 1980 at Hegeso village.

As I explained in *The Empty Place*, this song addresses the sun as a young girl, skipping down the sky. 'Don't set too quickly, Miss, I still have much work to do!' the singer is saying. (See Weiner 1991:120–26; for a textually simplified version of this song, see ibid. 1988a:134; finally, ibid. 1991:148–50 shows a transcription of this simplified version in Western music notation.) ♫ online example 1.

| | | | | | |
|---|---|---|---|---|---|
| 1. | *ira* wood | *abu-o*[2] mallet | | | |
| 2. | *biri* here | *huie* strike | | | |
| 3. | *ira* wood | *ka* woman | *wasa* mallet | | |
| 4. | *biri* here | *huma'ae* strike | | | |
| 5. | *duma* mountain | *haro* climbing | *hubu* struck | *kaboneo* Miss | *owa* owa |
| 6. | *meye* not yet | *wa'ayo'o* do not come | *owa* owa | | |
| 7. | *duma* mountain | *oro* top | *hubu* struck | *kabonere* Miss | *owa* owa |

---

1  The naming and numbering of songs here follows that used in *The Empty Place* (Weiner 1991). References to particular songs in that volume and other publications by Weiner are included in the notes prefacing the song texts.

2  The orthography used here is based on that initially developed by missionary linguist Murray Rule. For further details, see publications by Weiner (1988a:xvii–xviii; 1991:xi–xii) and Rule (1993:23–25). In particular, note that the apostrophe represents a glottal stop and that tildes indicate nasalisation of the vowels to which they are attached (ã, ẽ, ĩ, õ, ũ).

8.  *meye*       *wa'ayo'o*            *owa*
    not yet     do not come          *owa*

9.  *meye*       *wamone*             *owa*
    not yet     do not come          *owa*

10. *ibu*        *busu*               *humekerabo*   *kabonere*   *owa*
    river       dappled light        strike + put   Miss         *owa*

11. *meye*       *wa'ayo'o*            *owa*
    not yet     do not come          *owa*

12. *ibu*        *hohotogabo*         *kabo*         *na-o*       *owa*
    river       mirror               girl           I too        *owa*

13. *meye*       *wamone*             *owa*
    not yet     do not come          *owa*

14. *duma*       *humegenemodobo*     *kabonere*     *owa*
    mountain    to make dark         Miss           *owa*

15. *meye*       *wa'ayo'o*            *owa*
    not yet     do not come          *owa*

16. *ibu*        *anogo*              *hamayibu*     *kabonereo*  *owa*
    river       fish net             to have gaps   Miss         *owa*

17. *meya*       *wamona*             *owa*
    not yet     do not come          *owa*

18. *ibu*        *gikoba*             *humogoreye*   *ubu*        *kabonera*   *owa*
    river       butterflies          to scatter     go           Miss         *owa*

19. *meye*       *wa'ayo'o*            *owa*
    not yet     do not come          *owa*

20. *duma*       *haro*               *hubu*         *kabo*       *na'a*       *owa*
    mountain    climbing             struck         girl         you          *owa*

21. *meye*       *wamone*             *owa*
    not yet     do not come          *owa*

22. *meyere*     *eya*
    not yet     *eya*

| 23. | *nomo* | *ira* | *kabiri* | *ma'oyo'o* | *eya* |
|---|---|---|---|---|---|
| | my | tree | kabiri mallet | to take | *eya* |

| 24. | *meya'are* | *eya* |
|---|---|---|
| | not yet | *eya* |

| 25. | *gi* | *soboye* | *owa* |
|---|---|---|---|
| | ground | there | *owa* |

| 26. | *duma* | *haru* | *huaye* | *eya* |
|---|---|---|---|---|
| | mountain | hill | to leave | *eya* |

| 27. | *meya'a* | *umone* | *eya* |
|---|---|---|---|
| | not yet | do not go | *eya* |

| 28. | *ibu* | *damani* | *fufae* | *eya* |
|---|---|---|---|---|
| | river | Danimi | to fly | *eya* |

| 29. | *meya'a* | *o'oyo'o* | *eya* |
|---|---|---|---|
| | not yet | do not go | *eya* |

| 30. | *duma* | *sonobo* | *kigiri* | *hesae* | *eya* |
|---|---|---|---|---|---|
| | mountain | Yafua | base | to follow | *eya* |

| 31. | *meya'a* | *o'oyo'o* | *eya* |
|---|---|---|---|
| | not yet | do not go | *eya* |

| 32. | *duma* | *kanawebi* | *hesae* | *eya* |
|---|---|---|---|---|
| | mountain | Kagiri | to follow | *eya* |

| 33. | *meya* | *umona* | *eya* |
|---|---|---|---|
| | not yet | do not go | *eya* |

| 34. | *duma* | *gara* | *u'ubi* | *kigiri* | *hesae* | *eya* |
|---|---|---|---|---|---|---|
| | mountain | orphan | child | base | to follow | *eya* |

| 35. | *meya* | *o'oyo'o* | *eya* |
|---|---|---|---|
| | not yet | do not go | *eya* |

| 36. | *ibu* | *webiga* | *fufae* | *eya* |
|---|---|---|---|---|
| | river | Webi source | to fly | *eya* |

| 37. | *meye* | *umona* | *eya* |
|---|---|---|---|
| | not yet | do not go | *eya* |

38. *ira*          *tegare*        *gifubi-e*      *eya*
    tree          ko'oya          canopy          eya

39. *meya*         *degamone*      *eye*
    not yet        to hide         eye

40. *oro*          *yiyebi*        *oro*           *huae*          *eye*
    bamboo         small           top             strike          eye

41. *meye*         *o'oyo'o*       *dobo'o*        *eya*
    not yet        do not go       spoken          eya

42. *bi*           *yebimahone*    *eya*
    here           do not leave    eya

43. *kui*          *tuba*          *foraye*        *ma'ayo'o*      *eye*
    sago           hand            broken          to take         eye

44. *meya*         *o'oyo'o*       *eye*
    not yet        do not go       eye

45. *kui*          *hufuruwa*      *ma'ayo'o*      *eye*
    sago           to break apart  to take         eye

46. *ai*           *meya'are*      *eye*
    ai!            not yet         eye

47. *kui*          *ka'abe*        *ma'ayo'o*      *eye*
    sago           difficult       to take         eye

48. *meya'a*       *o'oyo'o*       *eye*
    not yet        do not go       eye

49. *kui*          *tirarudia*     *ma'ayo'o*      *eye*
    sago           to bundle       to take         eye

50. *meya'a*       *o'oyo'o*       *eye*
    not yet        do not go       eye

51. *kui*          *ka'abe*        *ma'oyo'o*      *eye*
    sago           difficult       to take         eye

52. *meye*         *umona*         *eye*
    not yet        do not go       eye

| 53. | *ibu* | *kosega* | *hubagiae* | *eye* |
|---|---|---|---|---|
| | river | phlegm | to spread | eye |

| 54. | *meye* | *umona* | *eye* |
|---|---|---|---|
| | not yet | do not go | eye |

| 55. | *ibu* | *hemomo'o* | *bagiae* | *eye* |
|---|---|---|---|---|
| | river | flotsam | to spread | eye |

| 56. | *meye* | *yebihamone* | *eye* |
|---|---|---|---|
| | not yet | to leave | eye |

1. Oh sago mallet

2. Strike this sago quickly

3. Miss Sago Mallet

4. Beat this sago quickly

5. You strike the mountain side as you set, Miss

6. Do not fall so quickly

7. You strike the top of the mountain as you sink

8. Do not fall yet

9. Do not come yet

10. You reflect in dappled sparkle off the river

11. Do not fall so quickly

12. You reflect off the river like my image, girl

13. Do not come yet

14. The mountain turns dark as you set, girl

15. Do not come yet

16. You shine through the holes in the fishing nets

17. Do not come yet

18. You scatter the butterflies on the river, Miss

19. Do not fall yet

20. You strike the side of the mountain as you fall

21. Do not come so quickly

22. Do not come yet

23. I still have to hold my mallet, girl

24. Not yet, girl!

25. Don't make this ground dark yet, girl

26. Don't leave this mountain yet, girl

27. Don't go yet

28. You fly down the Danimi Creek

29. Don't go yet

30. You fall towards the bottom of Mt Yafua

31. Don't leave me yet!

32. You follow the bottom of Mt Kagiri

33. Do not go yet

34. You follow the bottom of Mt Kagiri

35. Don't go yet

36. You fly towards the head of Webi Creek

37. Don't go yet

38. You shine through the top of the ko'oya tree

39. Don't hide from me yet

40. Shining through the bamboos on the mountain top

41. Don't go, I say

42. Don't leave me here

43. I have to still beat sago

44. Do not go yet

45. I have to bundle my sago up

46. Ai! Do not go yet

47. I have to wrap my sago

48. Do not go yet

49. I have to wrap up my sago

50. Do not go yet

51. I have a lot of work to do

52. Do not go yet

53. You spread along the river surface like froth

54. Do not go yet

55. You sparkle off the river flotsam

56. Do not leave me yet

---

# Sago Song 2

## Singer: Kunuhuaka. Recorded 26 November 1980 at Hegeso village.

A woman, angry that her husband berates her for not working, rebukes him in the following sago song. (Figure 2 in this volume is a music transcription of lines 10–14.) ♫ online example 2.

| | | | | | |
|---|---|---|---|---|---|
| 1. | *kare*<br>women's | *kui*<br>sago | *ini*<br>cook | *dobo'o*<br>spoken | *owa*<br>*owa* |
| 2. | *nena'a*<br>no reason | *doma'ae*<br>say | *owa*<br>*owa* | | |
| 3. | *wana'aro*<br>evening | *kui*<br>sago | *ini*<br>cook | *dobo'o*<br>spoken | *owa*<br>*owa* |
| 4. | *kama*<br>no reason | *doma'ae*<br>say | *eye*<br>*eye* | | |
| 5. | *nari*<br>*nari* pitpit | *hirima*<br>plant | *diburo*<br>talk | *owa*<br>*owa* | |
| 6. | *nena*<br>no reason | *doma'ae*<br>say | *owa*<br>*owa* | | |
| 7. | *senage*<br>*senage* pitpit | *hirima*<br>plant | *dibure*<br>said | *owa*<br>*owa* | |
| 8. | *kama*<br>mind | *dee*<br>say | *eye*<br>*eye* | | |

9. *dimu*    *hirima*    *dibure*    *oye*
    *dimu* pitpit    plant    said    *oye*

10. *kama*    *doma'ae*    *eye*
    mind    tell    *eye*

11. *sona*    *iburi*    *hirima*    *dibure*    *owa*
    *sona*    *iburi*    plant    said    *owa*

12. *nena'a*    *dee*    *eye*
    no reason    say    *eye*

13. *wãsia*    *diamoro*    *hirima*    *dibure*    *owa*
    pitpit    *diamoro*    plant    said    *owa*

14. *kama*    *doma'ae*    *eye*
    mind    tell    *eye*

15. *u'ubi*    *kama*    *ere*    *dibure*    *owa*
    children    female    mind    said    *owa*

16. *nena'a*    *doma'ae*    *doba'abe*    *eye*
    no reason    tell    should say    *eye*

17. *ira*    *do'a*    *ga*    *nereye*    *dibure*    *owa*
    tree    *do'a*    base    burn    said    *owa*

18. *kama'a*    *dee*    *eye*
    know    say    *eye*

19. *ira*    *ubi*    *ga*    *nereye*    *dibure*    *owa*
    tree    *ubi*    base    burn    said    *owa*

20. *nena'a*    *doma'ae*    *eye*
    no reason    say    *eye*

21. *ira*    *senage*    *ga*    *kea*    *diburo*    *owa*
    tree    *senage*    base    burn    talk    *owa*

22. *nena'a*    *doba'abe*    *eye*
    no reason    should say    *eye*

23. *ira*    *homono*    *ga*    *nareye*    *diburo*    *owa*
    tree    *homono*    base    burn    talk    *owa*

24. *kama'a*     *dee*     *eye*
     know     say     eye

25. *buru*     *kirari*     *ma*     *dibure*     *owa*
     black     rope     take     said     owa

26. *nena'a*     *doma'ae*     *eye*
     no reason     say     eye

27. *gãbu*     *kirari*     *ma*     *dibure*     *owa*
     piebald     rope     take     said     owa

28. *nena'a*     *dee*     *eye*
     no reason     say     eye

29. *wana'ari*     *kui*     *ini*     *dibure*     *owa*
     mid-day     sago     cook     said     owa

30. *kama'a*     *doma'ae*     *eye*
     know     tell     eye

31. *kusu*     *u'ubi*     *era*     *diburo*     *owa*
     cross-cousin     children     mind     talk     owa

32. *nena'a*     *dee*     *eye*
     no reason     say     eye

33. *ba'a*     *ga*     *kui*     *ini*     *dibureo*     *owa*
     boy     belongs to     sago     cook     spoken     owa

34. *nena'a*     *to*     *iba'ae*     *eye*
     no reason     this     is     eye

35. *magoro*     *kui*     *ini*     *diburo*     *owa*
     young man     sago     cook     talk     owa

36. *nena'a*     *dee*     *eye*
     no reason     say     eye

37. *ibu*     *viri*     *diburo*     *owa*
     water     fill up     talk     owa

38. *nena'a*     *doma'ae*     *eye*
     no reason     tell     eye

| 39. | *kumi* | *ka* | *era* | *dibure* | *owa* |
|-----|--------|------|-------|----------|-------|
|     | cross-cousin | wife | mind | said | *owa* |

| 40. | *nena'ae* | *dee* | *eye* |
|-----|-----------|-------|-------|
|     | for no reason | say | *eye* |

| 41. | *kuidobo* | *sa'abiyumo* | *owa* |
|-----|-----------|--------------|-------|
|     | kuidobo | Sa'abiyu | *owa* |

| 42. | *hua* | *mohũgaiye* | *eye* |
|-----|-------|-------------|-------|
|     | killed | discarded | *eye* |

| 43. | *yuaka* | *iribinunemo* | *owa* |
|-----|---------|---------------|-------|
|     | Yuaka | Iribinu | *owa* |

| 44. | *humofo'owaiye* | *eye* |
|-----|-----------------|-------|
|     | killed and thrown away | *eye* |

1.  'Cook my evening sago!' you say

2.  Without a care, you order me

3.  'Cook my quick sago!' you say

4.  For no reason you tell me

5.  Go plant the *nari* pitpit

6.  For no reason, tell me!

7.  Go plant the *senage* pitpit

8.  Thoughtlessly, you command me

9.  Go plant the *dimu* pitpit

10. Tell me you have a reason!

11. Go plant the *sona iburi* leaves, you say

12. Tell me for no reason

13. Go plant the *diamoro* pitpit, you say

14. You thoughtlessly tell me

15. Feed our little girls, you say

16. Without a care must you tell me

17. Burn the base of the *do'a* tree, you say

18. Tell me what you want

19. Burn the base of the *ubi* tree, you say

20. For no reason, tell me!

21. Burn the base of the *senage* tree, you say

22. You should tell me for no reason?

23. Burn the base of the *homono* tree, you say

24. You should tell me what you are thinking

25. Take the rope of the black pig, you say

26. For no reason, you tell me!

27. Take the rope of the piebald pig, you say

28. For no reason, you say to me

29. Cook my quick sago, you order me

30. Tell me what you are thinking

31. Mind your little cross-cousins, you say

32. For no reason, tell me

33. Mind your sister's child, you tell me

34. Is this for reason you say

35. Cook sago for the young men, you say

36. Say what you are thinking

37. Fetch water, you say

38. For no reason, tell me

39. Fetch water for your cross-cousins' wives, you say

40. For no reason, tell me

41. The Kuidobo man, Sa'abiyumo

42. Killed and left in the bush

43. His wife, Yuaka, daughter of Iribinu

44. Killed and thrown away

# Sago Song 3

## Singer: Gebo. Recorded 18 October 1980 at Hegeso village.

Gebo, an elderly widow, sang this song about her deceased husband, Kigiri. She recalls the places where her husband made traps, cut wood grubs, and dammed small creeks for fish. Because he can no longer go there, the bush and forest have obliterated the signs of human intervention. The final lines reference their two deceased children (although there were three other children living at the time). The lines also note that although Kigiri was genealogically of a So'onedobo clan lineage, he was adopted by the Orodobo clan and his children were also Orodobo. (See Weiner 1988a:132.) ♫ online example 3.

| | | | | | | |
|---|---|---|---|---|---|---|
| 1. | *ba'a* | *na'a* | *ira* | *sabe* | *hŭga* | *owe* |
| | boy | your | tree | sabe | larvae | owe |
| 2. | *aoda'ae* | | *owe* | | | |
| | bush covered up | | owe | | | |
| 3. | *ba'a* | *na'a* | *ira* | *dabi* | *bu'uni* | *derege* | *eya* |
| | boy | your | tree | dabi | deadfall | teach | eya |
| 4. | *kigiboba'ae* | | *owe* | | | |
| | tree covered | | owe | | | |
| 5. | *ba'a* | *na'a* | *sumaniyo* | *ibu* | *eya* | |
| | boy, | your | Sumani | Creek | eya | |
| 6. | *kigiboba'ae* | | *owe* | | | |
| | tree covered | | owe | | | |
| 7. | *ba'a* | *na'a* | *agegenebo* | *ibu* | *eya* | |
| | boy, | your | Agegenebo | Creek | eya | |
| 8. | *aoda'ae* | | *owe* | | | |
| | bush covered up | | owe | | | |
| 9. | *ba'a* | *na'a* | *gagihimu* | *ibu* | *eya* | |
| | boy | your | Gagihimu | Creek | eya | |

10. *kigiboba'ae*            *owe*
     tree covered            *owe*

11. *ba'a*       *na'a*       *yafua*       *duma*       *owe*
     boy         your        Yafua        mountain    *owe*

12. *ira*        *waboba'ae*          *owe*
     bush       has covered it up     *owe*

13. *ba'a*       *na'a*       *ira*         *waria*       *bu'uni*      *owe*
     boy         your        tree        *waria*       deadfall    *owe*

14. *aoda'ae*            *owe*
     bush covered up        *owe*

15. *agegenebo*    *ibu*       *owe*
     Agegenebo     Creek     *owe*

16. *aoda'ae*            *owe*
     bush covered up        *owe*

17. *ferorohimu*    *ibu*       *owe*
     Ferorohimu    Creek     *owe*

18. *kigiboba'ae*            *owe*
     tree covered            *owe*

19. *yahadenabo*    *ibu*       *owe*
     Yahadenabo    Creek     *owe*

20. *aoda'ae*            *owe*
     bush covered up        *owe*

21. *gorega*      *ibu*       *owe*
     Gorega      Creek     *owe*

22. *aoda'ae*            *owe*
     bush covered up        *owe*

23. *orodobo*    *ka*        *fumaruwame*   *ma'ame*    *eya*
     Orodobo    woman    Fumaruwame   thing      *eya*

24. *ba'a*       *aruweye*    *owe*
     boy         Aruweye    *owe*

| 25. | *ira* | *so'onedobo* | *bugimena* | *ma'ame* | *eya* |
|-----|-------|--------------|------------|----------|-------|
|     | line  | So'onedobo   | Bugimena   | thing    | *eya* |

| 26. | *kigiri-a* | *owe* |
|-----|-----------|-------|
|     | Kigiri    | owe   |

1. Boy, your *sabe* tree wood grubs

2. The bush has covered them up

3. Boy, the place where you showed [others] where you made your *dabi* tree traps

4. The bush has covered them up

5. Boy, your Sumani Creek

6. The bush has covered it up

7. Boy, your Agegenebo Creek

8. The bush has covered it up

9. Boy, your Gagihimu Creek

10. The bush has covered it up

11. Boy, your Yafua Mountain

12. The bush has covered it up

13. Boy, your *waria* tree deadfall

14. The bush has covered it up

15. Agegenebo Creek

16. The bush has covered it up

17. Ferorohimu Creek

18. The bush has covered it up

19. Yahadenabo Creek

20. The bush has covered it up

21. Gorega Creek

22. The bush has covered it up

23. (My) deceased Orodobo clan daughter Fumaruwame

24. (My) deceased son Aruweye

---

# Sago Song 4

## Singer: Kunuhuaka. Recorded 26 November 1980 at Hegeso village.

As I described in *The Empty Place*, Kunuhuaka's mother taught her this song. She composed it once when she was at Ayamo and her son Ta'anobo became lost. She called out to him at the places she searched for him, but only heard the sound of the birds calling, *i! i! wo! wo!* (See Weiner 1988a:132–33; 1991:20–22.) ♫ online example 4.

| | | | | | | |
|---|---|---|---|---|---|---|
| 1. | *me* | *huraro* | *ya* | *sisiyo* | *eye* | |
| | place | empty | bird | *sisiyo* | *eye* | |
| 2. | *me* | *odo'oiye* | | *eye* | | |
| | speech | cannot speak | | *eye* | | |
| 3. | *duma* | *hau* | *me* | *ya* | *u-o* | *eya* |
| | mountain | side | place | bird | *u* | *eye* |
| 4. | *me* | *odibikerayiye* | | *owa* | | |
| | speech | does not speak | | *owa* | | |
| 5. | *kui* | *yamo* | *ya* | *sisiye* | *eye* | |
| | sago | *yamo* | bird | *sisiyu* | *eye* | |
| 6. | *megenebo* | *deyiye* | | | | |
| | you only | do not speak | | | | |
| 7. | *kui* | *gabe* | *ya* | *muri-e* | *eye* | |
| | sago | *gabe* | bird | *muri* | *eye* | |
| 8. | *na'abo* | *deyiye* | | | | |
| | to you | do not speak | | | | |
| 9. | *ibu* | *ama'afu* | *geno* | *ya* | *sisiye* | |
| | creek | Ama'afu | river bend | bird | *sisiyu* | |

15

10. *nebo*      *deyiye*
    you alone   do not speak

11. *ibu*      *firigiri*     *tage*      *ya*      *u*
    creek      Firigiri      mouth      bird      *u*

12. *megenebo*   *deyiye*
    you only     do not speak

13. *ibu*      *segenabi*     *ya*      *u*
    creek      Segenabi      bird      *u*

14. *ne*      *odibikerayiye*
    you       do not speak

15. *ibu*      *saburuba*     *ya*      *muri-o*
    creek      Saburaba      bird      *muri*

16. *ne*      *odeyiye*
    you       do not speak

17. *ibu*      *dãri*      *ya*      *sisiye*
    creek      Dãri      bird      *sisiyu*

18. *ne*      *odeyiye*
    you       do not speak

19. *duma*     *sobore*     *kigiri*
    mountain   Sobore      base

20. *megene*    *odeyiye*
    you only     do not call out

21. *ibu*      *guratõa*     *tage*      *ya*      *u*
    creek      Guratõa      mouth      bird      *u*

22. *ne*      *odibikerayiye*
    you       do not call out

23. *kui*      *dãre*      *ya*      *sisiye-o*
    sago      *dãre*      bird      *sisiyu*

24. *ne*      *odibikiribubiye*
    you       do not speak out

25. *kui*      *yamo*      *ya*       *sisiye-o*
    sago      *yamo*      bird       *sisiyu*

26. *na'a*     *odeyiye*
    you       do not speak

27. *yegena*   *ya*        *muri-o*
    Yegena    bird        *muri*

28. *ne*       *odeyiye*
    you       do not call out

29. *sui*      *geroa*     *ya*       *muri-o*
    cane      *gerewa*    bird       *muri*

30. *ne*       *odeyiye*
    you       do not call out

31. *yegena*   *awa*       *ya*       *sisiye*
    Yegena    empty place bird       *sisiyu*

32. *mero*     *odo'oyiye*
    another   cannot call out

33. *duma*     *weyeru*    *ya*       *muri-o*
    mountain  Weyeru      bird       *muri*

34. *na*       *odibihayiye*
    you       do not call out

35. *ibu*      *ĩsa*       *ya*       *yiyo*
    creek     *Ĩsa*       bird       *yiyo*

36. *nere*     *odibihayiye*
    you alone do not call out

37. *ibu*      *dãri*      *ya*       *muri-o*
    creek     Dãri        bird       *muri*

38. *na'abore* *deyiye*
    you only  do not speak

39. *aboragemo* *ya*       *u*
    Aboragemo  bird        *u*

40. *nebo*      *dibihayiye*
    you alone   do not speak

41. *abu*       *biri-o*
    mallet      this

42. *a'a*       *huma'ae*
    quickly     strike

43. *ta'anobo*   *ma'ame*   *odibua*
    Ta'anobo     thing      calls out

44. *dibikerage*
    keeps calling out

45. *ya*        *ya'oe*      *ma'ame*   *diburo*
    bird        namesake     thing      talk

46. *dibihage*
    keeps calling out

1.  In this uninhabited place I hear the *sisiyu* bird

2.  But I hear no men

3.  The mountain side, the *u* bird

4.  But I hear no men's speech

5.  At the place of the *yamo* sago, the *sisiyu* bird

6.  But you only I hear not

7.  Where the *gabe* sago is, the *muri* bird

8.  But to me you do not speak

9.  At the bend in Ama'afu Creek, the *sisiyu* bird

10. But you alone do not speak

11. At the mouth of the Fifigiri Creek, the *u* bird

12. But you alone speak not

13. At Segenabi Creek, the *u* bird

14. But you do not call out

15. At Saburuba Creek, the *muri* bird

16. But you do not speak

17. At Dãri Creek, the *sisiyu* bird

18. But you do not speak

19. At the base of Mt Sobore

20. You only do not call out

21. At the mouth of Guratõa Creek, the *u* bird

22. But you do not sing out

23. At the place of the *dãre* sago, the *sisiyu* bird

24. But you do not speak

25. At the place of the *yamo* sago, the *sisiyu* bird

26. But you I hear not

27. At Yegena, the *muri* bird

28. But you do not call out

29. At the place of the *geroa* cane, the *muri* bird

30. But you do not call out

31. At the empty place Yegena, the *sisiyu* bird

32. But I hear no other sound

33. At Mt Weyeru, the *muri* bird

34. But you do not call out

35. At Ĩsa Creek, the *yiyo* bird

36. But you alone do not call out

37. At Dãri Creek, the *muri* bird

38. But you only do not speak

39. At Aboragemo Creek, the *u* bird

40. But you alone do not speak

41. This sago mallet

42. Strike quickly

43. Ta'anobo is calling out

44. He keeps calling out

45. Ta'anobo's namesake, the bird

46. He keeps calling out

# Sago Song 5

## Singer: Gebo. Recorded 18 October 1980 at Hegeso village.

In *The Empty Place*, I related how Gebo composed this song after her son, Yaroge, was taken to Mendi for questioning by the police following the suicide of his wife. As in the previous song, the silence of the addressed man is heightened in a dramatic way by contrasting it with the sound of something else, in this case, the aeroplane rather than birds. Gebo also refers to the white shirt and shoes which is the educated, white-collar Papua New Guinean's typical clothing. (See Weiner 1991:126–27, 139–41.) ♫ online example 5.

| 1. | *ba'a* | *na'a* | *bare* | *awa* | *hua* | *ubo'ora* | *eya* |
|----|--------|--------|--------|-------|-------|-----------|-------|
|    | boy | your | aeroplane | up | struck | gone | eya |

| 2. | *do'oyera* | | *owe* | | | | |
|----|------------|---|-------|---|---|---|---|
|    | did not tell | | owe | | | | |

| 3. | *ba'a* | *na'a* | *bare* | *kuabogabo'ore* | | *eya* | |
|----|--------|--------|--------|-----------------|---|-------|---|
|    | boy | you | aeroplane | hummed | | eya | |

| 4. | *dia* | *o'abibi-o* | *eya* | | | | |
|----|-------|-------------|-------|---|---|---|---|
|    | saying | wanted to | eya | | | | |

| 5. | *ba'a* | *na'a* | *kabe* | *ensu* | *ababo* | *hibabo'ore* | *owe* |
|----|--------|--------|--------|--------|---------|--------------|-------|
|    | boy | your | man | shoes | walk | embark | owe |

| 6. | *nabo* | *do'oyere* | *owe* | | | | |
|----|--------|------------|-------|---|---|---|---|
|    | to me | did not say | owe | | | | |

| 7. | *do'abibidobo* | | *owe* | | | | |
|----|----------------|---|-------|---|---|---|---|
|    | could not tell | | owe | | | | |

| 8. | *ba'a* | *na'a* | *kosa'a* | *fabo* | *hibabo'ore* | *eya* | |
|----|--------|--------|----------|--------|--------------|-------|---|
|    | boy | your | shirt | white | embark | eya | |

| 9. | *do'oyera* | | *owe* | | | | |
|----|------------|---|-------|---|---|---|---|
|    | did not tell | | owe | | | | |

| 10. | *ba'a* | *na'a* | *kosa'a* | *namuyu* | *ababo* | *hibabo'ore* | *eya* |
|-----|--------|--------|----------|----------|---------|--------------|-------|
|     | boy | your | shirt | cockatoo | walk | embark | eya |

11. *dia*     *o'oyera*     *owe*
    saying     did not go     owe

12. *ba'a*   *na'a*    *duma*    *a'o*    *hugoreye*   *ubo'ore*   *eya*
    boy     your     mountain   cloud    pierced     gone      eya

13. *dia*     *o'abibi-o*    *owe*
    saying     wanted to    owe

14. *fufu*    *masibu*    *hua*     *owe*
    neck     necklace    mother     owe

15. *do'oyera*           *owe*
    did not tell         owe

16. *ya*     *masibu*    *hua*     *owe*
    arm     necklace    mother     owe

17. *dia*     *u'abibio*    *owe*
    saying     should have   owe

18. *gõ*              *hage*    *hagikabo'ore*     *owe*
    string bag     two     carried         owe

19. *dia*     *o'abibi-o*    *owe*
    saying     wanted to    owe

20. *awa*    *masibu*    *hua*     *owe*
    hand     necklace    mother     owe

21. *dia*     *o'oyera*     *owe*
    saying     did not go     owe

22. *orodobo*   *ka*      *gebo*    *ma'ame*   *eya*
    Orodobo   woman     Gebo    thing     eya

23. *yaroge-o*   *owe*
    Yaroge     owe

24. *so'onedobo*         *kigirimone*     *owe*
    So'onedobo        Kigiri        owe

25. *ka'ariba*        *owe*
    Ka'ariba       owe

1. Boy, you have ascended in your aeroplane

2. But you didn't tell me

3. Boy, we heard your aeroplane hum as it flew away

4. You wanted to tell me but you didn't

5. You put on your shoes and embarked

6. But to me you said nothing

7. You wanted to tell me, but you could not

8. You put on your white shirt and embarked

9. But you did not tell me

10. You put on your shirt, white as a cockatoo, and left

11. But you didn't tell me before you left

12. You pierced the clouds as you flew away

13. You wanted to tell me but you couldn't

14. I am the mother of the widow's *kamora* necklace

15. You didn't tell me

16. I am the mother of the *kamora* wrist band

17. You should have told me before you left

18. You took your two suitcases

19. You wanted to tell me but you couldn't

20. I am the mother of the widow's *kamora*

21. You didn't tell me before you left

22. The Orodobo clan woman, Gebo

23. Yaroge

24. The So'onedobo man, Kigiri

25. Ka'ariba

# Sago Song 6

## Singer: Kunuhuaka (with Siyame).
## Recorded 23 March 1988 at Hegeso village.

This is another song addressing the sun maiden. This time, the singer, Kunuhuaka thinks about her eldest son, Bebe, who is assigned to a patrol boat with the Papua New Guinea Defence Force at Lombrum Patrol Base in Manus Province. She thinks of the sun shining off the guns on his ship and the ship's prow, even as it shines over Kunuhuaka's head while she is working. (See Weiner 1991:128–34; Figure 3 in this volume is a music transcription of lines 10–15.) ♫ online example 6.

1. *humotorohahaibi*      *weya'a*
   to break through      comes

2. *na'a*      *ibiba'ae*
   you      is

3. *eye*
   eye

4. *iri*      *fagi*      *si'abi*      *weya'a*
   tree      branches      to search for      comes

5. *ne*      *ibiba'ae*
   you      is

6. *eye*
   eye

7. *ira*      *so'oboro*      *sebe*      *weya'a*
   tree      canopy      search for      comes

8. *na'a*      *ibiba'ae*
   you      is

9. *eye*
   eye

10. *humeseseregaibi*      *weya'a*
    to shine      comes

11. *ne*      *ibiba'ae*
    you      is

12. *eye*
    eye

13. *kui*      *gaboba'ae*    *foraye*     *weya'a*
    sago     base-is      break through  comes

14. *na'a*    *ibiba'ae*
    you      is

15. *eye*
    eye

16. *ŭgi*      *abotu'u*     *kama'uri*    *meya'a*
    breadfruit  *abotu'u*     top        not yet

17. *na'a*    *ibiba'ae*
    you      is

18. *eye*
    eye

19. *humeseseregaibi*     *weya'a*
    to shine          comes

20. *na'a*    *ibiba'ae*
    you      is

21. *eye*
    eye

22. *kaubi*    *weya'a*
    region   comes

23. *ne*      *ibiba'ae*
    you      is

24. *eye*
    eye

25. *eresaibi*    *weya'a*
    to look after  comes

26. *na'a*     *ibiba'ae*
    you     is

27. *eye*
    eye

28. *humotorohahaibi*     *weya'a*
    to break through     comes

29. *ne*     *ibiba'ae*
    you     is

30. *eye*
    eye

31. *ira*     *so'oboro*     *sebe*     *weya'a*
    tree     canopy     search for     comes

32. *na'a*     *ibiba'ae*
    you     is

33. *eye*
    eye

34. *kui*     *gaboba'a*     *kamu'uri*     *meya'a*
    sago     base-is     top     not yet

35. *ne*     *ibiba'ae*
    you     is

36. *eye*
    eye

37. *sibi*     *arori*     *hiba'ane*     *uba'a*
    ship     prow     to embark     gone

38. *na'a*     *ibiba'ae*
    you     is

39. *eye*
    eye

40. *gagaruri*     *hiba'ane*     *uba'a*
    to carry     to embark     gone

41. *na'a*     *ibiba'ae*
    you       is

42. *eye*
    eye

43. *awa'a*    *bareri*    *hiba'ane*    *uba'a*
    sky       vessel    to embark    gone

44. *ne*      *ibiba'ae*
    you       is

45. *eye*
    eye

46. *borowame*         *humogore'ane*  *uba'ae*
    aquatic bird      to scatter    gone

47. *na'a*    *ibiba'ae*
    you       is

48. *eye*
    eye

49. *bagua*         *humogoreye*  *uba'a*
    aquatic bird     to scatter    gone

50. *na'a*    *ibiba'ae*
    you       is

51. *eye*
    eye

52. *e*      *kabo*    *sere-o*
    eh     girl      sun-o

53. *na'abo*    *dibu-o*
    to you    I speak

54. *eye*
    eye

55. *e*      *kabo*    *wãga-o*
    eh     girl      Clear-oh

56. *nebo*      *dibu-o*
    you alone   I speak

57. *eye*
    *eye*

58. *e*     *kabo*   *yuri-o*
    eh      girl     *Yuri-oh*

59. *na'abo*   *iba'ae*
    to you     is

60. *eye*
    *eye*

1.   You break through the clouds as you come

2.   It is you

3.   *eye*

4.   You peek through the tree branches as you come

5.   It is you

6.   *eye*

7.   You break through the tree canopy as you come

8.   It is you

9.   *eye*

10.  You shine as you come

11.  It is you

12.  *eye*

13.  You break through the sago palms as you come

14.  It is you

15.  *eye*

16.  Don't peek through the top of the *abotu'u* breadfruit yet

17.  It is you

18.  *eye*

19.  You shine as you come

20. It is you

21. *eye*

22. You look out over the whole land as you come

23. It is you

24. *eye*

25. You watch over the whole land as you come

26. It is you

27. *eye*

28. You break through the clouds as you come

29. It is you

30. *eye*

31. You peek through the top branches as you come

32. It is you

33. *eye*

34. Don't you light up the sago palms yet

35. It is you

36. *eye*

37. You light up the prow of his departing ship

38. It is you

39. *eye*

40. You light up the guns carried by his departing ship

41. It is you

42. *eye*

43. You light up the aeroplane as he embarked and left

44. It is you

45. *eye*

46. You cause the egrets to scatter over the Lake

47. It is you

48. *eye*

49. You cause the *bagua* birds to scatter over the Lake

50. It is you

51. *eye*

52. Oh, Miss Daytime

53. It is to you I am speaking

54. *eye*

55. Oh Miss Clear Light

56. To you alone I speak

57. *eye*

58. Oh, Miss Yuri

59. It is to you I speak

60. *eye*

---

# Sago Song 7

## Singer: Kunuhuaka (with Siyame). Recorded 23 March 1988 at Hegeso village.

Bebe's army uniforms, washed and hanging out to dry, remind Kunuhuaka of the leaf of the stinging nettle. She sings of these uniforms, and Bebe's hat, and rifle: 'are these things sufficient to replace your brothers and other relatives with whom you no longer live? Will they protect you as well as these relatives do?' (See Weiner 1991:134–38.) ♫ online example 7.

| | | | |
|---|---|---|---|
| 1. | *yengi* | *banima* | *ba* |
| | nettles | *banima* | that |
| | | | |
| 2. | *ba'a* | *na'a* | *hame* | *wae* |
| | boy | your | brother | not |
| | | | |
| 3. | *eye* | | |
| | *eye* | | |
| | | | |
| 4. | *yengi* | *boro* | *ba* |
| | nettles | *boro* | that |

| | | | | |
|---|---|---|---|---|
| 5. *ba'a*<br>boy | *na'a*<br>brother | *wame*<br>not | *wae* | |

| | |
|---|---|
| 6. *eye*<br>eye | |

| | | |
|---|---|---|
| 7. *yengi*<br>nettles | *gugabe*<br>flying fox | *ba*<br>that |

| | | | |
|---|---|---|---|
| 8. *ba'a*<br>boy | *na'a*<br>your | *base*<br>sister's husband | *wae*<br>not |

| | |
|---|---|
| 9. *eye*<br>eye | |

| | | | |
|---|---|---|---|
| 10. *ganuga*<br>hat | *boge*<br>club | *aba*<br>father | *ba*<br>that |

| | | | | |
|---|---|---|---|---|
| 11. *ba'a*<br>boy | *na'a*<br>your | *kabe*<br>man | *wame*<br>brother | *wae*<br>not |

| | |
|---|---|
| 12. *eye*<br>eye | |

| | | | |
|---|---|---|---|
| 13. *ganuga*<br>hat | *boge*<br>club | *aba*<br>father | *ba*<br>that |

| | | | |
|---|---|---|---|
| 14. *ba'a*<br>boy | *na'a*<br>your | *base*<br>sister's husband | *wae*<br>not |

| | |
|---|---|
| 15. *eye*<br>eye | |

| | | | |
|---|---|---|---|
| 16. *bi'a*<br>rifle | *fore*<br>large | *aba*<br>father | *ba*<br>that |

| | | | |
|---|---|---|---|
| 17. *ba'a*<br>boy | *na'a*<br>your | *aba*<br>father | *wae*<br>not |

| | |
|---|---|
| 18. *eye*<br>eye | |

| | | |
|---|---|---|
| 19. *bare*<br>canoe | *sibi*<br>ship | *ba*<br>that |

| 20. | *ba'a* | *na'a* | *hua* | *wae* |
|---|---|---|---|---|
| | boy | your | mother | not |

| 21. | *eye* |
|---|---|
| | eye |

| 22. | *sabe* | *sode* |
|---|---|---|
| | knife | sheath |

| 23. | *ba'a* | *na'a* | *ana* | *wae* |
|---|---|---|---|---|
| | boy | your | sister | not |

| 24. | *eye* |
|---|---|
| | eye |

| 25. | *oro* | *yerebi* | *ba'a* | *terewaro* |
|---|---|---|---|---|
| | bamboo | yerebi | boy | Terewaro |

| 26. | *na'abo* | *dibu-o* |
|---|---|---|
| | to you | I speak |

| 27. | *eye* |
|---|---|
| | eye |

| 28. | *kui* | *kenege* | *ba'a* | *bebe* |
|---|---|---|---|---|
| | sago | mid-rib | boy | Bebe |

| 29. | *na'abo* | *dibu-o* |
|---|---|---|
| | to you | I speak |

| 30. | *eye* |
|---|---|
| | eye |

1. Your *banima* nettles hanging there

2. It's not your brother

3. *eye*

4. Your *boro* nettles there

5. It's not your brother

6. *eye*

7. Your nettles hanging like flying foxes

8. It's not your brother-in-law

9. *eye*

10. The owner of the club-shaped army hat

11. It's not your Mister brother

12. *eye*

13. The owner of the club-shaped army hat

14. It's not your sister's husband

15. *eye*

16. The owner of your big rifle

17. It's not your father

18. *eye*

19. The sea going ship

20. It's not your mother

21. *eye*

22. Your bayonet sheath

23. It's not your sister

24. *eye*

25. The *yerebi* bamboo clan boy Terewaro

26. It is to you I am speaking

27. *eye*

28. The Sago mid-rib clan boy Bebe

29. It is you I am speaking

30. *eye*

# Men's Songs (*Sorohabora*)

## Men's Song 1

### Singers: Memene and Abeabo. Recorded 6 January 1985 at Hegeso village.

This song depicts the competition between the men of Hegeso and Barutage villages as they both prepare for a pig-kill. The subject of the song is revealed towards the end of it, in a section called *dawadobora*. The singing of the word *dawa* or *dawabo* is frequent at this point, as in verse four of this song. (See Weiner 1991:159–62.)

1.
| *ba'a* | *na'a* | *ẽ* | *siri* | *hubu* | *kegere* |
|---|---|---|---|---|---|
| boy | your | garden | large | struck | disparage |

*dibihamone*
do not speak (disparage)

| *ba'a* | *na'a* | *a* | *siri* | *hare* | *tegebu* | *kegere* |
|---|---|---|---|---|---|---|
| boy | your | house | large | doing | built | disparage |

*dibihamone*
do not speak (disparage)

2.
| *ba'a* | *na'a* | *buru* | *kirari* | *mabo* | *kegere* |
|---|---|---|---|---|---|
| boy | your | black | rope | taken | disparage |

*dibihamone*
do not say (disparage)

| *ba'a* | *na'a* | *ya'o* | | *kirari* | *mabo* | *kegere* |
|---|---|---|---|---|---|---|
| boy | your | many-coloured | | rope | taken | disparage |

*dia* *o'oyo'o*
saying do not go

3.
| *ba'a* | *na'a* | *ẽ* | *siri* | *hubu* | *kegere* |
|---|---|---|---|---|---|
| boy | your | garden | large | planted | disparage |

*dia* *o'oyo'o*
saying do not go

| ba'a | na'a | musu'uni | kamabo | kegere |
|------|------|----------|--------|--------|
| boy | your | smoke | rising | disparage |

*dibiha'oyo'o*
do not keep saying

4. 

| ya'a | amena | bariabe | sabe | u'ubi |
|------|-------|---------|------|-------|
| we | men | Bariabe | Ridge | children |

*dawabo*
*dawabo*

| ya'a | amena | ibu | faya'a | wabo |
|------|-------|-----|--------|------|
| we | men | river | Faya'a | coming |

*dawabo*
*dawabo*

5. 

| yiya | amena | ibu | faya'a | kege |
|------|-------|-----|--------|------|
| we | men | river | Faya'a | bank |

*dawabo*
*dawabo*

| yiya | amena | yagenebo | sabe | u'ubi |
|------|-------|----------|------|-------|
| we | men | Yagenebo | Ridge | children |

| ibu | dawabo |
|-----|--------|
| river | Dawabo |

---

1. Boy, you have made a big garden
   But don't disparage me

   Boy, you have built a great house
   But don't denigrate me

2. You hold the rope of the black pig
   But don't disparage me

   You hold the rope of the piebald pig
   But don't speak disrespectfully of me

3. You clear the bush to make a big garden
   But don't hold me cheaply

   The smoke rises from your new garden
   But don't disparage me

4.  We are the men of Bariabe Sabe
    *Dawabo*

    We are the men of the Faya'a Creek flowing
    *Dawabo*

5.  We are the men of the banks of the Faya'a Creek
    *Dawabo*

    We are the men of Yagenebo Sabe
    *Ibu Dawabo*

---

# Men's Song 2

## Singers: Memene and Abeabo. Recorded 6 January 1985 at Hegeso village.

Memene, a man of Hegeso village, learned this song, which commemorates a Wasemi man, when he was visiting at Lake Kutubu. (See Weiner 1991:83, 104.) ♫ online example 8.

1.  | *ibu* | *irama* | | *yibi* | *wabo'ore* |
    |---|---|---|---|---|
    | water | stick carrying | | sleep | if-gone |

    | *ai* | *na* | *go'o* | *dibige* | |
    |---|---|---|---|---|
    | ai! | I | also | stated | |

    | *ibu* | *ka'ayamikiribi* | | | *wabo'ore* |
    |---|---|---|---|---|
    | river | waves caused by moving canoe | | | come |

    | *ai* | *na* | *go'o* | *wabubege* | |
    |---|---|---|---|---|
    | ai! | I | also | am coming | |

2.  | *gera* | *kabera* | *waibo* | *ubo'ore* | |
    |---|---|---|---|---|
    | paddle | kabera | waibo | if-gone | |

    | *na-o* | *wa'anege* | | | |
    |---|---|---|---|---|
    | I too | will come | | | |

    | *ba'a* | *na'a* | *ira* | *waria* | *barebo'o* |
    |---|---|---|---|---|
    | boy | your | tree | waria | canoe-if |

    | *na* | *go'o* | *wasia* | *wa'anege* | |
    |---|---|---|---|---|
    | I | also | follow | will come | |

3. 

| ba'a | na'a | gesa | momabo | ubo'ore |
|------|------|------|--------|---------|
| boy | your | dog | Momabo | if-gone |

| na | go'o | wa'agerege |
|----|------|------------|
| I | also | will come |

| ba'a | na'a | gesa | sawabo | ubo'ore |
|------|------|------|--------|---------|
| boy | your | dog | Sawabo | if-gone |

| na-o | wa'anege |
|------|----------|
| I too | will come |

4. 

| orodobo | kabe | soaeyamo |
|---------|------|----------|
| Orodobo | man | Soaeya |

| kabe | kamuna |
|------|--------|
| man | Kamuna |

| orodobo | kabe | kamunamo |
|---------|------|----------|
| Orodobo | man | Kamuna |

| dawabo |
|--------|
| dawabo |

5. 

| ira | hagenamo | dobo | ba'a | faimano |
|-----|----------|------|------|---------|
| tree | Gnetum sp. | clan | boy | Faimano |

| kabe | seimano |
|------|---------|
| man | Seimano |

| ira | hagenamo | dobo | ba'a | faimano |
|-----|----------|------|------|---------|
| tree | Gnetum sp. | clan | boy | Faimano |

| kabe | seimano |
|------|---------|
| man | Seimano |

1.  The men who sleep near the fast flowing river
    Ai, I too am coming

    The waves caused by the canoe in motion
    Ai, I too am coming

2.  The *kabera* tree paddle which you used
    I too am coming

    Boy, your *waria* tree canoe
    I too am following you

3.  If you take your dog Moma
    I too want to come

    If you take your dog Sawabo
    I too will come

4.  The son of the Orodobo man Soaeya
    His son, Kamuna

    The Orodobo man Kamuna
    *Dawabo*

5.  The clan of the *hagenamo*, the boy Faimano
    His son, Seimano

    The Sanimahia clan, the boy Faimano
    His son, Seimano

---

# Men's Song 3

## Singers: Memene and Abeabo. Recorded 6 January 1985 at Hegeso village.

This song commemorates Dosabo, a man of Damayu village who was suspected of being a sorcerer, an accusation he denied before his death. The song speaks of a man who claimed never to have been taught these sorcery spells by the deceased before he died. (See Weiner 1991:47, 108–9, 171–75, 176–81 (music transcription); 2001:26; Figure 5 in this volume is a music transcription of verse 2.) ♫ online example 9.

1.  | *ba'a* | *na'a* | *ĩ* | *hone* | *ubu* | *kusa* | *do'ane* | *dobo'owua* |
    |--------|--------|-----|--------|-------|--------|----------|-------------|
    | boy | your | eye | dizzy | go | spell | to speak | recited |

    | *dia* | *ubo'oriye*[1] |
    |-------|-----------|
    | said | did not go |

---

1   The *-o'oriye* ending in *dia ubo'oriye* and, in the following verse, *dobo'oriye* indicates that the speaker learned of the action through indirect evidence or evidence no longer present, e.g. someone else informed him of an action that he himself lacks evidence of. In this case, he is singing, 'I have no evidence that you spoke to me about these spells before you died.'

| *ba'a* | *na'a* | *kigi* | *wara'obo* | | *kusa* | *do'ane* | *dobo'owua* |
|--------|--------|--------|-----------|---|--------|----------|-------------|
| boy | your | bone | weakness | | spell | to speak | recited |

| *dia* | *ubo'oriye* |
|-------|-------------|
| said | did not go |

2.
| *ba'a* | *na'a* | *ĩ* | *hone* | *ubu* | *kusa* | *do'ane* | *dobo'owa* |
|--------|--------|-----|--------|-------|--------|----------|-------------|
| boy | your | eye | dizzy | go | spell | to speak | recited |

| *dobo'oriye* |
|--------------|
| did not tell |

| *ba'a* | *na'a* | *ya* | *karo* | *kusa* | *do'ane* | | *dobo'owua* |
|--------|--------|------|--------|--------|----------|---|-------------|
| boy | your | arm | upper | spell | to speak | | recited |

| *dia* | *ubo'oriye* |
|-------|-------------|
| saying | did not go |

3.
| *ba'a* | *na'a* | *kõ* | | *tugame* | *kusa* | *do'ane* | *dobo'owa'a* |
|--------|--------|------|---|----------|--------|----------|--------------|
| boy | your | cordyline | | tugame | spell | to speak | recited |

| *dobo'oriye* |
|--------------|
| did not tell |

| *ba'a* | *na'a* | *ya* | *karo* | *kusa* | *do'ane* | | *dobo'owa* |
|--------|--------|------|--------|--------|----------|---|------------|
| boy | your | arm | upper | spell | to speak | | recited |

| *dia* | *ubo'oriye* |
|-------|-------------|
| saying | did not go |

4.
| *yia* | *amena* | *bi'a* | | *huba* |
|-------|---------|--------|---|--------|
| we | men | black palm | | huba |

| *ibudawabo* |
|-------------|
| ibudawabo |

| *yiya* | *amena* | *gesa* | *moma* |
|--------|---------|--------|--------|
| we | men | dog | Moma |

| *dawabo* |
|----------|
| dawabo |

5.
| *momahu'u* | | *isa'ibu* |
|------------|---|-----------|
| Momahu'u | | Isa'ibu |

| *kabe* | *bo* |
|--------|------|
| man | Bo |

*momahu'u*      *kabe*   *isa'ibu*
Momahu'u        man    Isa'ibu

*kabe*     *dosabo*
man     Dosabo

---

1.    Boy, your sleep-causing spell you used to recite
      You never told me before you left

      Boy, your weakness-causing spell you used to recite
      You never instructed me before you left

2.    Boy, your sleep-causing spell you used to recite
      You never told me before you left

      Boy, your wasting sickness spell you used to know
      You failed to pass it on to me before you left

3.    Boy, your spell of assassination you used to recite
      You never told me

      Boy, your wasting sickness spell you used to cast
      You never instructed me

4.    We are the men of the Huba Black Palm
      *Ibu Dawabo*

      We are the men of the dog Moma
      *Dawabo*

5.    The Momahu'u man Isa'ibu
      His son, Bo

      The Momahu'u man Isa'ibu
      His son, Dosabo

# Men's Song 4

## Singers: Memene and Abeabo. Recorded 1 January 1985 at Hegeso village.

This is a song about the tree kangaroo as it wanders through the forest. As with other marsupials and the cassowary, it seeks the fruit of the *baĩ* tree (a *Ficus* species), and the shoots of young bamboo. (See Weiner 1991:112–14.)

1.  | *kagi* | *aũwa* | *hubiwe'iya'are*[2] |
    | rain | softly | falling-come |

    | *ba'a* | *na'a* | *igebe* |
    | boy | you | is it? |

    | *kunu* | *kunuga* | *hubiwe'iya'are* |
    | palm wood | floor | rattling-come |

    | *ba'a* | *na'a* | *igebe* |
    | boy | you | is it? |

2.  | *kana* | *togebiwe'iya'are* |
    | stone | overturn-come |

    | *ba'a* | *na'a* | *iyo'oge*[3] |
    | boy | you | is |

    | *ira* | *waru* | *sina* | *irari* | *hubiwe'iya'are* |
    | tree | *waru* | shoots | dew | brushing-come |

    | *ba'a* | *na'a* | *iyo'oge* |
    | boy | you | is |

3.  | *kunuga* | *hubiwei'iya'are* |
    | floor | striking-come |

    | *ba'a* | *na'a* | *iyo'oge* |
    | boy | you | is |

---

2  *Hubiwe'iya'are*: the ending *-iya'are* is a nominalised form of the *-iyo'o* ending which indicates knowledge gained of a past action from present, sensible evidence (Weiner 1991:115, n. 4).
3  *-iyo'oge*: 'was that you? (based on the evidence I see myself as I walk through the bush).'

|  | *ira* | *baĩ* | *sina* | *irari* | *hubiwe'iya'are* |
|---|---|---|---|---|---|
|  | tree | baĩ | saplings | dew | brushing-come |

|  | *ba'a* | *na'a* | *iyo'oge* |
|---|---|---|---|
|  | boy | you | is |

| 4. | *oro* | *sina* | *ineri* | *hubiwe'iya'are* |
|---|---|---|---|---|
|  | bamboo | shoots | dew | brushing-come |

|  | *ba'a* | *na'a* | *iyo'oge* |
|---|---|---|---|
|  | boy | you | is |

|  | *ira* | *baĩ* | *sina* | *ireri* | *hubiwe'iya'are* |
|---|---|---|---|---|---|
|  | tree | baĩ | saplings | dew | brushing-come |

|  | *ba'a* | *na'a* | *iyo'oge* |
|---|---|---|---|
|  | boy | you | is |

| 5. | *duma* | *haro* | *sese* | *sone* |
|---|---|---|---|---|
|  | mountain | climbing | marsupial | Sone |

*dawabo*
*dawabo*

|  | *duma* | *hau* | *sese* | *sawa* |
|---|---|---|---|---|
|  | mountain | side | marsupial | Sawa |

*ibudawabo*
*ibudawabo*

| 6. | *duma* | *oro* | *sese* | *sawa* |
|---|---|---|---|---|
|  | mountain | top | marsupial | Sawa |

*dawabo*
*dawabo*

|  | *duma* | *fai* | *sese* | *sone* |
|---|---|---|---|---|
|  | mountain | side | marsupial | Sone |

*dawabo*
*dawabo*

1.  The sound of rain falling softly while someone approaches
    Boy, is that you?

    A sound like palm wood floor beams rattling as someone comes
    Boy, could that be you?

2.  You overturn the stones as you approach
    Boy, is that you?

    Your legs are wet like dew on the *waru* tree saplings
    Boy, could that be you?

3.  The sound of rattling as someone approaches
    Boy, is that you?

    Your legs are as wet as the *baĩ* saplings covered with dew
    Boy, could that be you?

4.  You brush the dew off the bamboo shoots as you come
    Boy, is that you?

    You are wet from the dew of the *baĩ* tree saplings
    Boy, could that be you?

5.  Along the hillside, the tree kangaroo named Sone walks
    *Dawabo*

    Along the side of the mountain, the tree kangaroo named Sawa wanders
    *Ibu Dawabo*

6.  At the crest of the mountain, Sawa wanders
    *Dawabo*

    Along the mountain sides, Sone travels
    *Dawabo*

# Men's Song 5

## Singers: Memene and Abeabo. Recorded 1 January 1985 at Hegeso village.

This song commemorates Mare of the Fo'omahu'u clan of Hegeso. The theme is a common one: a dead man can no longer go hunting. Men's songs 5 and 9 are alike in their use of the negative command form in the second line refrain. (See Weiner 1991:46, 110–12; 2001:25–26.)

1. | *se* | *duma* | *yibu* | *kunuga* |
   |------|--------|--------|----------|
   | marsupial | mountain | sleep | cave |

   *sebe'o'oyo'o*
   do not search

   | *sese* | *baro* | *yibu* | *kunuga* |
   |--------|--------|--------|----------|
   | marsupial | baro | sleep | cave |

   | *sia'* | *o'oyo'o* |
   |--------|-----------|
   | search | do not go |

2. | *sigina* | *daba* | *yibu* | *kunuga* |
   |----------|--------|--------|----------|
   | cassowary | large | sleep | cave |

   | *uaha* | *yiboba'ae* |
   |--------|-------------|
   | go-live | sleeps |

   | *sese* | *budu* | *yibu* | *kunuga* |
   |--------|--------|--------|----------|
   | marsupial | black | sleep | cave |

   *bereboba'ae*
   is lost

3. | *ya* | *dabura* | *hua* | *yibu* | *kunuga* |
   |------|----------|-------|--------|----------|
   | bird | red | mother | sleep | cave |

   | *sia* | *ubihamone* |
   |-------|-------------|
   | search | do not keep going |

   | *ya* | *gibi* | *hua* | *kunuga* |
   |------|--------|-------|----------|
   | bird | bush fowl | mother | cave |

   | *sia* | *o'oyo'o* |
   |-------|-----------|
   | search | do not go |

**43**

| 4. | *kuiyare* | *yibu* | *kunuga* | |
|---|---|---|---|---|
| | python | sleep | cave | |
| | *sia* | *o'oyo'o* | | |
| | search | do not go | | |
| | *tuba* | *budu* | *yibu* | *kunuga* |
| | tree kangaroo | black | sleep | cave |
| | *sebe'o'oyo'o* | | | |
| | do not search | | | |

| 5. | *yiya* | *amena* | *ira* | *ma'aru* |
|---|---|---|---|---|
| | we | men | tree | *ma'aru* |
| | *dawabo* | | | |
| | *dawabo* | | | |
| | *yiya* | *amena* | *ira* | *banamo* |
| | we | men | tree | *banamo* |
| | *dawabo* | | | |
| | *dawabo* | | | |

| 6. | *ira* | *ma'arudobo* | *meremo* | | |
|---|---|---|---|---|---|
| | tree | *ma'aru* clan | Mere's | | |
| | *ba'a* | *Mare* | | | |
| | boy | Mare | | | |
| | *ira* | *ma'arudobo* | *ba'a* | *mege* | *bamo* |
| | tree | *ma'aru* clan | boy | only | this |
| | *dawabo* | | | | |
| | *dawabo* | | | | |

1.  The *duma* marsupial which sleeps in the limestone caves
    Do not search for it

    The *baro* marsupial which sleeps in the caves
    Do not attempt to seek it

2.  The large cassowary which sleeps in the caves of stone
    He has gone away

The black marsupial of the stone caves
He too is lost

3. The bush fowl mother who sleeps in the cave
Do not go looking for her

The red bush fowl mother who sleeps in the cave
Do not seek her

4. The python who sleeps in the stone cave
Do not go looking for it

The black tree kangaroo who sleeps in the cave
Do not try and find it

5. We are the men of *ma'aru* tree clan
*Dawabo*

We are the men of the *banamo* tree clan
*Dawabo*

6. The *ma'aru* tree clan man, Mere
His son, Mare

The *ma'aru* tree clan, this only boy
*Dawabo*

# Men's Song 6

## Singers: Wa'o and Midibaru. Recorded 6 January 1985 at Hegeso village.

If in a dream, a man sees a large tree such as a *furubu* falling down, it portends the death of a headman. This song makes use of that common image to commemorate the death of the Hegeso headman Iraharabo, of the Tirifadobo (Ma'arudobo) clan. (See Weiner 1998a:339–40.)

1. *ira*      *furabu*      *derare*
   tree      *furabu*      that

   *forabibi'ae*
   fallen

| *ira* | *furabu* | *derare* |
|-------|----------|----------|
| tree  | furabu   | that     |

*formabibi'ae*
long fallen

2. 

| *ba'a* | *na'a* | *ao*  | *dumaro'o* |
|--------|--------|-------|------------|
| boy    | your   | bush  | mountain   |

*aodoboba'ae*
bush covered

| *ba'a* | *na'a* | *kõ*       | *tegeri* | *ma'ayaro'o* |
|--------|--------|------------|----------|--------------|
| boy    | your   | cordyline  | tegeri   | seeds        |

*foraboba'ae*
hand broken

3. 

| *ba'a* | *na'a* | *ira* | *furabu* | *derare* |
|--------|--------|-------|----------|----------|
| boy    | your   | tree  | furabu   | that     |

*forabi'ae*
fallen

| *ba'a* | *na'a* | *kegebe* | *abu* | *derare* |
|--------|--------|----------|-------|----------|
| boy    | your   | vine     | abu   | that     |

*forabo'owa'ae*
cut

4. 

| *wa'ari* | *hubobi* | *dobo* | *kabe* | *degayomore* |
|----------|----------|--------|--------|--------------|
| palm     | hubobi   | clan   | man    | Degayo       |

| *kabe* | *harabi* |
|--------|----------|
| man    | Harabi   |

| *wa'ari* | *hububi* | *dobo* | *kabe* | *mege* | *bamore* |
|----------|----------|--------|--------|--------|----------|
| palm     | hubobi   | clan   | man    | only   | that     |

| *kabe* | *iraharabo* |
|--------|-------------|
| man    | Iraharabo   |

5. 

| *yo* | *hua*  | *ka*  | *mege* | *bamo* |
|------|--------|-------|--------|--------|
| his  | mother | woman | only   | that   |

| *kabe* | *Iraharabo* |
|--------|-------------|
| man    | Iraharabo   |

46

| bi'a | huba | dobo | ka | mege | ba | ma'ame |
|------|------|------|------|------|------|--------|
| black palm | huba | clan | woman | only | that | thing |

| ba'a | Harabi |
|------|--------|
| boy | Harabi |

1. The tall *furabu* tree
   fallen

   The tall *furabo* tree
   long fallen

2. Your tree covered mountain
   Covered with bush

   Your *tegeri* cordyline seeds
   broken off

3. Your tall *furabu* tree
   fallen

   Your *abu* vine
   long cut down

4. He of the *hubobi* palm clan Degayo
   his son Harabi

   That sole man of the *hubobi* palm clan
   the man Iraharabo

5. That sole woman, his mother
   her son Iraharabo

   That only woman of the *huba* black-palm clan
   Her son, Harabi

# Men's Song 7

## Singers: Wa'o and Midibaru. Recorded 6 January 1985 at Hegeso village.

This song commemorates Sese, a man of Hegeso. The imagery is a very common one: a man is dead, and the forest has reclaimed those places which he used to frequent and upon which he left the imprint of human activity. The creeks referred to are at Ayamo in Banimahu'u clan territory. (See Weiner 1991:59, 101–2.) ♫ online example 8.

1. | ba'a | na'a | hagenamo | | mai | ira |
   |------|------|----------|---|-----|-----|
   | boy | your | Gnetum sp. | | mai | tree |

   *aodoba'aye*
   let bush covered

   | ba'a | na'a | mai | ira | bare |
   |------|------|-----|-----|------|
   | boy | your | mai | tree | that |

   *kigiba'aye*
   let strong bush

2. | ba'a | na'a | ibu | barua | ga | habo | duma |
   |------|------|-----|-------|-----|------|------|
   | boy | your | creek | Barua | source | flow into | mountain |

   *aodoba'aye*
   let bush covered

   | ba'a | na'a | ao | iburo'o |
   |------|------|-----|---------|
   | boy | your | bush | creek |

   *kigiba'aye*
   let strong bush

3. | ba'a | na'a | da'ari | fai | dumaro'o |
   |------|------|--------|-----|---------|
   | boy | your | stone | side | mountain |

   *abumaba'aye*
   let bank ground crumble

   | ba'a | na'a | aodumaro'o |
   |------|------|------------|
   | boy | your | bush covered mountain |

   | ira | wuba'aye |
   |-----|----------|
   | tree | let come |

4. 
| ya | banima | dobo | kabe | irihaimabo |
|----|--------|------|------|-----------|
| bird | banima | clan | man | Irihaimabo |

| kabe | tiraru |
|------|--------|
| man | Tiraru |

| ya | banima | dobo | kabe | irihaimabo |
|----|--------|------|------|-----------|
| bird | banima | clan | man | Irihaimabo |

| ibudawabo |
|-----------|
| ibudawabo |

5.
| kibudobo | ka | yamo |
|----------|-----|------|
| Kibudobo | woman | Ya |

| kabe | kunugamena |
|------|-----------|
| man | Kunugamena |

| kibudobo | ka | mege | bamo |
|----------|-----|------|------|
| Kibudobo | woman | only | that |

| kabe | Sese |
|------|------|
| man | Sese |

1. Boy, your *mai hagenamo* tree
   Has been covered over with bush

   Boy, that *hagenamo* tree of yours
   Has been reclaimed by the forest

2. Boy, your Baruaga Creek flowing into the mountain
   The bush has covered it over

   Boy, your tiny creek
   The forest has claimed it back

3. Boy, your stone banked mountain creek
   The ground crumbles from its banks

   Boy, your mountain place in the forest
   Let the trees take it back

4. The clan of the *banima* bird, the man Irihaimabo
   His son, Tiraru

   The clan of the *banima* bird, the man Irihaimabo
   *Ibu Dawabo*

5.  The Kibudobo clan, the woman Ya
    Her son's hidden name, Kanugamena

    The Kibudobo clan this only woman
    Her son Sese

---

# Men's Song 8

## Singers: Wa'o and Midibaru. Recorded 6 January 1985 at Hegeso village.

This song commemorates a man of the So'onedobo clan of Hegeso, Yabokigi. The dead man is likened to a bird who drops to earth with a broken wing. The Sulphur-crested Cockatoo is one of the main totems of the So'onedobo clan. The leaves of the *so'one* and *furabu* trees, the former a totem of the So'onedobo clan, the latter associated with headmen, are broken off by the flapping wings of birds; the leaves are the men of a clan as they die and drop off or are broken off. (See Weiner 1991:17–19, 94–95, 97, 171–75, 176–81 (music transcription).) ♫ online example 9.

1.  | *duma* | *yefua* | *sabe* | *ya* | *erege* |
    | --- | --- | --- | --- | --- |
    | mountain | Yefua | ridge | bird | cockatoo |

    | *auwa* | *fore* | *iba'ae* |
    | --- | --- | --- |
    | wing | broken | is |

    | *ibu* | *sumane* | *habo* | *ya* | *namuyu* |
    | --- | --- | --- | --- | --- |
    | creek | Sumane | water end | bird | cockatoo |

    | *vira* | *hua* | *uboba'a* |
    | --- | --- | --- |
    | shot | struck | gone |

2.  | *duma* | *faĩ* | *hesabo* | *ya* | *erege* |
    | --- | --- | --- | --- | --- |
    | mountain | side | following | bird | cockatoo |

    | *auwa* | *forabo'owa'ae* |
    | --- | --- |
    | wing | broken |

    | *duma* | *ka'afa* | *hesabo* | *ya* | *namuyu* |
    | --- | --- | --- | --- | --- |
    | mountain | edge | following | bird | cockatoo |

    | *vira* | *huiba'ae* |
    | --- | --- |
    | shot | killed |

3. 

| *ira* | *farabo* | *haũ* | *bobo* | *ya* | *namuyu* |
|---|---|---|---|---|---|
| tree | *farabo* | break off | leaves | bird | cockatoo |

| *auwa* | *gefodiyo'owa'ae* |
|---|---|
| wing | spear pierced |

| *ira* | *sonane* | *haũ* | *bobo* | *ya* | *namuyu* |
|---|---|---|---|---|---|
| tree | *sonane* | break off | leaves | bird | cockatoo |

| *auwa* | *fore* | *iba'ae* |
|---|---|---|
| wing | broken | is |

4. 

| *yiya* | *amena* | *ira* | *so'one* |
|---|---|---|---|
| we | men | tree | *so'one* |

| *hedawabo* |
|---|
| *dawabo* |

| *yiya* | *amena* | *ira* | *namani* |
|---|---|---|---|
| we | men | tree | *namani* |

| *dawabo* |
|---|
| *dawabo* |

5. 

| *yo* | *hua* | *ka* | *mege* | *bamo* |
|---|---|---|---|---|
| his | mother | woman | only | that |

| *kabe* | *Suibu* |
|---|---|
| man | Sui |

| *yo* | *hua* | *ka* | *mege* | *bamo* |
|---|---|---|---|---|
| his | mother | woman | only | that |

| *kabe* | *Sui* |
|---|---|
| man | Sui |

1. The ridge of Mt Yefua, the Sulphur-crested Cockatoo
   Its wing is broken

   At Sumani Creek as it flows underground, the cockatoo
   Its wing is broken

2. Following the side of the mountain, the cockatoo
   Its wing broken

Along the edge of the mountain's base, the cockatoo
Arrow shot and killed

3.  The cockatoo breaks off the leaves of the *farabo* tree as it flies
    Its wing broken

    The leaves of the *so'one* tree, broken off by the cockatoo's flapping wings
    Its wing broken

4.  We are the men of the *so'one* tree clan
    *Ibu Dawabo*

    We are the men of the *namani* tree clan
    *Dawabo*

5.  His mother, the only woman
    Her son, Sui

    His mother, the only women
    Her son, Sui

# Men's Song 9

## Singers: Kora and Garibi. Recorded 6 January 1985 at Hegeso village.

This song for Hibare, a So'onedobo man of Hegeso, appeared in abbreviated form in *The Heart of the Pearl Shell* (Weiner 1988a:284). A man moves from place to place during his life, and these places constitute a spatial record of his temporal life span. So too do the remembered bodies of discourse which were attributed to him during his life—such as myths. Insofar as speaking is a bodily activity, a person's utterances outline his or her body and give some clue as to its components, physical and social. In its illustrative use of discursive detotalisation, the following song indicates how literally the Foi are apt to consider that image. (See Weiner 1991:47, 162–64; 2001:26.) ♫ online example 8.

| 1. | *ba'a* | *na'a* | *ĩ* | *mano* | *tuniro'o* |
|----|--------|--------|-----|--------|------------|
|    | boy    | your   | eye | small  | myth       |

| *dibiha'adiye* |
|----------------|
| can not recite |

| | | | | | |
|---|---|---|---|---|---|
| | *ba'a*<br>boy | *na'a*<br>your | *ya*<br>arm | *karo*<br>upper | *tuniro'o*<br>myth |
| | *do'odiye*<br>cannot say | | | | |
| 2. | *ba'a*<br>boy | *na'a*<br>your | *ĩ*<br>eye | *mano*<br>small | *tuniro'o*<br>myth |
| | *dibihamone*<br>do not recite | | | | |
| | *ba'a*<br>boy | *na'a*<br>your | *ya*<br>arm | *karo*<br>upper | *tuniro'o*<br>myth |
| | *dibihamone*<br>do not recite | | | | |
| 3. | *ba'a*<br>boy | *na'a*<br>your | *ĩ*<br>eye | *mano*<br>small | *tuniro'o*<br>myth |
| | *dibihamone*<br>do not recite | | | | |
| | *ba'a*<br>boy | *na'a*<br>your | *ya*<br>arm | *karo*<br>upper | *tuniro'o*<br>myth |
| | *dibihamone*<br>do not recite | | | | |
| 4. | *oro*<br>bamboo | *yerebi*<br>*yerebi* | *dobo*<br>clan | *ka*<br>woman | *fumarewamemo*<br>Fumarewame |
| | *kabe*<br>man | *hibare*<br>Hibare | | | |
| | *ira*<br>tree | *namani*<br>*namani* | *dobo*<br>clan | *bugimenamo*<br>Bugimena | |
| | *kabe*<br>man | *dabiyayo*<br>Dabiyayo | | | |
| 5. | *ira*<br>tree | *namani*<br>*namani* | *dobo*<br>clan | *bugimenamo*<br>Bugimena | |
| | *ba'a*<br>boy | *dabiyayo*<br>Dabiyayo | | | |

| *oro* | *yerebi* | *dobo* | *ka* | *fumarewamemo* |
|-------|----------|--------|------|----------------|
| bamboo | *yerebi* | clan | woman | Fumarewame |

| *ba'a* | *Hibare* |
|--------|----------|
| boy | Hibare |

1.   Boy, your 'Little Eye' myth
     You can no longer tell

     Boy, your 'Upper Arm' myth
     How can you tell it

2.   Boy, your 'Little Eye' myth
     Do not recite it

     Boy, your 'Upper Arm' myth
     Do not recite it

3.   Boy, your 'Little Eye' myth
     Do not recite it

     Boy, your 'Upper Arm' myth
     Do not recite it

4.   The clan of the *yerebi* bamboo, the woman Fumaruwame
     Her son, Hibare

     The clan of the *namani* tree, the man Bugimena
     His son, Dabiyayo

5.   The *namani* tree clan, the man Bugimena
     The boy Dabiyayo

     The *yerebi* bamboo clan, the woman Fumaruwame
     The boy Hibare

# Men's Song 10

## Singers: Kora and Garibi. Recorded 6 January 1985 at Hegeso village.

Cordyline, whether worn as a rear covering by men, or as shrubs planted around a house, is intimately associated indexically and metonymically with men. Hence, a broken cordyline shrub is an oft-used image for a dead man, as this memorial song for the Orodobo man Kawaru demonstrates. The shoots or regrowth which appear on cordyline and on the trees mentioned in the song are also likened to living, growing children, and are used in this song to depict the death of Kawaru. (See Weiner 1991:171–75, 176–81 (music transcription).) ♫ online example 9.

| 1. | *ba'a* | *na'a* | *kõ* | *tegeri* | *ma'aya* | *dera* |
|---|---|---|---|---|---|---|
|  | boy | your | cordyline | *tegeri* | seeds | those |

| | *foraboba'ae* | | | | | |
|---|---|---|---|---|---|---|
| | broken off | | | | | |

| | *ba'a* | *na'a* | *wagebo* | *kegebe* | *ma'aya* | *dera* |
|---|---|---|---|---|---|---|
| | boy | your | cane | vine | seeds | those |

| | *debema* | | *uboba'ae* | | | |
|---|---|---|---|---|---|---|
| | broken off-taken | | gone | | | |

| 2. | *kõ* | *aboduri* | *ma'aya* | *dera* |
|---|---|---|---|---|
|  | cordyline | *aboduri* | seeds | those |

| | *fore* | *iba'ae* |
|---|---|---|
| | broken | are |

| | *ira* | *tu'u* | *sĩ* | *dera* |
|---|---|---|---|---|
| | tree | *tu'u* | regrowth | that |

| | *debeya* | *iba'ae* |
|---|---|---|
| | broken | is |

| 3. | *ba'a* | *na'a* | *ira* | *waru* | *ma'aya* | *dera* |
|---|---|---|---|---|---|---|
|  | boy | your | tree | *waru* | seeds | those |

| | *forabo'owa'ae* | | | | | |
|---|---|---|---|---|---|---|
| | broken | | | | | |

| | *ba'a* | *na'a* | *ira* | *baĩ* | *ma'aya* | *dera* |
|---|---|---|---|---|---|---|
| | boy | your | tree | *baĩ* | seeds | those |

| | *forebiba'ae* | | | | | |
|---|---|---|---|---|---|---|
| | broken off | | | | | |

| 4. | *momahu'u* | *ka* | *fofo* |
|---|---|---|---|
|  | Momahu'u | woman | Fofo |

| | *kabe* | *kawaru* |
|---|---|---|
| | man | Kawaru |

| *oro* | *yerebi* | *dobo* | *kabe* | *waria* |
|-------|----------|--------|--------|---------|
| bamboo | yerebi | clan | man | Waria |

| *kabe* | *baya* |
|--------|--------|
| man | Baya |

5.

| *oro* | *yerebi* | *dobo* | *wariamo* |
|-------|----------|--------|-----------|
| bamboo | yerebi | clan | Waria |

| *kabe* | *baya* |
|--------|--------|
| man | Baya |

| *yo* | *hua* | *ka* | *fofomo* |
|------|-------|------|----------|
| his | mother | woman | Fofo |

| *kabe* | *kawaru* |
|--------|----------|
| man | Kawaru |

1.  Boy, your *tegeri* cordyline shoots
    Have been broken off

    Boy, your *kegebe* vine shoots
    Someone has broken them off and taken them away

2.  Those *aboduri* shoots of yours
    Have been broken off

    The regrowth on the *tu'u* tree
    Someone has taken them away

3.  Boy, your *waru* tree shoots
    Have long been broken off

    Boy, your *baĩ* tree shoots
    Are broken off

4.  The Momahu'u clan woman, Fofo
    Her son, Kawaru

    The *yerebi* bamboo clan man, Waria
    His son, Baya

5.  The *yerebi* bamboo clan man Waria
    His son, Baya

    His mother, the woman Fofo
    Her son, Kawaru

# Men's Song 11

## Singers: Gesa and Sariaba. Recorded 7 January 1985 at Barutage village.

This song commemorates Baruma, a man of Barutage. The rhetorical use of the command verb endings evokes indignation and sorrow at the death of Baruma. (See Weiner 1991:95–97, 105–6; 1998a:339.) ♫ online example 10.

1. | *ibu* | *barua* | *ga* | *iga* |
   |-------|---------|------|-------|
   | creek | Barua | source | path |

   | *iga* | *ere'e* |
   |-------|---------|
   | path | look! |

   | *kumagi* | *iga* |
   |----------|-------|
   | Kumagi | path |

   | *iga* | *ereyiya'abe* |
   |-------|----------------|
   | path | do you not see? |

2. | *ba'a* | *na'a* | *ibu* | *faya'a* | *ga* | *iga* |
   |--------|--------|-------|----------|------|-------|
   | boy | your | river | Faya'a | source | path |

   | *iga* | *ere'e* |
   |-------|---------|
   | path | look! |

   | *ba'a* | *na'a* | *ibu* | *faya'a* | *ga* | *iga* |
   |--------|--------|-------|----------|------|-------|
   | boy | your | river | Faya'a | source | path |

   | *iga* | *ere'e* |
   |-------|---------|
   | path | look! |

3. | *kumagi tage* | *iga* |
   |---------------|-------|
   | Kumagi-mouth | path |

   | *iga* | *kigiba'ae* |
   |-------|-------------|
   | path | bush covered |

   | *sese* | *faiyu* | *wabu* | *iga* |
   |--------|---------|--------|-------|
   | marsupial | faiyu | coming | path |

   | *iga* | *aodiba'ae* |
   |-------|-------------|
   | path | tree covered |

4.  *orodobo*    *meremo*
    Orodobo     Mere's

    *ba'a*       *baruma*
    boy          Baruma

    *tirifadobo*  *ka*      *gairame*
    Tirifadobo    woman     Gairame

    *kabe*       *memenemabo*
    man          Memenemabo

5.  *tirifadobo*  *ka*      *gairame*
    Tirifadobo    woman     Gairame

    *kabe*       *daribu*
    man          Daribu

    *orodobo*    *mere*
    Orodobo      Mere

    *kabe*       *Baruma*
    man          Baruma


1.  The path to Baruaga Creek
    Look at the path!

    The path to Kumagi Creek
    Do you not see it?

2.  Boy, the head of the Faya'a River
    Look at it now!

    Boy, your Faya'a River source land
    Just see what it looks like now!

3.  The path leading to the mouth of the Kumagi Creek
    It is covered with bush

    The path along which the *faiyu* marsupial travels
    Has been covered over with bush

4.  The Orodobo man, Mere
    His son, Baruma

    The Tirifadobo woman Gairame
    Her son, Memenemabo

5.  The Tirifadobo woman Gairame
    Her son, Daribu

    The Orodobo man Mere
    His son Baruma

# Men's Song 12

## Singers: Gesa and Sariaba. Recorded 7 January 1985 at Barutage village.

This song commemorates the man Duri of Barutage. There is often a sense of mingled resentfulness and fatalism when men sing, 'let another man steal your sago palms your garden land' in regard to the productive acts the deceased leaves behind.

1.  | *ba'a* | *na'a* | *abamo* | *sobore* | *duma* |
    |---|---|---|---|---|
    | boy | your | father's | Sobore | mountain |

    *kigiba'aye*
    let strong bush

    | *ba'a* | *na'a* | *asibaye* | *ira* |
    |---|---|---|---|
    | boy | your | sago | tree |

    | *memo* | *noba'aye* |
    |---|---|
    | another | let eat |

2.  | *damanibugai* | *duma* |
    |---|---|
    | Damanibugai | mountain |

    *aodibarabe*
    bush covered

    | *duma* | *soa* | *dumaro'o* |
    |---|---|---|
    | mountain | Soa | mountain |

    *aginibarabe*
    stolen eaten

3. | *orodobo* | *mogebo* | | | |
|---|---|---|---|---|
| Orodobo | Mogebo | | | |
| *kabe* | *duri* | | | |
| man | Duri | | | |
| *ira* | *yĩa* | *dobo* | *ka* | *bae* |
| tree | yĩa | clan | woman | Bae |
| *ba'a* | *kubira* | | | |
| boy | Kubira | | | |

4. | *ira* | *onono* | *dobo* | *kabo* | *wasiano* |
|---|---|---|---|---|
| tree | onono | clan | woman | Wasiano |
| *ba'a* | *duri* | | | |
| boy | Duri | | | |
| *oro* | *yerebi* | *dobo* | *kabe* | *bae* |
| bamboo | yerebi | clan | man | Bae |
| *ira* | *kubira* | *hoaborabo* | | |
| tree | kubira | dawabo | | |

1. Boy, your father's Mt Sobore
   Let the bush cover it up

   Boy, your sago palms
   Another man has eaten them

2. Your Mt Damanibugai
   Let the bush obliterate it

   Your Mt Soa
   Let another man steal it

3. The Orodobo man Mogebo
   His son Duri

   The clan of the *yĩa* tree, the man Bae
   His son Kubira

4. The clan of the *onobo* tree, the woman Wasiano
   Her son Duri

   The clan of the *yerebi* bamboo, the man Bae
   His son, the *kubira* tree

# Men's Song 13

## Singers: Nabu and Bogo. Recorded 7 January 1985 at Barutage village.

The butterflies referred to in this song are those such as the rhinoceros beetle that leave edible larvae. The dead man is likened to a fallen tree visited by egg-laying insects, suggesting regeneration from death. (See Weiner 1991:97–99.) ♫ online example 10.

| | | | | | | |
|---|---|---|---|---|---|---|
| 1. | *ba'a*<br>boy | *bamo*<br>this | *ira*<br>tree | *huba*<br>huba | *gugu*<br>flower | *biri*<br>here |
| | *hŭga*<br>larvae | *afu*<br>butterfly | *wahuge*<br>alight | | | |
| | *ba'a*<br>boy | *bamo*<br>this | *ira*<br>tree | *kabare*<br>kabare | *gugu*<br>flower | *biri*<br>here |
| | *hŭga*<br>larvae | *none*<br>bumblebee | *wahuge*<br>alight | | | |
| 2. | *ba'a*<br>boy | *na'a*<br>your | *ira*<br>tree | *fayane*<br>fayane | *gugu*<br>flower | *biri*<br>here |
| | *hŭga*<br>larvae | *afu*<br>butterfly | *wahuge*<br>alight | | | |
| | *ba'a*<br>boy | *na'a*<br>your | *hefa*<br>vine | *bari*<br>bari | *gugu*<br>flower | *biri*<br>here |
| | *hŭga*<br>larvae | *none*<br>bumblebee | *wahuge*<br>alight | | | |
| 3. | *ba'a*<br>boy | *na'a*<br>your | *ira*<br>tree | *huba*<br>huba | *gugu*<br>flower | *biri*<br>here |
| | *hŭga*<br>larvae | *afu*<br>butterfly | *wahuge*<br>alight | | | |
| | *ba'a*<br>boy | *na'a*<br>your | *ira*<br>tree | *fayare*<br>fayare | *gugu*<br>flower | *biri*<br>here |
| | *hŭga*<br>larvae | *none*<br>bumblebee | *wahuge*<br>alight | | | |

4.  

| *aidobo* | *ba'a* | *bereromo* | *u'ubi* |
|---|---|---|---|
| Aidobo | boy | Berero's | child |

| *ba'a* | *howare* |
|---|---|
| boy | Howare |

| *momahu'u* | *ka* | *genemo* |
|---|---|---|
| Momahu'u | woman | Genemo |

*dawa*
dawabo

5.  

| *momahu'u* | *kabo* | *genemoka* |
|---|---|---|
| Momahu'u | girl | Genemoka |

| *ba'a* | *herere* |
|---|---|
| boy | Herere |

| *aidobo* | *berero* |
|---|---|
| Aidobo | Berero |

| *kabe* | *Howare* |
|---|---|
| man | Howare |


1.  On the flowers of your *huba* palm
    The *afu* butterfly alights

    On the flowers of your *kabare* tree
    The *none* bumblebee alights

2.  On the flowers of your *fayane* tree
    The *afu* butterfly alights

    On the flowers of your *hefa bari* vine
    The *none* bumblebee alights

3.  On the flowers of your *huba* palm
    The *afu* butterfly alights

    On the flowers of your *fayare* tree
    The *none* bumblebee alights

4.  The Aidobo clan, the man Berero
    His son Howare

    The Momahu'u clan woman Genemo
    *Dawa*

5.  The Momahu'u clan woman Genemoka
    Her son Herere

    The man of the Aidobo clan, Berero
    His son Howare

---

# Men's Song 14

## Singers: Nabu and Bogo. Recorded 7 January 1985 at Barutage village.

Visits by men and women of other longhouses are often encounters comprising equal parts of affability, neighbourliness, and the nervous competitiveness of hosts and visitors alike. This song, sung by two young Barutage men, mocks the Hegeso men's insults directed towards Barutage. 'Are we women that you should tell us to make gardens and cook sago,' the song is saying. Hegeso longhouse lies upstream of Barutage longhouse along the Mubi River. 'First' sago refers to what the Foi call *kare kui*, 'woman's sago,' the sago that a woman cooks first when she is preparing the evening meal, and which she eats first. (See Weiner 1991:165–67.)

1.
| *ẽ* | *siri* | *hubu* | *kegere* |
|---|---|---|---|
| garden | large | planted | disparage |
| *dia* | *ubuyebe* | | |
| saying | is it going? | | |
| *kare* | *kui* | *meke'abo* | *kegere* |
| women's | sago | ought to cook | disparage |
| *dia* | *ubu* | *korobore* | |
| saying | going | close upstream | |

2.
| *ẽ* | *siri* | *hubu* | *kegere* |
|---|---|---|---|
| garden | large | planted | disparage |
| *dia* | *uboba'ae* | | |
| saying | is going | | |
| *kare* | *kui* | *meke'abo* | *kegere* |
| women's | sago | ought to cook | disparage |
| *dia* | *ubu* | *korobore* | |
| saying | going | close upstream | |

3.
| *yiya* | *amena* | *ibu* | *faya'a* | *wagibu* |
|---|---|---|---|---|
| we | men | river | Faya'a | mouth |

*dawabo*
*dawabo*

| *yiya* | *amena* | *igiri* | *sabe* | *na'abo* |
|---|---|---|---|---|
| we | men | Igiri | Ridge | to you |

*dawabo*
*dawabo*

4.
| *amena* | *yagenebo* | *sabe* |
|---|---|---|
| men | Yagenebo | Ridge |

*dawabo*
*dawabo*

| *amena* | *igiri* | *sabe* |
|---|---|---|
| men | Igiri | Ridge |

*ibudawabo*
*dawabo*

1. You should plant a big garden, you jeer at me
   Is this what you are saying?

   You should be cooking First sago, you insult me
   People pass this talk as they go upstream[4]

2. I should plant a big garden, you derogate me
   This is what you are saying

   I ought to cook First sago, you insult me
   People are talking about me as they go upstream

3. We sing of you men of the Faya'a Creek mouth
   *Dawabo*

   You men of Sorofigitono
   *Dawabo*

---

4  'Talk going upstream': people spreading a story as they paddle back to their bush houses upon leaving the longhouses (applies to Hegeso and Barutage only; Herebo bush houses are mostly downstream from the longhouse).

4.  We sing of you men of Yagenebo Ridge
    *Dawabo*

    You men of Igiri Ridge
    *Ibu Dawabo*

---

# Men's Song 15

## Singers: Nabu and Bogo. Recorded 7 January 1985 at Barutage village.

When men beat the drums during the *Usane habora* night-time dancing, women are supposed to be irresistably drawn romantically to the male performers. Women, as they make sago, very commonly sing to their husbands, 'don't come around with your sweet-talking drum and try to entice me away from work.' (See Weiner 1991:167–69.)

1.  | *ira* | *tengo* | *so'a* | *nomo* |
    |---|---|---|---|
    | tree | *tengo* | drum | to me |

    *odibihamone*
    do not call out

    | *ira* | *sugu* | *so'a* | *nomo* |
    |---|---|---|---|
    | tree | *sugu* | drum | to me |

    *odobobareo*
    shouldn't call out

2.  | *ira* | *sugu* | *sa'o* | *nomo* |
    |---|---|---|---|
    | tree | *sugu* | drum | to me |

    *odibihamone*
    do not call out

    | *ira* | *suabo* | *sa'o* | *nomo* |
    |---|---|---|---|
    | tree | *suabo* | drum | to me |

    *odobobarebe*
    shouldn't call out

3. | yiya | amena | sorofigi | tono |
|---|---|---|---|
| we | men | Sorofigi | Ridge |

*dawabo*
*dawabo*

| yiya | amena | yabagamu |
|---|---|---|
| we | men | Yabagamu |

*ibudawabo*
*ibudawabo*

4. | amena | yabagamu |
|---|---|
| men | Yabagamu |

*dawabo*
*dawabo*

| amena | kana | derege |
|---|---|---|
| men | stone | side |

*dawabo*
*dawabo*

---

1. Your *tengo* tree drum
Don't call out to me

Your *sugu* tree drum
You shouldn't call to me

2. Your *sugu* tree drum
Don't cry out to me

Your *suabo* tree drum
Don't call out my name

3. We are the men of Sorofigitono
*Dawabo*

We are the men of Yabagamu
*Ibu Dawabo*

4. We are the men of Yabagamu
*Dawabo*

We are the men of the mountain side
*Dawabo*

# Men's Song 16

## Singers: Oromene and Fahaisabo. Recorded 7 January 1985 at Barutage village.

The deceased, who died from sorcery and was characteristically emaciated upon death, is described in terms of his now ill-fitting clothing, hanging loose upon his frame. The song also refers to the accusations of sorcery that invariably occur at these times. In this case, a Banimahu'u clan man was accused of complicity in the man's death. (See Weiner 1991:109–10.)

1. | *ba'a* | *na'a* | *ira* | *nabi* | *tera'a* | *bunubidobo'ore* |
   |--------|--------|-------|--------|----------|------------------|
   | boy | your | tree | nabi | bark | if emaciated |

   | *ai* | *na* | *do'oyo'o* |
   |------|------|-----------|
   | ai! | to me | do not speak |

   | *ba'a* | *na'a* | *ira* | *tera'a* | *yafubidobo'ore* |
   |--------|--------|-------|----------|------------------|
   | boy | your | tree | bark | if loose |

   | *ai* | *na* | *do'oyo'o* |
   |------|------|-----------|
   | ai! | to me | do not speak |

2. | *ba'a* | *na'a* | *ira* | *bodo* | *yafu* | *soabidobo'ore* |
   |--------|--------|-------|--------|--------|------------------|
   | boy | your | tree | bodo | belt | if descends |

   | *ai* | *nane* | *wae* | *dibubege* |
   |------|--------|-------|-----------|
   | ai! | I | no | saying |

   | *ira* | *kaema* | *bunu* | *soabidobo'ore* |
   |-------|---------|--------|------------------|
   | tree | burnt | black | if descends |

   | *tare* | *na'a* | *kabe* | *ibu* | *do'obege* |
   |--------|--------|--------|-------|-----------|
   | then | you | man | who | are speaking |

3. | *turu* | *ya* | *banima* | *dobo* | *u'ubi-o* |
   |--------|------|----------|--------|----------|
   | sky | bird | banima | clan | children |

   | *dawa* | *dibubege* |
   |--------|-----------|
   | dawabo | saying |

   | *yiya* | *amena* | *karewayu* |
   |--------|---------|-----------|
   | we | men | banimahu'u clan |

   | *ibu* | *dawabo* |
   |-------|----------|
   | water | dawabo |

4. | *yiya* | *amena* | *karewayu* | | | |
|---|---|---|---|---|---|
| we | men | banimahu'u clan | | | |

| *kabe* | *dawa* | *dibubege* | | | |
|---|---|---|---|---|---|
| man | dawabo | saying | | | |

| *yiya* | *amena* | *ya* | *banima* | *dobo* | *u'ubi* |
|---|---|---|---|---|---|
| we | men | bird | banima | clan | children |

| *ibu* | *dawabo* | | | | |
|---|---|---|---|---|---|
| water | dawabo | | | | |

1. Boy, your *nabi* tree bark belt grown loose around your waste
   But do not tell me about it

   Boy, your bark belt hangs loose around your thin waist
   But why tell me about it?

2. Boy, your *bodo* tree bark belt slips down your waist
   But it is not me

   Boy, your dredlocks have become dirty and scanty
   But who is it you are accusing?

3. We are the men of the high flying *banima* bird
   *Dawa* we say

   We are the men of the Kareweyu clan
   *Ibu Dawabo*

4. We are the men of the Kareweyu clan
   The man *Dawa* we are saying

   We are the children of the Banimadobo clan
   *Ibu Dawabo*

# Men's Song 17

## Singers: Oromene and Fahaisabo. Recorded 7 January 1985 at Barutage village.

The Barutage man Ya'asa struck his wife on the hand during an argument. A woman sang of this mistreatment in a sago melody, and the men adopted it as a *sorohabora*. ♫ online example 10.

1. | *ira* | *kabiri* | *maibiyiya* | | | |
   |------|----------|------------|--|--|--|
   | tree | *kabiri* mallet | want to take | | | |

   | *ai* | *na* | *ya* | *dibige* |
   |------|------|------|----------|
   | ai! | my | arm | stated |

   | *ira* | *abu* | *biri* | *maibiyiya* |
   |-------|-------|--------|-------------|
   | tree | mallet | here | want to take |

   | *ai* | *na* | *ya* | *forage* |
   |------|------|------|----------|
   | ai! | my | arm | broken |

2. | *kabo* | *bamo* | *kui* | *ya* | *ka'uye* | *maibiyiya* |
   |--------|--------|-------|------|----------|-------------|
   | girl | this | sago | hand | fill | want to take |

   | *ya* | *derege* |
   |------|----------|
   | arm | motionless |

   | *kabo* | *bamo* | *abu* | *biri* | *maibiyiya* |
   |--------|--------|-------|--------|-------------|
   | girl | this | mallet | here | want to take |

   | *ya* | *kinage* |
   |------|----------|
   | arm | stiff |

3. | *hua* | *nomo* | *ira* | *subiwae* | *yerihabibiyiya* | *wasio* |
   |-------|--------|-------|-----------|------------------|--------|
   | mother | my | tree | paddle | hold with hand | well |

   | *ya* | *wayobibi'e* |
   |------|--------------|
   | arm | motionless |

   | *hua* | *nomo* | *ira* | *baifarira* | *maibibiya* | *dibige* |
   |-------|--------|-------|-------------|-------------|----------|
   | mother | my | tree | sago beater | want to take | stated |

   | *nomo* | *ya* | *forage* |
   |--------|------|----------|
   | my | arm | broken |

4. | gesadobo | ba'a | webi | | |
   |----------|------|------|--|--|
   | Gesadobo | boy | Webi | | |

   | ya'asa | doba'abe | | | |
   |--------|----------|--|--|--|
   | Ya'asa | may we speak | | | |

   | hãyadobo | ka | mege | ba | dibige |
   |----------|------|------|------|--------|
   | Hãyadobo | woman | only | that | stated |

   | ba'a | ya'asa | iba'ae | | |
   |------|--------|--------|--|--|
   | boy | Ya'asa | is | | |

5. | amena | gesa | moma | dobo | u'ubi |
   |-------|------|------|------|-------|
   | men | dog | Moma | clan | children |

   | kabe | dawa | dibige | | |
   |------|------|--------|--|--|
   | man | dawabo | stated | | |

   | amena | hãyadobo | ka | mege | ba |
   |-------|----------|------|------|-----|
   | men | Hãyadobo | woman | only | that |

   | kabe | ya'asa | | | |
   |------|--------|--|--|--|
   | man | Ya'asa | | | |

1. I want to take my *kabiri* wood sago mallet
   But my hand is broken and lifeless

   I want to make sago with my *abu* mallet
   Ai, my hand is broken and useless

2. This girl wants to fill her basket with sago
   But her hand is stiff and motionless

   This girl wants to take her sago mallet
   But her hand is stiff and dead

3. Mother, I want to to hold my canoe paddle strongly
   But my hand is dead

   Mother, I want to take my sago beating stick
   But my hand cannot grasp it

4. The man of the Gesadobo clan, Webi
   May we speak of his son, Ya'asa

   The woman of the Hãyadobo clan
   It is her son, Ya'asa

5. The men of the dog Moma's clan
   The man *Dawa* we are saying

   The woman of the Hãyadobo clan
   Ya'asa, her son

---

# Men's Song 18

## Singers: Oromene and Fahaisabo. Recorded 7 January 1985 at Barutage village.

This song nicely summarises the characteristics of a headman: he who helps others get married, raises many pigs, plants large gardens, and so forth. When such a man dies, his 'hand' becomes weak and lifeless. (See Weiner 1991:169–71.)

1. | *ka* | *sabora* | *tabeyabo* | *ya* | *dibige* | | |
   |---|---|---|---|---|---|---|
   | woman | maiden | headman[5] | hand | stated | | |

   | *ya* | *wãyoiba'ae* | | | | | |
   |---|---|---|---|---|---|---|
   | hand | limp, pliant | | | | | |

   | *ba'a* | *bamo* | *kirari* | *mabuya* | *mege'ame* | | |
   |---|---|---|---|---|---|---|
   | boy | this | rope | held | only perhaps | | |

   | *ya* | *kinayo'o* | *dibige* | | | | |
   |---|---|---|---|---|---|---|
   | hand | stale | stated | | | | |

2. | *ẽ* | *siri* | *hubu* | *ya* | *dibige* | | |
   |---|---|---|---|---|---|---|
   | garden | large | planted | hand | stated | | |

   | *ya* | *derege*[6] | | | | | |
   |---|---|---|---|---|---|---|
   | hand | stone-like | | | | | |

   | *ba'a* | *na'a* | *kui* | *ka'amea* | *kiginimabo* | *ya* | *dibige* |
   |---|---|---|---|---|---|---|
   | boy | your | sago | *ka'amea* | scraps | hand | stated |

   | *ya* | *kinage* | | | | | |
   |---|---|---|---|---|---|---|
   | hand | stiff | | | | | |

---

5   *Kabe tabeyabo*: a man who habitually raises the wealth for many men's bridewealth payments; i.e. a headman (cf. Weiner 1992:170).
6   *Derege*: as in *kana derege*, stone cliff face.

3.  | *yadobo* | *kabo* | *ãyabo* | | |
    | --- | --- | --- | --- | --- |
    | Yadobo | girl | Ãyabo | | |
    | | | | | |
    | *ba'a* | *deya* | | | |
    | boy | Deya | | | |
    | | | | | |
    | *yiya* | *amena* | *kui* | *inibi* | *dibige* |
    | we | men | sago | cooked-eaten | stated |
    | | | | | |
    | *yiya* | *hedawa* | *dibige* | | |
    | we | dawabo | stated | | |

4.  | *kui* | *kenege* | *dobo* | *kabe* | *fasu'u'ubi* |
    | --- | --- | --- | --- | --- |
    | sago | mid-rib | clan | man | Fasu'u'ubi |
    | | | | | |
    | *kabe* | *deya* | *dibubega* | | |
    | man | Deya | speaking | | |
    | | | | | |
    | *yiya* | *amena* | *kui* | *kenege* | |
    | we | men | sago | mid-rib | |
    | | | | | |
    | *dawa* | *dibubega* | | | |
    | dawabo | speaking | | | |

1.  The man who fastens a wife for others with his own hand
    That hand is now weak

    The man who holds the rope of the black pig
    His hand is limp and weak

2.  The man who cleared a great garden
    His hand is stiff and lifeless

    The man who gatherd *ka'amea* sago scraps for his many pigs
    His hand is weak now

3.  The Yadobo woman Ãyabo
    Her son Deya

    We are the men of Cooked Sago clan
    *Hedawa* we say

4.  The man of the Sago Rib clan, Fasu'u'ubi
    Deya, we say

    We are the men of the Sago Rib clan
    *Dawa*

# Men's Song 19

## Singers: Muya and Agiri. Recorded 7 January 1985 at Barutage village.

This is a particularly beautiful song in Foi, making use of the imagery of cloud-covered mountains and limestone-littered paths so beloved by Foi singers. (See Weiner 1991:61.) ♫ online example 10.

1. | *duma* | *a'o* | *figibiwe'iya'are* | |
   |--------|-------|-------------------|--|
   | mountain | cloud | part-climb-come | |
   | | | | |
   | *ba'a* | *na'a* | *igebe* | |
   | boy | you | is it? | |
   | | | | |
   | *duma* | *kana* | *togebiwe'iya'are* | |
   | mountain | stone | overturn-come | |
   | | | | |
   | *ba'a* | *na'a* | *egebe* | |
   | boy | you | is it? | |

2. | *duma* | *kana* | *togebiwe'iya'are* | |
   |--------|--------|--------------------|--|
   | mountain | stone | remove-come | |
   | | | | |
   | *ba'a* | *na'a* | *igebe* | |
   | boy | you | is it? | |
   | | | | |
   | *duma* | *haru* | *hubiwe'iya'are* | |
   | mountain | hill | breaking-come | |
   | | | | |
   | *ba'a* | *na'agebe* | | |
   | boy | is it you? | | |

3. | *duma* | *busu* | *humekiribi* | *waba'are* |
   |--------|--------|-------------|-----------|
   | mountain | dappled light | break through | come |
   | | | | |
   | *ba'a* | *na'a* | *igebe* | |
   | boy | you | is it? | |
   | | | | |
   | *duma* | *kana* | *togebi* | *waba'are* |
   | mountain | stone | overturn | come |
   | | | | |
   | *ba'a* | *na'agebe* | | |
   | boy | is it you? | | |

| 4. | *duma* | *haru* | *hubu* | *se* | *sawa* |
|---|---|---|---|---|---|
| | mountain | climb | parted | marsupial | Sawa |

*dawabo*
*dawabo*

| | *duma* | *hau* | *sese* | *sone* | |
|---|---|---|---|---|---|
| | mountain | side | marsupial | Sone | |

*dawabo*
*dawabo*

| 5. | *duma* | *hau* | *se* | *sawa* | |
|---|---|---|---|---|---|
| | mountain | side | marsupial | Sawa | |

*dawabo*
*dawabo*

| | *duma* | *haru* | *se* | *sawa* | |
|---|---|---|---|---|---|
| | mountain | hill | marsupial | Sawa | |

*dawabo*
*dawabo*

1. The mist covering the mountain parts as you come
   Little one is that you?

   The mountain stones move aside as you come
   Boy, is that you?

2. You move the mountain stones as you come
   Boy, is that you?

   You part the forest as you come down the mountain
   Little one, is it you?

3. You break through the dappled sunlight on the hillside
   Boy, is it you?

   You part the stones as you come down the mountain
   Is that you little one?

4. The mountain climber, stone mover, Sawa the marsupial
   *Dawabo*

   The mountainside dweller, Sone the marsupial
   *Dawabo*

5.   Mountain side, marsupial Sawa
     *Dawabo*

     Mountain climber, marsupial Sawa
     *Dawabo*

---

# Men's Song 20

## Singers: Oromene and Fahaisabo. Recorded 5 January 1985 at Barutage village.

This song makes use of the most popular landscape imagery for the Foi: the sounds made by swiftly flowing water. The contrast between the exuberance and ceaselessness of water and the finality and stillness of death is most poignantly expressed here. (See Weiner 1991:46, 104–5; 2001:26.) ♩ online example 11.[7]

| | | | | |
|---|---|---|---|---|
| 1. | *ibu*<br>river | *hekoro*<br>bank | *yibumena*<br>sleep-man | |
| | *bereye*<br>lost | *yibo'oge*<br>sleeps | | |
| | *ibu*<br>river | *hekoro*<br>bank | *bagia*[7]<br>debris island | *yibumena*<br>sleep-man |
| | *bereye*<br>lost | *yibo'oge*<br>sleeps | | |
| 2. | *ibu*<br>river | *ya*<br>hand | *ka'uye*<br>together | *ma*<br>takes | *yibumena*<br>sleep-man |
| | *ua*<br>gone | *ha*<br>is | *yiboba'ae*<br>sleeps | | |
| | *ibu*<br>river | *ira*<br>tree | *ma*<br>takes | *yibumena*<br>sleep-man | |
| | *nomaye*<br>how | *ebo'oge*<br>is | | | |

---

7   *Bagia-*: to divide into parts; hence, anything that branches out, like tree roots. And in this case, a clot of debris in the middle of a river causing the water to divide into two or more streams.

3. | *ibu* | *dimani* | *hua* | *yibumena* |
   |---|---|---|---|
   | river | rushing | strikes | sleep-man |
   | *kabe* | *nabo'oge* | | |
   | man | what (has happened) | | |
   | *ibu* | *hefofore* | *hua* | *yibumena* |
   | river | bank | strikes | sleep-man |
   | *kabe* | *bereye* | *yiboba'ae* | |
   | man | lost | sleeps | |

4. | *kabo* | *heko'onomo* | *yo* | *aba-o* |
   |---|---|---|---|
   | girl | Heko'ono | her | father, oh! |
   | *ibudawabo* | | | |
   | *ibudawabo* | | | |
   | *ba'a* | *bugimena* | *yo* | *aba-o* |
   | boy | Bugimena | his | father, oh! |
   | *ibuhedawabo* | | | |
   | *dawabo* | | | |

5. | *ba'a* | *bugimena* | *yo* | *aba-o* |
   |---|---|---|---|
   | boy | Bugimena | his | father, oh! |
   | *ibudawabo* | | | |
   | *ibudawabo* | | | |
   | *kabo* | *heko'onomo* | *yo* | *aba-o* |
   | girl | Heko'ono | her | father, oh! |
   | *ibudawabo* | | | |
   | *ibudawabo* | | | |

1. The man who sleeps by the bank of the rushing water
   He is lost now

   Twigs and branches clot in the swift flowing water
   But he who sleeps there is lost

2. The man who catches fish from the water with his hand
   He has gone somewhere else to sleep

   The man who takes the fish from the water with his hands

What has happened to him?

3. The beautiful hissing sound of rapid water
   But you who slept there, what of you?

   The bank of the rushing water
   The man who slept there is lost

4. The father of the girl Heko'ono
   *Ibu Dawabo*

   The father of the boy Bugimena
   *Ibu hedawabo*

5. The father of Bugimena
   *Ibu Dawabo*

   The father of Heko'ono
   *Ibu Dawabo*

# Men's Song 21

## Singers: Muya and Agiri. Recorded 5 January 1985 at Barutage village.

This song likens the deceased to a marsupial in the forest, and recites the names of the places the marsupial travelled and slept in the hunting forest. ♫ online example 11.

1. *duma*       *masiba*       *dumaro'o*
   mountain     Masiba         mountain

   *aodibihaboro*
   bush covered

   *duma*       *ao*           *dumaro'o*
   mountain     bush           mountain

   *aodoboro*
   jungle covered

2.  | ba'a | na'a | metega | yibu | kanega |
    |------|------|--------|------|--------|
    | boy | your | hidden | sleep | cave |

    *aodoboro*
    jungle covered

    | ba'a | na'a | kubarihimu | iga |
    |------|------|------------|-----|
    | boy | your | Kubarihimu[8] | path |

    *aodoboro*
    jungle covered

3.  | ibu | damekebo | fera | igaro'o |
    |-----|----------|------|---------|
    | river | Damekebo[9] | space | path |

    | aodia | yibi | haboba'a |
    |-------|------|----------|
    | bush covered | sleep | remains |

    | duma | masiba | duma |
    |------|--------|------|
    | mountain | Masiba | mountain |

    | aodia | yibi | haboba'a |
    |-------|------|----------|
    | bush covered | sleep | remains |

4.  | egadobo | humane |
    |---------|--------|
    | Egadobo | Humane |

    | ba'a | hagiabe |
    |------|---------|
    | boy | Hagiabe |

    | ira | onobo | dobo | ka | horaro(e) |
    |-----|-------|------|-----|-----------|
    | tree | onobo | clan | woman | Horaro(e) |

    | ba'a | sera |
    |------|------|
    | boy | Sera |

---

8   *Kubarihimu* = 'kubaru tree cut', i.e. named after a spot where a *kubaru* tree was cut down.

9   *Damekebo* = 'salt cooked', i.e. named after a place where vegetable salt was prepared.

| | | | | |
|---|---|---|---|---|
| 5. *ira* | *onobo* | *dobo* | *kabo* | *horare* |
| tree | *onobo* | clan | girl | Horare |
| | | | | |
| *ba'a* | *hagiabe* | | | |
| boy | Hagiabe | | | |
| | | | | |
| *egadobo* | *humane* | | | |
| Egadobo | Humane | | | |
| | | | | |
| *ba'a* | *sera* | | | |
| boy | Sera | | | |

1. The mountain Masiba
Is covered with bush

   The forest covered mountain
Reclaimed by the bush

2. Boy, your hidden cave in which you slept
Is covered over by the jungle

   Boy, your path to Kubarihimu Creek
Has been taken back by the bush

3. The Damekebo path which cuts its way through the mountain
Is covered over by the jungle

   The mountain Masiba
Has been covered over by the bush

4. Humane of the Egadobo clan
His son, Hagiabe

   The woman of the *onobo* tree clan, Horare
Her son, Sera

5. The *onobo* clan woman Horare
Her son Hagiabe

   The man of the Egadobo clan, Humane
His son, Sera

# Men's Song 22

## Singers: Muya and Agiri. Recorded 5 January 1985 at Barutage village.

The dogs named Awaro and Kimi appear in the myth 'Moon-man and Sun-girl', concerning the origin of the sun and moon, originally collected by F. E. Williams (1940–42:149–51; 1977:317–20). They seem to be unspecific names for dogs, much as 'Fido' is for Americans. (See Weiner 1991:47; 2001:26.) ♩ online example 12.

1. *awaro*   *yiadira'ame*
  Awaro   cries out perhaps

  *naye*    *uge*
  how    gone

  *kimi*    *yiadira'ame*
  Kimi    cries out perhaps

  *naye*    *uge*
  how    gone

2. *duma*   *vivi*   *gari*   *vira*
  mountain  Vivi   base   gone

  *naye*    *ubihage*
  how    habitually go

  *kabosa*   *gari*   *vira*
  *kabosa* tree  base   gone

  *naye*    *viye*
  how    go

3. *ibu*    *namasa'a* *gari*   *vira*
  creek   Namasa'a  head   gone

  *naye*    *ubihage*
  how    habitually go

  *duma*   *vivi*   *gari*   *vira*
  mountain  Vivi   base   gone

  *naye*    *ubihage*
  how    habitually go

4.  *abaru*            *yiadira*
    Abaru             cries out

    *naye*             *ubiremo*
    how               his going

    *kimi*             *yiadira*
    Kimi              cries out

    *naye*             *ubiremo*
    how               his going

5.  *ira*          *kibudobo*      *kabe*        *vibu*
    tree          Kibudobo        man          Vibu

    *dawabo*
    dawabo

    *ira*          *kibudobo*      *kabe*        *vibu*
    tree          Kibudobo        man          Vibu

    *dawabo*
    dawabo

6.  *orodobo*      *ka*            *bononobo*
    Orodobo       woman           Bononobo

    *ba'a*         *gamabo*
    boy           Gamabo

    *ira*          *kibudobo*      *kabe*        *vibu*
    tree          Kibudobo        man          Vibu

    *ba'a*         *gamabo*
    boy           Gamabo

1.  The dog Awaro cries out
    How will it find the way now?

    The dog Kimi cries out
    How will it go?

2.  To the base of Mt Vivi
    How can he keep going?

    To the base of the *kabosa* tree
    How can it find the way?

3.  To the source of the Namasa'a Creek
    How will he go?

    To the base of the mountain Vivi
    How will he keep going there?

4.  The sound of Abaru's barking
    'How will I go?' it is saying

    The sound of Kimi's barking
    'How will I go?' it is saying

5.  The Kibudobo man, Vibu
    *Dawabo*

    The Kibudobo man, Vibu
    *Dawabo*

6.  The Orodobo woman Bononobo
    Her son, Gamabo

    The clan of *kibu* tree, the man Vibu
    His son, Gamabo

# Men's Song 23

## Singers: Habeyu and Hira. Recorded 7 January 1985 at Barutage village.

This is a woman's sago song that was performed without any changes as a men's *sorohabora*. A woman is pounding sago and she hears the sound of the *obo* and *sisi* birds singing from a tree nearby. She pretends it is her sweetheart, and she answers back, 'Don't bother me now, I am making sago!'

1.  | *ira* | *fagiweĩ* | *yĩyĩ* | *bi* | *erakera'ame* |
    |---|---|---|---|---|
    | tree | twisted-come | branches | there | sitting perhaps |

    | *odomone* |
    |---|
    | do not call |

    | *ira* | *tu'u* | *yĩyĩ* | *bi* | *erakerare'ame* |
    |---|---|---|---|---|
    | tree | tu'u | branches | there | sitting perhaps |

    | *tawadomone* |
    |---|
    | do not call out |

| 2. | *ira*<br>tree | *fayare*<br>*fayare* | *yĩyĩ*<br>branches | *bi*<br>there | *erakera'ame*<br>sitting perhaps |
|----|---------------|----------------------|--------------------|---------------|----------------------------------|

*odomone*
do not call

| | *ira*<br>tree | *koage*<br>*koage* | *yĩyĩ*<br>branches | *bi*<br>there | *erakera'ame*<br>sitting perhaps |
|----|---------------|--------------------|--------------------|---------------|----------------------------------|

| *aba-o*<br>father, oh! | *odomone*<br>do not call |
|------------------------|--------------------------|

| 3. | *aya*<br>sky | *ya*<br>bird | *obo*<br>*obo* |
|----|--------------|--------------|----------------|

*awara'abo*
*dawabo*

| | *aya*<br>sky | *ya*<br>bird | *sisi*<br>*sisi* |
|----|--------------|--------------|------------------|

*dawabo*
*dawabo*

| 4. | *aya*<br>sky | *ya*<br>bird | *obo*<br>*obo* |
|----|--------------|--------------|----------------|

*dawabo*
*dawabo*

| | *aya*<br>sky | *ya*<br>bird | *sisi*<br>*sisi* |
|----|--------------|--------------|------------------|

*dawabo*
*dawabo*

1. Is it on the twisted branches of the tree above you are sitting?
   Don't call out to me

   Are you perhaps on the *tu'u* tree bracnhes?
   Don't call out to me

2. Perhaps you are sitting on the *fayare* tree branches
   But don't call out my name

Are you sitting on the *koage* tree branches perhaps?
'Sister!' don't call to me

3.  The *obo* bird above
    *Awara'abo*

    The *sisi* bird above
    *Dawabo*

4.  The *obo* bird in the sky
    *Dawabo*

    The *sisi* bird above
    *Dawabo*

---

# Men's Song 24

## Singers: Mare and Maniname. Recorded 7 January 1985 at Barutage village.

This song begins as a repeated woman's sago melody with a familiar theme; it ends with the men's *dawabo*.

1.  | *nomo* | *kui* | *hua* | *mabo* | *ti* |
    |--------|-------|-------|--------|------|
    | my | sago | pounding | taken | here |

    *kaubihamone*
    do not fence (me)

    | *nomo* | *kui* | *dage* | *mabo* | *ti* |
    |--------|-------|--------|--------|------|
    | my | sago | pounded | taken | here |

    *kaumone*
    do not encircle

2.  | *ira* | *gibi* | *sa'o* | *nomo* |
    |-------|--------|--------|--------|
    | tree | gibi | drum | to me |

    *odibihamone*
    do not call out

    | *ira* | *tiraru* | *sa'o* | *nomo* |
    |-------|----------|--------|--------|
    | tree | tiraru | drum | to me |

*odomone*
do not call

3. | *yiya* | *amena* | *nanumi* | *hubu* | |
|---|---|---|---|---|
| we | men | Nanumi | strongly | |

*dawabo*
*dawabo*

| *yiya* | *amena* | *nanumi* | *hubu* | *ku'ubaĩ* |
|---|---|---|---|---|
| we | men | Nanumi | strongly | beautiful |

*dawabo*
*dawabo*

4. | *yiya* | *amena* | *sorofigi* | *tono* |
|---|---|---|---|
| we | men | Sorofigi | Hill |

*dawabo*
*dawabo*

| *yiya* | *amena* | *sorofigi* | *tono* |
|---|---|---|---|
| we | men | Sorofigi | Hill |

*dawabo*
*dawabo*

1. I am working here at my sago trough
Don't crowd me here

I have my sago to pound now
Don't bother me

2. With your *gibi* tree-made drum
Don't sing out to me

With your *tiruru* tree-made drum
Don't call out my name

3. We are the men of the swiftly flowing Nanumi River
*Dawabo*

We are the men of the fiercely flowing Baru River
*Dawabo*

4.  We are the men of Sorofigitono
    *Dawabo*

    We are the men of Sorofigitono
    *Dawabo*

---

# Men's Song 25

## Singers: Gofe and Hobe. Recorded 7 January 1985 at Barutage village.

A dead man leaves behind children, as this song commemorates. The children are referred to by reference to their toys and clothing. But the deceased is also referred to as a boy who himself has left these toys behind.

1.  | *ba'a* | *na'a* | *ira* | *sõga* | *bi'a* | *mano* | *mogoreye* |
    |--------|--------|-------|--------|--------|--------|-----------|
    | boy    | your   | tree  | stem   | arrow  | small  | left      |

    | *ua*   | *hai*  | *yiboro* |
    |--------|--------|----------|
    | gone   | lives  | sleeps   |

    | *ira*  | *mamage*  | *mefese'ame*   |
    |--------|-----------|----------------|
    | tree   | toy bow   | left perhaps   |

    | *bereboba'ae* |
    |---------------|
    | is lost       |

2.  | *ba'a* | *na'a* | *ira* | *kotono* | *gaĩya* | *mano* | *sina'ame*         |
    |--------|--------|-------|----------|---------|--------|-------------------|
    | boy    | your   | tree  | kotono   | skirt   | small  | abandoned perhaps |

    | *ua*   | *ha*   | *yiboba'ae* |
    |--------|--------|-------------|
    | gone   | is     | sleeps      |

    | *ba'a* | *na'a* | *ira* | *tera'a* | *yefu* | *sina'ame*        |
    |--------|--------|-------|----------|--------|-------------------|
    | boy    | your   | tree  | bark     | belt   | abandoned perhaps |

    | *ua*   | *ha*   | *visomoro* |
    |--------|--------|------------|
    | gone   | is     | went       |

3.  | *ira*  | *so'one* | *dobo* | *kabo* | *fana'ayome*  |
    |--------|----------|--------|--------|---------------|
    | tree   | *so'one* | clan   | girl   | Fana'ayome    |

    | *ba'a* | *derabore* |
    |--------|------------|
    | boy    | Derabore   |

| *yo* | *hua* | *ka* | *moruame* | | |
|------|-------|------|-----------|--|--|
| his | mother | woman | Moruame | | |

*ibudawabo*
*ibudawabo*

4. 

| *yiya* | *amena* | *kibudobo* | | *ba'a* | *hogebomo* |
|--------|---------|------------|--|--------|------------|
| we | men | Kibudobo | | boy | Hogebo |

| *yo* | *hua* | *ka* | *moruame* | | |
|------|-------|------|-----------|--|--|
| his | mother | woman | Moruame | | |

| *yo* | *aba* | *ba'a* | *yafo* | *dawabo* | |
|------|-------|--------|--------|----------|--|
| his | son | boy | name | *dawabo* | |

| *ba'a* | *derabore* | | | | |
|--------|------------|--|--|--|--|
| boy | Derabore | | | | |

---

1. Boy, you have left behind your toy bow and arrow
   It is lost

   You have left behind your *mamage* wood toy bow and arrow
   Now it is lost

2. Boy, you have left your little girl's *kotono* string skirt
   Abandoning it, it is lost

   Your little boy's *tera'a* bark belt
   You have left it behind

3. The *so'one* tree clan woman Fana'ayome
   Her son Derabore

   His mother Moruame
   *Ibu Dawabo*

4. His father Kibudobo man Hogebo
   His mother Moruame

   Their child whose name we call so sweetly
   Derabore

---

# Men's Song 26

## Singers: Dunubu and Abuyu. Recorded 4 December 1984 at Hegeso village.

This song makes use of the polysemy of the Foi word *hua*, which means 'struck' (from the verb *hu-*, to strike, kill, hit); 'planted' (from the same verb, *mohu-*); and, with the addition of nasalisation on the *u* (*hũa*), 'mother.' Crashing, rushing water strikes the stones in creek and river beds. Also, men must plant the stakes with which they construct fish dams across the mouths of small creeks. Finally, large bodies of water, like the Mubi, Baru, Yo'oro Rivers, and Lake Kutubu, are called *ibu hũa*, the 'mother' of waters, as in any particularly large specimen of any category (hence, *a hũa* 'mother of houses', i.e. the longhouse).

*Hemomo'o* is a detritus, and flotsam collects as it flows downstream. It also means, 'froth, scum', etc. The verb *hubagia-* means two things: (1) to push aside logs and flotsam as one paddles a canoe; (2) to spread fish poison in dammed water. This fine verse thus compresses the image of spreading fish poison in still water, with that of the man threading a canoe through debris-laden water. (See Weiner 1991:60, 83, 102–4.)

| | | | | |
|---|---|---|---|---|
| 1. | *ibu*<br>creek | *dufu*<br>dam | *hua*<br>planted | *yibumena*<br>sleep-man |
| | *uaha*<br>go-live | *yiboba'ae*<br>sleeps | | |
| | *ibu*<br>creek | *dufu*<br>dam | *hua*<br>planted | *yibumena*<br>sleep-man |
| | *uaha*<br>go-live | *yiboba'ae*<br>sleeps | | |
| 2. | *ibu*<br>creek | *dufu*<br>dam | *hua*<br>planted | *yibumena*<br>sleep-man |
| | *uaha*<br>go-live | *yiboba'ae*<br>sleeps | | |
| | *ibu*<br>creek | *dufu*<br>dam | *hua*<br>planted | *yibumena*<br>sleep-man |
| | *uaha*<br>go-live | *yiboba'ae*<br>sleeps | | |

3. 

| ibu | dimani | hua | yibumena |
|-----|--------|-----|----------|
| water | rushing | strikes | sleep-man |

| uaha | yiboba'ae |
|------|-----------|
| go-live | sleeps |

| ibu | ãgu | hua | yibumena |
|-----|-----|-----|----------|
| water | swiftly | strikes | sleep-man |

| bereboba'ae | |
|-------------|--|
| is lost | |

4. 

| ibu | hua | yibumena |
|-----|-----|----------|
| water | mother | sleep-man |

| uaha | yiboba'ae |
|------|-----------|
| go-live | sleeps |

| ibu | ka'asubagedia | yibumena |
|-----|---------------|----------|
| water | crashing | sleep-man |

| bereboba'ae | |
|-------------|--|
| is lost | |

5. 

| ibu | hemomo'o | hubagia | yibumena |
|-----|----------|---------|----------|
| water | flotsam | remove | sleep-man |

| uaha | yiboba'ae |
|------|-----------|
| go-live | sleeps |

| ibu | ãgu | hua | yibumena |
|-----|-----|-----|----------|
| water | swiftly | mother | sleep-man |

| bereboba'ae | |
|-------------|--|
| is lost | |

6. 

| nami | ko'onomo | yo | aba-o |
|------|----------|-----|-------|
| pig | Ko'ono | its | father, oh! |

| dawabo |
|--------|
| dawabo |

| gesa | sawa | yo | aba-o |
|------|------|-----|-------|
| dog | Sawa | its | father, oh! |

| dawabo |
|--------|
| dawabo |

| 7. | *nami* | *duni* | *yo* | *aba* |
|----|--------|--------|------|-------|
|    | pig    | many   | their | father |

*dawabo*
*dawabo*

| | *gesa* | *sawa* | *yo* | *aba* |
|---|--------|--------|------|-------|
| | dog    | Sawa   | his  | father |

*dawabo*
*dawabo*

1.  Near the fish dam where you habitually sleep
    There you have gone to rest

    Near the fish dam where you are wont to stay
    There you have gone to sleep the night

2.  Near the fish dam where you habitually sleep
    There you have gone to rest

    Near the fish dam where you are wont to stay
    There you have gone to sleep the night

3.  He who sleeps near the rushing water
    There he silently sleeps

    Near the rushing hissing water
    Only the river's sound we hear

4.  The man who sleeps near the sibilant water
    He has gone to rest there

    The soft crash of rushing water
    But he is lost

5.  He who removed the flotsam as he paddled
    He has gone there to sleep

    Near the splashing rushing water
    He is lost

6.  The father of the pig Ko'onobo
    *Dawabo*

    The father of the dog Sawa
    *Dawabo*

7.  The man who cared for many pigs
    *Dawabo*

    He who cared for the dog Sawa
    *Dawabo*

---

# Men's Song 27

## Singers: Kora and Abeabo.[10] Recorded 4 December 1984 at Hegeso village.

The gentle up-and-down movement of a canoe as it moves through water is evoked in this song. (See Weiner 1991:99–101.)

1.  | *ba'a* | *na'a* | *bare* | *ga* | *burayodi* | *dibiri* |
    |---|---|---|---|---|---|
    | boy | your | canoe | prow | rise from water | curved |

    | *na-o* | *mihiba'ane* | *we* |
    |---|---|---|
    | I | to embark | come! |

    | *ba'a* | *na'a* | *bare* | *ga* | *yõdibi* |
    |---|---|---|---|---|
    | boy | your | canoe | prow | dips into water |

    | *na-o* | *moware* | *do'ane* | *we* |
    |---|---|---|---|
    | I too | to embark | to speak | come! |

2.  | *ba'a* | *na'a* | *bare* | *ga* | *ya* | *sabeyu* | *arumaibi* |
    |---|---|---|---|---|---|---|
    | boy | your | canoe | prow | bird | cockatoo | tongue-taken |

    | *na-o* | *moware* | *do'ane* | *we* |
    |---|---|---|---|
    | I too | to embark | to speak | come! |

    | *ba'a* | *na'a* | *bare* | *ga* | *ya* | *sabeyu* | *arumaibi* |
    |---|---|---|---|---|---|---|
    | boy | your | canoe | prow | bird | cockatoo | tongue-taken |

    | *na-o* | *moware* | *do'ane* | *we* |
    |---|---|---|---|
    | I too | to embark | to speak | come! |

3–4. [verse 2 repeated two more times]

---

10  As well as being skilled singers and close friends, Kora Midibaru and Abeabo Waibo were my field assistants, helping me to translate many of the songs in this volume (Weiner 1991:ii, xiii).

5. 

| *ba'a* | *na'a* | *ibu* | *faya'a* | *wagibu* |
|---|---|---|---|---|
| boy | your | river | Faya'a | mouth |

*ibudawabo*
*ibudawabo*

| *yiya* | *amena* | *ibu* | *hesa* | *wagibu* |
|---|---|---|---|---|
| we | men | creek | Hesa | mouth |

*dawabo*
*dawabo*

6. 

| *yiya* | *amena* | *ĩbariabe* | *sabe* | *u'ubi* |
|---|---|---|---|---|
| we | men | Ĩbariabe | Ridge | children |

*dawabo*
*dawabo*

| *yiya* | *amena* | *kana* | *deregebo* |
|---|---|---|---|
| we | men | stone | cliff face |

*dawabo*
*dawabo*

1. Boy, the curved prow of your canoe lifts gently from the water
Come fetch me too

   The bow of your canoe dips gracefully back into the water
Oh come and let me embark too!

2. Boy, your cockatoo-tongued canoe prow
Come and get me, I say!

   Boy, your canoe prow as beautiful as the cockatoo's tongue
I too want to get in your canoe

3–4. [verse 2 repeated 2 more times]

5. Boy, your Faya'a Creek flowing into the Mubi
*Ibu Dawabo*

   We are the men of the mouth of Hesa Creek
*Dawabo*

6.  We are the children of Ĩbariabe Hill
    *Dawabo*

    We are the men of the stone lined mountain
    *Dawabo*

---

# Men's Song 28

## Singers: Hasuabo and Kuri. Recorded 2 January 1985 at Hegeso village.

This song was sung in memory of a Wage River man who migrated to Hegeso village and remained there for the rest of his life. His name was Ayamena, which literally means 'above man'. Like most Highlands men, he wore a knitted cap, and after his death, this cap was likened to a cassowary's crest. Denabuyu and Kinabo were Ayamena's mother and father respectively; Ayamena's name itself is not mentioned in the *dawa*.

1.  *togeganuga*
    cassowary crest

    | | |
    |---|---|
    | *ira* | *waboba* |
    | tree | come |
    | *iburi* | *yage* |
    | water | drowned |
    | *aodiba* | |
    | bush covered | |

2.  | *ira* | *gua* | *duru* |
    |---|---|---|
    | tree | *gua* | fence |
    | *foraye* | *uboba'a* | |
    | broken | has gone | |
    | *masene* | *dogo* | |
    | arrow | bundle | |
    | *foroma* | *uboba'a* | |
    | broken + take | has gone | |

3. | *ibu* | *wage* | *kabo* | *denabuyu* |
| river | Wage | girl | Denabuyu |

| *ba'a* | *kinabo* | | |
| boy | Kinabo | | |

| *ibu* | *wage* | *kabo* | *denabuyu* |
| river | Wage | girl | Denabuyu |

| *ba'a* | *daribu* | | |
| boy | Daribu | | |

4. | *ibu* | *wage* | *kabo* | *denabuyu* |
| river | Wage | girl | Denabuyu |

| *ba'a* | *kinabo* | | |
| boy | Kinabo | | |

| *ibu* | *wage* | *kabo* | *denabuyu* |
| river | Wage | girl | Denabuyu |

| *ba'a* | *daribu* | | |
| boy | Daribu | | |

1. The man of the cassowary crest
   The bush has covered him over

   Drowned in the river
   The trees have hidden him

2. The Highlands' *gua* tree fence
   Has been broken off

   The Highlands's *masene* arrow bundle
   Has been snapped in two

3. The woman of the Wage River, Denabuyu
   The boy Kinabo

   The woman of the Wage River, Denabuyu
   The boy Kinabo

4. The woman of the Wage River, Denabuyu
   The boy Kinabo

   The woman of the Wage River, Denabuyu
   The boy Kinabo

# Men's Song 29

## Singers: Hasuabo and Kuri. Recorded 2 January 1985 at Hegeso village.

A man's trees, flowers, and garden vegetables become prey to wild animals and birds and to furtive humans after he has died. The signs of life and regeneration of a man's plantings gradually are consumed, by animals or people as well as the bush itself, after the man has died.

1.  *kõ*            *tegeri*        *agiri'ameo*
    cordyline       *tegeri*        stolen perhaps

    *virima*        *uboba'ae*
    shot + taken    has gone

    *kõ*            *tegeri*        *agiri'ameo*
    cordyline       *tegeri*        stolen perhaps

    *virima*        *uboba'ae*
    shot + taken    has gone

2.  *ba'a*          *na'a*          *ga*            *mohagi*
    boy             your            banana          hanging

    *agiri*         *hua*           *uboba'ae*
    stolen          struck          has gone

    *ba'a*          *na'a*          *hãya*          *auwa*
    boy             your            Ficus           auwa

    *agiri*         *vira*          *uboba'ae*
    stolen          shot            has gone

3.  *hãya*          *auwa*          *agiri'ame*
    Ficus           *auwa*          stolen perhaps

    *hua*           *uboba'ae*
    struck          has gone

    *hãya*          *su'uri*        *agiri'ame*
    Ficus           *su'uri*        stolen perhaps

    *viri*          *uboba'ae*
    shot            has gone

95

4. | *aya* | *ya* | *unubu* |
   | sky | bird | flying fox |

   *dawabo*
   *dawabo*

   | *aya* | *ya* | *gugabe* |
   | sky | bird | flying fox |

   *dawabo*
   *dawabo*

5. | *aya* | *ya* | *unubu* |
   | sky | bird | flying fox |

   *dawabo*
   *dawabo*

   | *aya* | *ya* | *gugabe* |
   | sky | bird | flying fox |

   *dawabo*
   *dawabo*

1. Perhaps your *tegeri* cordyline has been stolen
   They struck it and left

   Perhaps your *tegeri* cordyline has been stolen
   They struck it and left

2. Boy, your banana hanging there
   Perhaps the flying foxes have eaten and stolen it

   Boy, your *auwa* Ficus leaves
   Perhaps the flying foxes have shot it and left

3. Your *auwa* Ficus leaves
   They have struck them and left

   Your *su'uri* Ficus leaves
   They have shot them and left

4. The flying fox high in the sky
   *Dawabo*

   The sky bird, the flying fox
   *Dawabo*

5.  The flying fox high in the sky
    *Dawabo*

    The sky bird, the flying fox
    *Dawabo*

---

# Men's Song 30

## Singers: Viya and Komo'o. Recorded 2 January 1985 at Hegeso village.

When the subject of this song, Sega, was mortally ill, he was flown to the hospital in Mendi. He eventually was flown back to Pimaga, and he died in Hegeso. This song makes use of the aeroplane image. (See Weiner 1991:47; 2001:26.)

1.  | *turu* | *mogo* | *bagia* | *vira* |
    |---|---|---|---|
    | sky | mist | divides | shot |

    *iribiwae*
    saw not

    | *bare* | *ŭdia* | *vira* |
    |---|---|---|
    | aeroplane | hummed | gone |

    *iribiwae*
    saw not

2.  | *turu* | *mogo* | *bagia* | *vira* |
    |---|---|---|---|
    | sky | mist | divides | shot |

    *iribiwae*
    saw not

    | *bare* | *ŭdia* | *vira* |
    |---|---|---|
    | aeroplane | hummed | gone |

    *iribiwae*
    saw not

3.  | *bare* | *ŭdia* | *vira* |
    |---|---|---|
    | aeroplane | droned | went |

    | *nabo* | *dibiwae* |
    |---|---|
    | to me | said not |

Songs of the Empty Place

| | | |
|---|---|---|
| *bare* | *õdia* | *vira* |
| aeroplane | droned | went |
| *nabo* | *dibiwae* | |
| to me | said not | |

| | | | |
|---|---|---|---|
| 4. *wa'aridobo* | *ka* | *hasobe* | |
| Wa'aridobo | woman | Hasobe | |
| *ba'a* | *sega* | | |
| boy | Sega | | |
| *ira* | *namani* | *dobo* | *yarogemo* |
| tree | namani | clan | Yaroge |
| *ba'a* | *fu'ubuĩ* | | |
| boy | Fu'ubuĩ | | |

| | | | |
|---|---|---|---|
| 5. *wa'aridobo* | *ka* | *hasobe* | |
| Wa'aridobo | woman | Hasobe | |
| *ba'a* | *sega* | | |
| boy | Sega | | |
| *ira* | *namani* | *dobo* | *yarogemo* |
| tree | namani | clan | Yaroge |
| *ba'a* | *fu'ubuĩ* | | |
| boy | Fu'ubuĩ | | |

1. Through the cloud-covered mountains you flew
   But we did not see you

   The aeroplane droned as it disappeared
   But we saw you not

2. Through the cloud-covered mountains you flew
   But we did not see you

   The aeroplane droned as it disappeared
   But we saw you not

3. The aeroplane buzzed as it flew away
   But you said nothing to us

The aeroplane hummed as it disappeared through the cloud
But to us you said nothing

4.  The Wa'aridobo woman, Hasobe
    Her son Sega

    The clan of the *namani* tree, the man Yaroge
    His son, Fu'u'ubi

5.  The Wa'aridobo woman, Hasobe
    Her son Sega

    The clan of the *namani* tree, the man Yaroge
    His son, Fu'u'ubi

---

# Men's Song 31

## Singers: Viya and Komo'o. Recorded 2 January 1985 at Hegeso village.

In January 1985 the Hegeso men held their pig-kill. This song, composed some months before by one of the Hegeso women, expressed the uncertainties that surround the planning of such a pig-kill. The verse concerning the bird feathers refers to the placing of such feathers in mens' headdresses.

1.  *ira*        *nabu*        *gugu'anegebe*
    tree       casuarina    will it flower?

    *dobo'owa*    *togebe*
    spoken of      is this it?

    *ira*        *sonane*     *gugu'anegebe*
    tree       *sonane*     will it flower?

    *dobo'owa*    *togebe*
    spoken of      is this it?

2.  *sui*       *gerewa*     *hae*      *do'ane*     *dobo'owa*
    cane      *gerewa*     fruit     to speak   spoken of

    *togebe*
    is this it?

| | | | | |
|---|---|---|---|---|
| *ira* | *gua* | *hae* | *gugu'ane* | *dobo'owa* |
| tree | gua | fruit | to flower | spoken of |

| |
|---|
| *togebe* |
| is this it? |

3. 

| | | | |
|---|---|---|---|
| *ya* | *furu* | *sae* | *ho'ane* |
| bird | furu | feathers | to insert |

| | |
|---|---|
| *dobo'owa* | *togebe* |
| spoke of | is this it? |

| | | | |
|---|---|---|---|
| *ya* | *garobo* | *sae* | *ho'ane* |
| bird | garobo | feathers | to insert |

| | |
|---|---|
| *dobo'owa* | *togebe* |
| spoken of | is this it? |

4. 

| | | | |
|---|---|---|---|
| *amena* | *ibu* | *faya'a* | *wagibu* |
| men | river | Faya'a | mouth |

| |
|---|
| *dawabo* |
| dawabo |

| | | | |
|---|---|---|---|
| *amena* | *ibu* | *hesa* | *tage* |
| men | creek | Hesa | mouth |

| |
|---|
| *dawabo* |
| dawabo |

5. 

| | | | |
|---|---|---|---|
| *amena* | *koroba* | *sabe* | *u'ubi-o* |
| men | Koroba | Ridge[11] | children |

| |
|---|
| *dawabo* |
| dawabo |

| | | | |
|---|---|---|---|
| *amena* | *baiga* | *sabe* | *u'ubi* |
| men | Baiga | Ridge[12] | children |

| |
|---|
| *dawabo* |
| dawabo |

---

11  Site of the Herebo longhouse.
12  Site of the Barutage longhouse.

1. The casuarina tree that we have been speaking of
   Will it flower?

   The flower of the *sonane* tree
   Will it appear as we said it would?

2. Will the fruit of the *gerewa* cane
   Appear as we spoke of?

   Will the *gua* tree flower appear
   That which we have been speaking of for so long?

3. The *furu* bird feathers that we wanted to plant
   Is it these that we see before us?

   The *garobo* bird feathers which we wanted to plant
   Is it these here?

4. We are the men of the end of the Faya'a Creek
   *Dawabo*

   We are the men of the end of the Hesa Creek
   *Dawabo*

5. We are the men of Koroba Ridge
   *Dawabo*

   We are the men of Baiga Ridge
   *Dawabo*

---

# Men's Song 32

## Singers: Viya and Komo'o. Recorded 2 January 1985 at Hegeso village.

A man is angry at the birds who eat his bananas and other fruit. He addresses them, 'we didn't plant these things together; they're not yours.'

1. | *ga* | *dõbe* | *hiri* | *bare* |
   |------|--------|--------|--------|
   | banana | *dõbe* | planted | that |

   | *yage* | *wae* |
   |--------|-------|
   | ours | no |

|   | | | | |
|---|---|---|---|---|
|   | *ira*<br>tree | *bai*<br>bai | *duru*<br>fence | *bare*<br>that |
|   | *yagemo*<br>ours | *wae*<br>not | | |
| 2. | *ga*<br>banana | *mahagi*<br>mahagi | *hiri*<br>planted | |
|   | *yagemo*<br>our | *ga*<br>belongs to | *wae*<br>not | |
|   | *ira*<br>tree | *onobo*<br>onobo | *duru*<br>fence | |
|   | *yagemo*<br>ours | *ga*<br>belongs to | *wae*<br>not | |
| 3. | *ira*<br>tree | *bai*<br>bai | *duru*<br>fence | *bare*<br>that |
|   | *yagemo*<br>ours | *wae*<br>not | | |
|   | *wãsia*<br>pitpit | *kamua*<br>kamua | *hiri*<br>planted | *bare*<br>that |
|   | *yagemo*<br>ours | *wae*<br>not | | |
| 4. | *ga*<br>banana | *dõbe*<br>*dõbe* | *hiri*<br>planted | *tore*<br>this |
|   | *yagemo*<br>ours | *mohobiwae*<br>planted not | | |
|   | *ira*<br>tree | *bai*<br>bai | *duru*<br>fence | *tore*<br>this |
|   | *yagemo*<br>ours | *wae*<br>not | | |
| 5. | *yiya*<br>we | *amena*<br>men | *ya*<br>bird | *ganiyu*<br>*ganiyu* |
|   | *dawabo*<br>*dawabo* | | | |

| yiya | amena | ya | dẽse |
|---|---|---|---|
| we | men | bird | dẽse |

*dawabo*
*dawabo*

6.
| yiya | amena | ya | ga | nobo |
|---|---|---|---|---|
| we | men | bird | banana | eaten |

*dawabo*
*dawabo*

| yiya | amena | ya | ganiyu |
|---|---|---|---|
| we | men | bird | ganiyu |

*dawabo*
*dawabo*

---

1.  These *dobe* bananas here
    We didn't plant them

    This fence of *bai* wood around my garden
    You didn't help me make it

2.  This *mahagi* banana here
    It is not ours

    This *onobo* tree wood fence
    It doesn't belong to *us*

3.  This *bai* wood fence
    It is not the two of ours

    This *kamua* pitpit here
    It is not ours

4.  This *dobe* banana here
    We didn't plant is together

    This *bai* wood fence
    We didn't build it together

5.  We are the *ganiyu* birds
    *Dawabo*

    We are the *dẽse* parrots
    *Dawabo*

6.  We are the banana eating birds
    *Dawabo*

    We are the *ganiyu* birds
    *Dawabo*

---

# Men's Song 33

## Singers: Sega and Abeabo. Recorded 31 December 1983 at Hegeso village by Kora Midibaru.

A woman from Ibutaba longhouse, east of Hegeso, composed this song, in which she complains about the unfair treatment she has been subject to at the hands of her husband. The second verse refers to the beatings she has endured with certain hardwood sticks her husband used.

1.  | *buru* | *kirari* | *ma* | *diburo* | | |
    |--------|----------|------|----------|--|--|
    | black | rope | take | talk | | |
    | *kama* | *dibibie* | | | | |
    | mind | did not speak | | | | |
    | *kare* | *kui* | *mekea* | *diburo* | | |
    | women's | sago | cook | talk | | |
    | *koremo* | *do'ora* | | | | |
    | with mouth | not said | | | | |

2.  | *ba'a* | *na'a* | *ira* | *waru* | *fura* | *bamo* |
    |--------|--------|-------|--------|--------|--------|
    | boy | your | tree | *waru* | stick | that |
    | *ai* | *nano* | *gariko-e* | | | |
    | ai! | my | neck-oh! | | | |
    | *ba'a* | *na'a* | *ira* | *mono* | *fura* | *bamo* |
    | boy | your | tree | *mono* | stick | that |
    | *ai* | *nano* | *tui-e* | | | |
    | ai! | my | ribs-oh! | | | |

3.  | *ya* | *karirima* | *diburo* | | | |
    |------|-----------|----------|--|--|--|
    | hand | rope | talk | | | |

| | | | | |
|---|---|---|---|---|
| *kama* | *dibubi'e* | | | |
| mind | did not speak | | | |

| | | | |
|---|---|---|---|
| *kare* | *kui* | *mekea* | *diburo* |
| women's | sago | cook | talk |

| | |
|---|---|
| *dase* | *do'abobi'o* |
| talk | should have said |

4.

| *oro* | *yerebi* | *dobo* | *ba'a* | *baihaehubu* |
|---|---|---|---|---|
| bamboo | yerebi | clan | boy | Baihaehubu |

| *ba'a* | *guma* |
|---|---|
| boy | Guma |

| *kui* | *inibi* | *dobo* | *kabo* | *isanoka* |
|---|---|---|---|---|
| sago | cooked-eaten | clan | girl | Isanoka |

| *ba'a* | *herebo* |
|---|---|
| boy | Herebo |

5.

| *kui* | *inibi* | *dobo* | *kabo* | *isanoka* |
|---|---|---|---|---|
| sago | cooked-eaten | clan | girl | Isanoka |

| *ba'a* | *herebo* |
|---|---|
| boy | Herebo |

| *kui* | *inibi* | *dobo* | *kabo* | *mege* | *ba-o* |
|---|---|---|---|---|---|
| sago | cooked-eaten | clan | girl | only | that |

| *ba'a* | *guma* |
|---|---|
| boy | Guma |

1.  You did not tell me to hold the rope of the black pig
    How should I know what you want of me?

    You didn't tell me to cook afternoon sago
    How can I tell what your thoughts are?

2.  Boy, your *waru* tree stick there
    Oh, my poor neck!

    Boy, your *mono* tree stick there
    Ai, my poor rib-cage!

3.  To take the pig's rope with my hands, you did not say

You didn't tell me what you were thinking

To cook afternoon sago, you did not say
You should have told me with words

4.   The man of the *yerebi* bamboo clan, Baihaihubu
His son, Guma

The Cooked Sago clan woman Isanoka
Her son, Herebo

5.   The Cooked Sago clan woman Isanoka
Her son Herebo

The Cooked Sago woman only
Her son Guma

# Men's Song 34

## Singers: Ayadobo and Damu. Recorded 31 December 1983 at Hegeso village by Kora Midibaru.

This is a common sago melody. The two men who sang this song, instead of calling out the name of a commemorated man in the *dawa*, sang 'sago clan', as a rendition of the subject of this woman's sago song.

1.   | *na'a* | *huamo* | *kui* | *huamaba'ayo'o* |
     |--------|---------|-------|----------------|
     | your   | mother's | sago | strike-take    |

*gibihamone*
do not keep crying

| *na'a* | *huamo* | *kui* | *yuaemaba'ayo'o* |
|--------|---------|-------|------------------|
| your   | mother's | sago | wash-take        |

*gemone*
do not cry

2.   | *na'a* | *huamo* | *abu* | *biri* | *maba'ayo'o* |
     |--------|---------|-------|--------|--------------|
     | your   | mother's | mallet | this  | to take      |

*gibihamone*
do not keep crying

|  | *na'a* | *huamo* | *kui* | *huamaba'ayo'o* |  |
|--|--------|---------|-------|-----------------|--|
|  | your | mother's | sago | strike-take |  |

*gemone*
do not cry

| 3. | *na'a* | *huamo* | *kui* | *gesamaba'ayo'o* |  |
|----|--------|---------|-------|------------------|--|
|    | your | mother's | sago | remove pith |  |

*hirabumone*
do not cry

|  | *na'a* | *huamo* | *kui* | *ya* | *forayemaba'ayo'o* |
|--|--------|---------|-------|------|--------------------|
|  | your | mother's | sago | hand | snap-take |

*gibihamone*
do not keep crying

| 4. | *amena* | *kui* | *hebo* |
|----|---------|-------|--------|
|    | men | sago | *hebo* |

*dawarabo*
*dawabo*

|  | *amena* | *kui* | *kenege* |
|--|---------|-------|----------|
|  | men | sago | mid-rib |

*ibuhebo*
*dawabo*

| 5. | *amena* | *kui* | *hebo* |
|----|---------|-------|--------|
|    | men | sago | *hebo* |

*dawarabo*
*dawabo*

|  | *amena* | *kui* | *kenege* |
|--|---------|-------|----------|
|  | men | sago | mid-rib |

*ibuhebo*
*dawabo*

1. Child, let your mother beat her sago
   Don't keep crying

   Child, let your mother wash her sago
   Do not cry

2. Let your mother take her sago mallet
   Child, stop crying

   Let your mother keep pounding sago
   Child, do not cry

3. Child, let your mother remove the pith
   Do not keep crying

   Let your mother snap her wrists
   Do not cry so

4. We are the men of the *hebo* Sago clan
   *Dawarabo*

   We are the men of the *kenege* Sago clan
   *Ibu Hebo*

5. We are the men of the *hebo* Sago clan
   *Dawarabo*

   We are the men of the *kenege* Sago clan
   *Ibu Hebo*

# Men's Song 35

## Singers: Tari and Abuyu. Recorded 31 December 1983 at Hegeso village by Kora Midibaru.

This is also a common woman's sago song. A woman's child cries out 'like a hornbill' to be fed while she is busy making sago. As with men's song 34, this *sorohabora* is not a commemorative song per se, but an untransformed rendition of a common woman's sago song. In the *dawa*, the men sing 'hornbill clan' to mark the imagery the woman uses for her child. The verb ending used in the second line of each couplet, *-yebe*, is an interrogative particle with sarcastic overtones. The woman is thus singing, 'So, you are crying out heartily that I have not given you sago. What do you think I do all day?!' (See Weiner 1991:154.)

1. *wana'ari*    *kui*      *migi'orebo'o*
   mid-day      sago       have not given

   *dibuyebe*
   are you saying?

   *kare*        *kui*      *migi'orebo'o*
   women's     sago       have not given

   *tawadibuyebe*
   are you complaining?

2. *kare*        *kui*      *migi'orebo'o*
   women's     sago       have not given

   *odibuyebe*
   are you calling out?

   *tãbura*      *kui*      *migi'orebo'o*
   bamboo filled  sago       have not given

   *tawadibuyebe*
   are you complaining?

3. *tãbura*      *kui*      *migi'orebo'o*
   bamboo filled  sago       have not given

   *hirabubuyebe*
   are you crying?

   *kare*        *kui*      *migi'orebo'o*
   women's     sago       have not given

   *dibuyebe*
   are you saying?

4. *yiya*      *amena*     *ya*      *ware*
   we        men       bird     hornbill

   *dawabo*
   dawabo

   *yiya*      *amena*     *ya*      *weigo*
   we        men       bird     hornbill

   *dawara'abo*
   dawabo

| 5. | *yiya* | *amena* | *ya* | *ware* |
|----|--------|---------|------|--------|
|    | we     | men     | bird | hornbill |

*dawabo*
*dawabo*

| | *yiya* | *amena* | *ya* | *weigo* |
|---|--------|---------|------|---------|
| | we     | men     | bird | hornbill |

*dawara'abo*
*dawabo*

1. So I haven't given you your mid-day sago
   Is that what you think you're telling me?

   So I haven't given you your evening sago
   Is that what you're complaining about?

2. I haven't given you your evening sago
   Is that why your calling out to me?

   Sago cooked in a new bamboo tube you haven't received
   Is that what I hear you complaining about?

3. Your new bamboo cooked sago you haven't eaten yet
   Is this what you're crying about?

   Your evening sago you haven't eaten yet
   Is this what you're saying to me?

4. We are the men of the hornbill
   *Dawabo*

   We are the men of Ayayewego, the hornbill
   *Dawara'abo*

5. We are the men of the hornbill
   *Dawabo*

   We are the men of Ayayewego, the hornbill
   *Dawara'abo*

# Men's Song 36

## Singers: Kusabuyu and Webirabo. Recorded 31 December 1983 at Hegeso village by Kora Midibaru.

This song likens the deceased Hegeso headman Iriharabu to a bird with a broken wing, which crippled, falls to earth.

1.
| *ibu* | *uri* | *gakobo*[13] | *ya* | *fifinu* |
|-------|-------|---------|------|---------|
| creek | Uri | source | bird | *fifinu* |

| *auwa* | *forage* |
|--------|----------|
| wing | broken |

| *ibu* | *uri* | *gakobo* | *ya* | *aiyabe* |
|-------|-------|----------|------|----------|
| creek | Uri | source | bird | hawk |

| *auwa* | *forage* |
|--------|----------|
| wing | broken |

2.
| *ibu* | *uri* | *ga* | *tegare* |
|-------|-------|------|---------|
| creek | Uri | source | *ko'oya* tree |

| *foraboba'ae* |
|---------------|
| cut down |

| *ibu* | *uri* | *ga* | *ira* | *fore* |
|-------|-------|------|-------|--------|
| creek | Uri | source | tree | large |

| *daria* | *uboba'ae* |
|---------|-----------|
| uprooted | gone |

3.
| *ibu* | *kumagi* | *ya* | *aiyabe* |
|-------|----------|------|----------|
| creek | Kumagi | bird | hawk |

| *viramaiba'ae* |
|----------------|
| shot-taken |

| *ibu* | *uri* | *ya* | *fifinu* |
|-------|-------|------|---------|
| creek | uri | bird | *fifinu* |

| *vira* | *uboro* |
|--------|---------|
| shot | gone |

---

13   *Gakobo* is a contraction of *ga korobo*: 'source upstream'. The source of the Uri Creek is 'upstream', in Ayamo country. This song, like men's song 6, is about the former headman Iraharabo of Hegeso, and makes use of the same imagery.

4.  | *wa'aridobo* | *kabe* | *degayo* |
    | palm clan | man | Degayo |

    | *kabe* | *iraharabo* |
    | man | Iraharabo |

    | *wa'aridobo* | *kabe* | *mege* | *bamo* |
    | palm clan | man | only | that |

    | *kabe* | *iraharabo* |
    | man | Iraharabo |

5.  | *wa'aridobo* | *kabe* | *mege* | *bamo* |
    | palm clan | man | only | that |

    | *dawabo* |
    | dawabo |

    | *wa'aridobo* | *kabe* | *mege* | *bamo* |
    | palm clan | man | only | that |

    | *dawabo* |
    | dawabo |

---

1.  At the source of the Uri Creek, the *fifinu* bird
    Broken winged

    At the head of the Uri Creek, the hawk
    Cripple winged

2.  At the source of the Uri Creek, the *ko'oya* tree
    Cut down

    At the origin of the Uri water, the large *tegare* tree
    The wind has uprooted it

3.  At the Kumagi Creek, the hawk
    Long time shot

    At the Uri Creek, the *fifinu* bird
    Shot and taken

4.  The man of the *wa'ari* palm clan, Degayo
    His son, Iraharabo

The lonely man of the *wa'ari* palm clan
Iraharabo

5. This man only of the Wa'aridobo clan
   *Dawabo*

   This man only of the Wa'aridobo clan
   *Dawabo*

---

# Men's Song 37

## Singers: Sega and Abeabo. Recorded 31 December 1983 at Hegeso village by Kora Midibaru.

Highlands men cover their pearl shells with red ochre. The woman singing of the dead man Terewaro, a Highlander who came to live in a Foi village, remembered seeing his red pearl shells and composed this song.

1. | *nomo* | *gi* | *hare* | *dogo* |
   |--------|------|--------|--------|
   | my | ochre | red | bundle |

   *fisige*
   removed

   | *nomo* | *gi* | *damani* | *dogo* |
   |--------|------|----------|--------|
   | my | ochre | red | bundle |

   *fisige*
   removed

2. | *gi* | *hare* | *dogo* |
   |------|--------|--------|
   | ochre | red | bundle |

   *fisige*
   removed

   | *ba'a* | *na'a* | *gi* | *damani* | *dogo* |
   |--------|--------|------|----------|--------|
   | boy | your | ochre | red | bundle |

   *fisige*
   removed

3. | *amena* | *ibu* | *wage* | *habu* |
|---|---|---|---|
| men | river | Wage | lived |

*dawabo*
*dawabo*

| *amena* | *duma* | *dira* | *wagibu* |
|---|---|---|---|
| men | mountain | Dira | ending |

*dawabo*
*dawabo*

4. | *yiya* | *amena* | *ba'a* | *terewaro* |
|---|---|---|---|
| we | men | boy | Terewaro |

*dawabo*
*dawabo*

| *yiya* | *amena* | *ba'a* | *terewaro* |
|---|---|---|---|
| we | men | boy | Terewaro |

*dawabo*
*dawabo*

---

1. My bundle of red ochre
   Has been removed

   My parcel of red ochre
   Has been taken

2. The red ochre bundle
   Taken

   Boy, your red ochre parcel
   Removed

3. The men who lived near the Wage River
   *Dawabo*

   The men who live at the end of Mt Dira
   *Dawabo*

4. We are Terewaro's men
   *Dawabo*

   We are Terewaro's men
   *Dawabo*

# Men's Song 38

## Singers: Memene and Abeabo. Recorded 16 March 1988 at Hegeso village.

This song commemorates all the headmen who died in Hegeso's recent past. The places referred to are spots owned by previous Hegeso headmen.

1. | *hiba'aweĩ* | *merabe* | | |
   |---|---|---|---|
   | Hiba'aweĩ | harbour | | |

   *aodoboba'ae*
   bush covered

   | *nomo* | *ibu* | *faya'a* | *geno* |
   |---|---|---|---|
   | my | river | Faya'a | riverbend |

   *kigiboba'ae*
   tree covered

2. | *nomo* | *ira* | *fiwa* | *dera* |
   |---|---|---|---|
   | my | tree | fiwa | that |

   *forabi'ae*
   fallen

   | *nomo* | *ira* | *furabo* | *dera* |
   |---|---|---|---|
   | my | tree | furabo | that |

   *foramaibi'ae*
   fallen down

3. | *nomo* | *kosa'a* | *buru* | *ga* | *merabe* |
   |---|---|---|---|---|
   | my | Ficus | black | base | harbour |

   *kigiboba'a*
   tree covered

   | *nomo* | *ira* | *furubu* | *ga* | *merabe* |
   |---|---|---|---|---|
   | my | tree | furubu | base | harbour |

   *aodoboba'a*
   bush covered

4. 
| nomo | ibu | faya'a | tage | geno |
|------|-----|--------|------|------|
| my | river | Faya'a | mouth | riverbend |

*kigiboba'ae*
tree covered

| nomo | ira | furubu | dera | |
|------|-----|--------|------|--|
| my | tree | furubu | that | |

*foramaboba'ae*
fallen down

5. 
| yiya | amena | ĩbariabe | sabe | u'ubi |
|------|-------|----------|------|-------|
| we | men | Ĩbariabe | Ridge | children |

*dawabo*
dawabo

| yiya | amena | yageneboro | sabe | u'ubi |
|------|-------|------------|------|-------|
| we | men | Yagenebo | Ridge | children |

*ibuhebo*
dawabo

6. 
| yiya | amena | hiba'aweĩ | merabe | iba'ae |
|------|-------|-----------|--------|--------|
| we | men | Hiba'aweĩ | harbour | are |

*ibudawabo*
ibudawabo

| yiya | amena | yageneboro | sabe | |
|------|-------|------------|------|--|
| we | men | Yagenebo | Ridge | |

*dawabo*
dawabo

---

1.  Hiba'aweĩ Harbour
    The bush has hidden it

    My Faya'a Creek whirlpool
    The trees have covered it over

2.  My *fiwa* tree there
    Has fallen by itself

My *furabo* tree there
Has fallen down

3.  My harbour near the base of the *kosa'a buru* tree
    The forest has reclaimed it

    My harbour near the base of the *furubu* tree
    The bush has obliterated it

4.  The still water near the mouth of the Faya'a
    The forest has taken it back

    My *furubu* tree there
    Has fallen down

5.  We are the children of Ĩbariabe Ridge
    *Dawabo*

    We are the children of Yegenebo Ridge
    *Ibu hebo*

6.  We are the men of Hiba'aweĩ Harbour
    *Ibu Dawabo*

    We are the men of Yagenebo Ridge
    *Dawabo*

# Men's Song 39

## Singers: Kora and Abeabo. Recorded 16 March 1988 at Hegeso village.

Kora heard his wife's mother singing this song. She had married the man Waria as an aged widow, and he used to beat her repeatedly, claiming she was no good for anything. The woman refers to the nettles she must rub against her brusied skin and the walking stick she must use because of her sore limbs. (See Weiner 1991:142–44.)

1.  | *nane* | *yengi* | *baya'a* | *dogo* | *hua* | *iyo'o* |
    |---|---|---|---|---|---|
    | I | nettles | *baya'a* | bundle | mother | am |

    | *ba'a* | *na'a* | *dibiyebe* |
    |---|---|---|
    | boy | you | not saying? |

| nane | yengi | fagena | dogo | hua | iyo'o |
|------|-------|--------|------|-----|-------|
| I | nettles | fagena | bundle | mother | am |

| dibiyebe |
|----------|
| not saying? |

2.

| nane | ira | waru | tãbu | hua | iyo'o |
|------|-----|------|------|-----|-------|
| I | tree | waru | stick | mother | am |

| ba'a | na'a | ka'arubidibiyebe |
|------|------|------------------|
| boy | you | not complaining? |

| nane | ira | mono | tãbu | hua | iyo'o |
|------|-----|------|------|-----|-------|
| I | tree | mono | stick | mother | am |

| ba'a | na'a | tenewanedibiyebe |
|------|------|------------------|
| boy | you | not muttering? |

3.

| budu | kirari | ma'aboya'ayo'o |
|------|--------|----------------|
| black | rope | should take |

| ba'a | na'a | ho'obuyebe |
|------|------|------------|
| boy | you | not dislike? |

| kare | kui | ino'oya'ayo'o |
|------|-----|---------------|
| women's | sago | should cook |

| ba'a | na'a | tenewanedibuyebe |
|------|------|------------------|
| boy | you | not muttering? |

4.

| abu | biri | mayiye | diburo |
|-----|------|--------|--------|
| mallet | here | haven't taken | talk |

| ba'a | na'a | dibuyebe |
|------|------|----------|
| boy | you | are you saying? |

| abu | wasa | mayiye | dibure |
|-----|------|--------|--------|
| abu | wasa | haven't taken | said |

| ba'a | na'a | dibuyebe |
|------|------|----------|
| boy | you | are you saying? |

5.

| yo | hua | kabo | keborame |
|----|-----|------|----------|
| his | mother | girl | Keborame |

| kabe | waria |
|------|-------|
| man | Waria |

| *yo* | *hua* | *ka* | *mege* | *bamo* |
|------|-------|------|--------|--------|
| his | mother | woman | only | that |

| *kabe* | *waria* |
|--------|---------|
| man | Waria |

6. 

| *kibudobo* | *kabe* | *tonebo* |
|------------|--------|----------|
| Kibudobo | man | Tonebo |

| *kabe* | *waria* |
|--------|---------|
| man | Waria |

| *yo* | *hua* | *kabo* | *keborame* |
|------|-------|--------|------------|
| his | mother | girl | Keborame |

| *kabe* | *yamagi* |
|--------|----------|
| man | Yamagi |

---

1. My parcel of stinging nettles I carry
   Now what do you say to me?

   I carry my little package of *fagena* nettles
   Boy, what do you say about me now?

2. I am the mother of the *waru* wood walking stick
   Boy, are you criticising me now?

   I am the mother of the *mono* wood walking stick
   Are you muttering under your breath about me?

3. So, I am not taking the rope of the black pig
   Is that what you dislike about me?

   Evening sago I am unable to cook
   Is that what you are swearing about under your breath?

4. I haven't taken my sago mallet
   Come now boy, is that what you are saying?

   I haven't taken my sago hammer
   Is that what you are saying?

5. His mother, the woman Keborame
   The man Waria

   His mother, the only woman
   The man Waria

6.  The Kibudobo man, Tonebo
    His son, Waria

    His mother, the woman Keborame
    Her son, Yamagi

---

# Men's Song 40

## Singers: Sega and Kora. Recorded October 1982 at Hegeso village by Kora Midibaru.

Men themselves—sadly, a dead man's own clansmen—are most instrumental in obliterating the signs of that man's productive life after his death, as this song alludes to. (See Weiner 1991:106–8.)

1.  | *ba'a* | *na'a* | *yebibu* | *ibu* |
    |--------|--------|----------|-------|
    | boy    | your   | Yebibu   | creek |

    *aginoba'aye*
    let another steal it

    | *ba'a* | *na'a* | *yefua* | *duma*   |
    |--------|--------|---------|----------|
    | boy    | your   | Yefua   | mountain |

    *aodoba'aye*
    let bush cover it

2.  | *ba'a* | *na'a* | *yebibu* | *ibu* |
    |--------|--------|----------|-------|
    | boy    | your   | Yebibu   | creek |

    *aginoba'aye*
    let another steal it

    | *ba'a* | *na'a* | *yefua* | *duma*   |
    |--------|--------|---------|----------|
    | boy    | your   | Yefua   | mountain |

    *aodoba'aye*
    let bush cover it

3.  | *na'a* | *huamo*  | *ibu* | *sumaniyu* |
    |--------|----------|-------|------------|
    | your   | mother's | creek | Sumaniyu   |

    | *ibu* | *aginoboba'ae* |
    |-------|----------------|
    | creek | stolen eaten   |

120

| | | | |
|---|---|---|---|
| *ba'a* | *bamo* | *yahadenabo* | |
| boy | that | Yahadenabo | |
| | | | |
| *ibu* | *aodoba'aye* | | |
| water | let bush cover it | | |

4.
| | | | |
|---|---|---|---|
| *ba'a* | *na'a* | *ibu* | *agegenebo* |
| boy | your | creek | Agegenebo |
| | | | |
| *ibu* | *aodoba'aye* | | |
| creek | let bush cover it | | |
| | | | |
| *ba'a* | *na'a* | *yebibu* | *ibu* |
| boy | your | Yebibu | creek |
| | | | |
| *ira* | *waba'aye* | | |
| tree | let come | | |

5.
| | | | |
|---|---|---|---|
| *ba'a* | *na'a* | *sonobo* | *duma* |
| boy | your | Sonobo | mountain |
| | | | |
| *aodoboba'ae* | | | |
| bush covered | | | |
| | | | |
| *ba'a* | *na'a* | *yefua* | *duma* |
| boy | your | Yefua | mountain |
| | | | |
| *kigiboba'ae* | | | |
| tree covered | | | |

6.
| | | | | | |
|---|---|---|---|---|---|
| *oro* | *yerebi* | *dobo* | *ba'a* | *hamabo* | |
| bamboo | *yerebi* | clan | boy | Hamabo | |
| | | | | | |
| *kabe* | *kabusa* | | | | |
| man | Kabusa | | | | |
| | | | | | |
| *oro* | *yerebi* | *dobo* | *kabe* | *mege* | *bamo* |
| bamboo | *yerebi* | clan | man | only | this |
| | | | | | |
| *ba'a* | *dãwano* | | | | |
| boy | Dãwano | | | | |

7.
| | | | |
|---|---|---|---|
| *kuidobo* | *ka* | *enegoaimo* | |
| Sago clan | woman | Enegoai | |
| | | | |
| *ba'a* | *kabusa* | | |
| boy | Kabusa | | |

| *yo* | *hua* | *ka* | *mege* | *bamo* |
|------|-------|------|--------|--------|
| his  | mother | woman | only | this |

| *ba'a* | *dãwano* |
|--------|----------|
| boy    | Dãwano   |

1.  Boy, your Yebibu Creek
    Let another man eat it

    Boy, your Yefua Ridge
    Let the bush cover it over

2.  Boy, your Yebibu Creek
    Let another man eat it

    Boy, your Yefua Ridge
    Let the bush cover it over

3.  Your Sumaniyu Creek
    This creek, let another man steal it

    This boy's Yahadenabo Creek
    Let the bush cover it over

4.  Boy, your Agegenebo Creek
    Let the forest reclaim it

    Boy, your Yebibu Creek
    Let the trees cover it up

5.  Boy, your Sonobo Ridge
    Let the bush cover it

    Boy, your Yefua Ridge
    The forest will be allowed to hide it

6.  The clan of the *yerebi* bamboo, the man Hamabo
    His son, Kabosa

    The clan of the *yerebi* bamboo, this only man
    His son, Dãwano

7.  The Kuidobo clan woman Enegoai
    Her son, Kabosa

    His mother, the only woman
    Her son, Dãwane

# Men's Song 41

## Singers: Kora and Webirabo. Recorded 16 March 1988 at Hegeso village.

This song illustrates one of the commonest images used in these songs: a man's inhabited places become reclaimed by the forest after his death, when he is no longer able to maintain them as sites of human intervention. (See Weiner 2001:39–42.)

1. | *ba'a* | *na'a* | *namikiribibi* | *iga* |
   |--------|--------|----------------|------|
   | boy    | your   | Namikiribibi   | path |

   | *iga* | *aodiba'ae*  |
   |-------|--------------|
   | path  | tree covered |

   | *ba'a* | *na'a* | *tigifu* | *iga* |
   |--------|--------|----------|-------|
   | boy    | your   | Tigifu   | path  |

   | *iga* | *aodiba'ae*  |
   |-------|--------------|
   | path  | tree covered |

2. | *ba'a* | *bamo* | *waya'arihabo* | *iburo'o* |
   |--------|--------|----------------|----------|
   | boy    | this   | Waya'arihabo   | creek    |

   | *aodibihaba'aye*    |
   |---------------------|
   | let the bush cover it |

   | *ba'a* | *bamo* | *domege* | *ibu* |
   |--------|--------|----------|-------|
   | boy    | this   | Domege   | creek |

   | *aodoba'aye*      |
   |-------------------|
   | let bush cover it |

3. | *ba'a* | *na'a* | *duma*   | *orege* | *duma*   |
   |--------|--------|----------|---------|----------|
   | boy    | your   | mountain | Orege   | mountain |

   | *memo*  | *aginoba'aye* |
   |---------|---------------|
   | another | let steal it  |

   | *ba'a* | *na'a* | *sõa* | *duma*   |
   |--------|--------|-------|----------|
   | boy    | your   | Sõa   | mountain |

   | *memo*  | *aginoba'aye* |
   |---------|---------------|
   | another | let steal it  |

4. | kibudobo | ka | yamo |
   |----------|-----|------|
   | Kibudobo | woman | Ya |

   | kabe | sese |
   |------|------|
   | man | Sese |

   | banimahu'u | | kabe | irahaimabomo |
   |------------|---|------|--------------|
   | Banimahu'u | | man | Irahaimabo |

   | kabe | sisu'umena |
   |------|-----------|
   | man | Sisu'umena |

5. | turu | ya | bari | dobo | ba'a | irahaimabo |
   |------|-----|------|------|------|------------|
   | sky | bird | banima | clan | boy | Irahaimabo |

   | kabe | sese |
   |------|------|
   | man | Sese |

   | kibudobo | ka | yamo |
   |----------|-----|------|
   | Kibudobo | woman | Ya |

   | kabe | sisu'umena |
   |------|-----------|
   | man | Sisu'umena |

6. | yo | hua | ka | mege | bamo |
   |-----|--------|-------|------|------|
   | his | mother | woman | only | that |

   | kabe | sese-o |
   |------|--------|
   | man | Sese |

   | yo | hua | ka | mege | bamo |
   |-----|--------|-------|------|------|
   | his | mother | woman | only | this |

   | ibudawabo |
   |-----------|
   | ibudawabo |

1. Boy, your Namikiribi path
   That path is covered over

   Boy, your Tigifu path
   That path is hidden by the forest

2. This boy's Waya'arihabo Creek
   It is obliterated by trees

This man's Domege Creek
Is covered over by the jungle

3. Boy, your Orege Mountain
Let another man steal it

    Boy your Sõa Mountain
    Let another man steal it

4. The Kibudobo woman Ya
Her son Sese

    The Banimahu'u man Irihaimabo
    His son Sisu'umena

5. The clan of the high flying *banima* bird, Irihaimabo
His son Sese

    The Kibudobo woman Ya
    Her son Sisu'umena

6. His mother, this woman alone
Her son Sese

    His mother, this lonely woman
    *Ibu Dawabo*

# Men's Song 42

## Singers: Fahaisabo and Oromene. Recorded 5 January 1985 at Barutage village.

This song capitalises on the lexical meaning of the deceased's hidden name, Tĩbu, which is the name of a variety of cane. The phrase 'cane water' refers to a creek or river alongside which cassowary snares have been set. In common with other Fringe Highlands hunters of this area, the Foi set their traps near known drinking and eating places of animals, and place snares and deadfalls near discovered tracks of animals near the various watercourses and trees in fruit. The elements of haiku are especially noteworthy in the terseness of the phrasing here. ♫ online example 12.

1. *ba'a*       *na'a*       *sui*       *ko'ome*       *ibu*
   boy       your       cane       *ko'ome*       water

| | | | | |
|---|---|---|---|---|
| *ibu* water | *weigebe* has it come? | | | |
| *ba'a* boy | *na'a* your | *sui* cane | *gagi* gagi | *ibu* water |
| *ibu* water | *weiba'ae* has come | | | |

2. 
| | | | |
|---|---|---|---|
| *sui* cane | *dabe* dabe | *ibu* water | *wa* come |
| *konaye* full | *iba'ae* is | | |
| *sui* cane | *gerewa* gerewa | *ibu* water | *wa* come |
| *konaye* full | *ba'ae* is | | |

3. 
| | | |
|---|---|---|
| *sui* cane | *tĩbu* tĩbu | *ibu* water |
| *konabo'o* full | *dibiga* stated | |
| *sui* cane | *ko'ome* ko'ome | *ibu* water |
| *yiragedobo'o* coming down from mountain | | *dibiga* stated |

4. 
| | | |
|---|---|---|
| *sui* cane | *ko'ome* ko'ome | *ibu* water |
| *konabo'o* full | *dibige* stated | |
| *sui* cane | *wa* come | *ibu* water |
| *konabo'o* full | *dibige* stated | |

5. 
| | | |
|---|---|---|
| *orodobo* Orodobo | *ka* woman | *wa'ane* Wa'ane |

| | | | | |
|---|---|---|---|---|
| *ba'a*<br>boy | *ayamena*<br>Ayamena | | | |
| *banimahu'u*<br>Banimahu'u | *ba'a*<br>boy | *yore*<br>Yore | | |
| *kabe*<br>man | *tĩbu*<br>Tĩbu | | | |

6. 
| | | | | |
|---|---|---|---|---|
| *karewẽyudobo*<br>Banimahu'u | *kabe*<br>man | *mege*<br>only | *ba*<br>that | *ma'ame*<br>thing |
| *ba'a*<br>boy | *ayamena*<br>Ayamena | | | |
| *oro*<br>bamboo | *taru*<br>great | *dobo*<br>clan | *ka*<br>woman | *wa'anemo*<br>Wa'ane |
| *ba'a*<br>boy | *tĩbu*<br>Tĩbu | | | |

1. Boy, your *ko'ome* cane snare creek
   Is the water coming?

   Boy, your *gagi* cane snare creek
   Water is coming

2. *Dabe* cane snare water coming
   Water is full

   *Gerewa* cane snare water coming
   Full

3. *Tĩbu* cane water
   Full

   *Ko'ome* cane creek
   Out of the mouth of the mountain

4. *Ko'ome* cane creek
   Full, we say

   Cane coming creek
   Full, we say

5. Orodobo woman Wa'ane
   The boy Ayamena

Banimahu'u boy Yore
The man Tĩbu

6.  The Karewẽyudobo clan man only
The boy Ayamena

The Great Bamboo clan woman Wa'ane
The boy Tĩbu

---

# Men's Song 43

## Singers: Abeabo and Gobero. Recorded 2 January 1985 at Hegeso village.

Places in the deep bush, where hunting and fishing activities characteristically take place, are the most common places associated with a man after death, as the imagery in this song depicts.

1.  | *ya* | *koa* | | *duma* | |
    |---|---|---|---|---|
    | bird | bird of paradise | | mountain | |

    *aodibihaboba'a*
    bush covered

    | *yefua* | *duma* |
    |---|---|
    | Yefua | mountain |

    | *ira* | *waboba'a* |
    |---|---|
    | tree | come |

2.  | *ba'a* | *na'a* | *kana* | *ibu* | *dera* |
    |---|---|---|---|---|
    | boy | your | stone | creek | that |

    *aodoboba'ae*
    bush covered

    | *ba'a* | *na'a* | *suanobo* | *ibu* |
    |---|---|---|---|
    | boy | your | fish dammed | creek |

    *kigiboba'ae*
    tree covered

3.  | *yo* | *hua* | *ka* | *fofo* |
    |---|---|---|---|
    | his | mother | woman | Fofo |

|  |  |  |  |
|---|---|---|---|
| *ba'a* | *kawaru* | | |
| boy | Kawaru | | |
| *momahu'u* | *ka* | *fofomo* | |
| Momahu'u | woman | Fofo | |
| *ba'a* | *baya* | | |
| boy | Baya | | |

4.
|  |  |  |  |
|---|---|---|---|
| *yo* | *hua* | *ka* | *fofo* |
| his | mother | woman | Fofo |
| *ba'a* | *kawaru* | | |
| boy | Kawaru | | |
| *momahu'u* | *ka* | *fofomo* | |
| Momahu'u | woman | Fofo | |
| *ba'a* | *baya* | | |
| boy | Baya | | |

1.  Bird-of-Paradise mountain
    Bush covered

    Yefua Mountain
    Trees come

2.  Boy your stony creek
    Bush covered

    Boy your fish dammed creek
    Strongly covered

3.  His mother, Fofo
    The boy Kawaru

    The Momahu'u clan woman Fofo
    The boy Baya

4.  His mother, Fofo
    The boy Kawaru

    The Momahu'u clan woman Fofo
    The boy Baya

# Men's Song 44

## Singers: Kora and Webirabo. Recorded 16 March 1988 at Hegeso village.

As I described in *The Empty Place*, during a man's life, he leaves imprints or traces on the land, made for example by setting animal traps or constructing fish dams. When a man dies, the bush begins to cover over these traces and erase them, out of which the Foi construe an image of the most common results of a man's death.

1. *ba'a*     *na'a*     *masiba*     *duma*
   boy,     your     Masiba     mountain

   *aodoba'aye*
   let the bush cover it

   *ba'a*     *na'a*     *dagina*     *ibu*
   boy,     your     Dagina     creek

   *kigiba'aye*
   let the strong trees claim it

2. *ba'a*     *na'a*     *duma*     *bugi*     *duma*
   boy,     your     mountain     Bugi     mountain

   *aginoba'aye*
   let another man steal it

   *ba'a*     *na'a*     *masiba*     *duma*
   boy,     your     Masiba     mountain

   *aginoba'aye*
   let another man steal it

3. *ba'a*     *bamo*     *dagina*     *ibu*
   this     boy's     Dagina     creek

   *aginoba'aye*
   let another man eat it

   *ba'a*     *bamo*     *kubarohimu*     *ibu*
   this     boy's     Kubarihimu     creek

   *aodoba'aye*
   let the bush cover it

4. | ba'a | bamo | asiba[14] | honamo | ira |
   |------|------|----------|--------|-----|
   | this | boy's | sago | honamo | sago |

   *aodoba'aye*
   let the bush cover it

   | ba'a | bamo | asiba | yora | ira |
   |------|------|-------|------|-----|
   | this | boy's | sago | yora | sago |

   *irawaba'ame*
   let the trees come and cover it

5. | wa'aridobo | | ka | hasebameno |
   |------------|--|-----|------------|
   | wa'ari palm clan | | woman, | Hasebame |

   | kabe | fumena[15] |
   |------|-----------|
   | her son, | Fumena |

   | ira | namanidobo | yarogeno |
   |-----|-----------|----------|
   | the | namani tree clan man, | Yaroge |

   | kabe | sega |
   |------|------|
   | his son, | Sega |

6. | ira | namanidobo | yarogemo |
   |-----|-----------|----------|
   | the | namani tree clan | Yaroge |

   | kabe | sega |
   |------|------|
   | his son, | Sega |

   | yo | hua | ka | hasebame |
   |----|-----|-----|----------|
   | his | mother, | woman | Hasebame |

   | kabe | fumene |
   |------|--------|
   | the man | Fumene |

---

1. Boy, your Masiba Mountain
   Let the bush cover it

   Boy, your Dagina Creek
   Let the strong trees claim it

---

14   *Asiba* or *asipa* is the Fasu term for 'sago' (May and Loeweke 1981:19).
15   Sega's 'hidden' name.

131

2.   Boy, your Bugi Mountain
     Let another man steal it

     Boy, your Masiba Mountain
     Let another man steal it

3.   This boy's Dagina Creek
     Let another man eat it

     This boy's Kubarihimu Creek
     Let the bush cover it

4.   This boy's *honamo* sago
     Let the bush cover it

     This boy's *yora* sago
     Let the trees come and cover it

5.   The *wa'ari* palm clan woman, Hasebame
     Her son, Fumena

     The *namani* tree clan man, Yaroge
     His son, Sega

6.   The *namani* tree clan Yaroge
     His son, Sega

     His mother, the woman Hasebame
     The man Fumene

# Women's Songs (*Sorohabora*)

## Women's Song 1

### Singers: Kunuhuaka and Wa'abiyu. Recorded 4 November 1984 at Hegeso village.

These songs were performed shortly before the Hegeso men's pig-kill. The first one refers to the dancing that is anticipated after the distribution of the pork. Note that the male singers are likened to birds, a metaphor that is widespread in the ceremonial life throughout the Mt Bosavi–Lake Kutubu area of the Southern Highlands of Papua New Guinea. ♫ online example 13.

1. | *wabo* | *medo'ane* | *dobo'owua* |
   |---|---|---|
   | *wabo* bird | to sing | spoken of |

   *togebe*
   is this it?

2. | *bi'a* | *medo'ane* | *dobo'owua* |
   |---|---|---|
   | *bi'a* bird | to sing | spoken of |

   *togebe*
   is this it?

3. | *ya* | *koa* | *ũbo* | *so'ane* | *dobo'owua* |
   |---|---|---|---|---|
   | bird | Raggianna | headdress | to hang down | spoken of |

   *togebe*
   is this it?

4. | *fore* | *me* | *ya* | *sore* | *medo'ane* | *dobo'owua* |
   |---|---|---|---|---|---|
   | hornbill | sings | bird | sore | to sing | spoken of |

   *togebe*
   is this it?

5. | *hubage* | *ũ* | *ho'ane* | *dobo'owua* |
   |---|---|---|---|
   | feathers | head | to insert | spoken of |

   *togebe*
   is this it?

6. | *furubu* | *gugu'anege* | *dobo'owua* |
   | *furubu* | to flower | spoken of |

   *togebe*
   is this it?

7. | *ya* | *bi'a* | *medo'ane* | *dobo'owua* |
   | bird | *bi'a* | to sing | spoken of |

   *togebe*
   is this it?

8. | *ya* | *sore* | *medo'ane* | *dobo'owua* |
   | bird | *sore* | to sing | spoken of |

   *togebe*
   is this it?

9. | *amena* | *yagenebo* | *u'ubi* |
   | men | Yagenebo | children |

   *dawa-o*
   *dawabo*

10. | *kaibutage* | *u'ubi* |
    | Kaibutage | children |

    *dawa-o*
    *dawabo*

11. | *baiga* | *sabe* | *u'ubi* |
    | Baiga | Ridge | children |

    *dawa-o*
    *dawabo*

1. The *wabo* bird that we have been speaking of for so long
   Is this it?

2. The *bi'a* bird we have been speaking of
   Is this bird singing now?

3. The bird-of-paradise feathers that hang down
   Is it these here?

4.   The hornbill and *sore* bird
     Is it they who are singing now?

5.   The Chimbu men's black head feathers
     Are these hanging from men's heads?

6.   They have been saying that the *furubu* tree will carry many flowers
     Is it now going to happen?

7.   The *bi'a* bird we have been speaking of
     Is this bird singing now?

8.   The *sore* bird that has been singing
     Is it this one singing now?

9.   The children of Yagenebo
     *Dawa*

10.  The children of the mouth of the Kaibu River
     *Dawa*

11.  The children of Baiga Ridge
     *Dawa*

# Women's Song 2

## Singers: Kunuhuaka and Wa'abiyu. Recorded 4 November 1984 at Hegeso village.

Kunuhuaka's eldest son, Bebe, joined the Papua New Guinea Defence Force and eventually was stationed in Manus Island. This song, one of many that Kunuhuaka composed for her son, describes his departure. Traditionally, enemies were referred to as 'wasps' and as hawks and other birds of prey. (Figure 6 in this volume is a music transcription of lines 8–11.) ♩ online example 14.

| 1. | *tĩngi* | *burusumaremo* | *ari* | *viba'ae* |
|    | wasp | *burusama* | house | gone |
|    |  |  |  |  |
|    | *bi* | *sinae* |  |  |
|    | here | abandoned |  |  |

| 2. | *tĩngi*<br>wasp | *so'aremo*<br>*so'a* | *ari*<br>house | *viba'ae*<br>gone |
|---|---|---|---|---|
| | *bi*<br>here | *mo'aye*<br>left | | |

| 3. | *ya*<br>bird | *aiyaberemo*<br>hawk | *ari*<br>house | *viba'ae*<br>gone |
|---|---|---|---|---|
| | *bi*<br>here | *sinae*<br>abandoned | | |

| 4. | *tĩngi*<br>wasp | *ka'oremo*<br>*ka'o* | *ari*<br>house | *viba'ae*<br>gone |
|---|---|---|---|---|
| | *bi*<br>here | *tinae*<br>abandoned | | |

| 5. | *ya*<br>bird | *ibibiremo*<br>*ibibi* | *ari*<br>house | *viba'ae*<br>gone |
|---|---|---|---|---|
| | *bi*<br>here | *mo'aye*<br>left | | |

| 6. | *ya*<br>bird | *ãgegaremo*<br>hawk | *ari*<br>house | *viba'ae*<br>gone |
|---|---|---|---|---|
| | *bi*<br>here | *mo'aye*<br>left | | |

| 7. | *tĩngi*<br>wasp | *burusumaremo*<br>*burusama* | *ari*<br>house | *viba'ae*<br>gone |
|---|---|---|---|---|
| | *bi*<br>here | *sinae*<br>abandoned | | |

| 8. | *bi'a*<br>rifle | *foreremo*<br>large | *ari*<br>house | *viba'ae*<br>gone |
|---|---|---|---|---|
| | *bi*<br>here | *tinae*<br>abandoned | | |

| 9. | *bi'a*<br>black palm | *ka'aroremo*<br>bow and arrow | *ari*<br>house | *viba'ae*<br>gone |
|---|---|---|---|---|
| | *bi*<br>here | *mo'aye*<br>left | | |

| 10. | *amena* | *yiya* | *kui* | *kenege* |
|-----|---------|--------|-------|----------|
|     | men     | we     | sago  | mid-rib  |

*dawa-o*
*dawabo*

| 11. | *amena* | *oro*   | *yerebi* | *ibuhe'o* |
|-----|---------|---------|----------|-----------|
|     | men     | bamboo  | *yerebi* | *dawabo*  |

*dawa-o*
*dawabo*

1. Into the house of the *burusama* wasps you have gone
   Abandoning this place

2. Into the house of the wasps larvae you have gone
   Leaving here

3. Into the hawk's house you have entered
   Departing

4. Into the *ka'o* wasps house you have gone
   Abandoning this place

5. Into the house of the *ibibi* hawk you have entered
   Left here

6. Into the house of the *ãgega* hawk
   You have abandoned this place

7. Into the house of the *burusama* wasps you have gone
   Abandoning this place

8. Into the house of the big rifle
   You have left here

9. Into the house of the metal bow and arrow
   You have gone, leaving this place

10. We are the men of the Sago Bark clan
    *Dawa*

11. We are the men of the *yerebi* bamboo clan
    *Ibu he'o dawa*

# Women's Song 3

## Singers: Kunuhuaka and Wa'abiyu. Recorded 4 November 1984 at Hegeso village.

This song describes the aeroplane that took Kunuhuaka's son Bebe away from Hegeso and to his posting with the Papua New Guinea Defence Force. The Foi term *bare,* which means 'canoe', became used for any motorised vehicle they came to know, most commonly the aeroplane, and in this song, Kunuhuaka comments on the relationship between canoe and aeroplane. ♫ online example 15.

1. *bare*     *yuramaboba'ae*
   canoe     pull + take

   *bi*     *mo'aye*
   here     left

2. *bare*     *arurudiba'ae*
   canoe     crooked

   *bi*     *tinae*
   here     abandoned

3. *duma*     *hunabu*     *orori*     *huboba'ae*
   mountain     Hunabu     peak     pierced

   *bi*     *tinae*
   here     abandoned

4. *duma*     *dagerabo*     *orori*     *huboba'ae*
   mountain     Dagerabo     peak     pierced

   *bi*     *mo'aye*
   here     left

5. *ibu*     *suki*     *fufaboba'ae*
   river     Suki     fly away

   *bi*     *sinae*
   here     abandoned

6. *duma*     *a'o*     *hua*     *uboba'ae*
   mountain     cloud     pierced     has gone

   *bi*     *sinae*
   here     abandoned

| 7. | *duma* | *buru* | *orori* | *huboba'ae* |
|---|---|---|---|---|
| | mountain | black | peak | pierced |

| | *bi* | *mo'aye* |
|---|---|---|
| | here | left |

| 8. | *bare* | *arurudiba'ae* |
|---|---|---|
| | canoe | crooked |

| | *bi* | *tinae* |
|---|---|---|
| | here | abandoned |

| 9. | *bare* | *yura* | *uboba'ae* |
|---|---|---|---|
| | canoe | pulled | has gone |

| | *bi* | *sinae* |
|---|---|---|
| | here | abandoned |

| 10. | *kui* | *kenege* | *dobo* | *ka* | *bamo* |
|---|---|---|---|---|---|
| | sago | mid-rib | clan | woman | *that* |

| | *ba'a* | *terewaro* |
|---|---|---|
| | boy | Terewaro |

| 11. | *oro* | *yerebi* | *dobo* | *ba'a* | *bamo* |
|---|---|---|---|---|---|
| | bamboo | *yerebi* | clan | boy | that |

| | *dawabo* |
|---|---|
| | *dawabo* |

1. The aeroplane pulled him inside
   He has left this place

2. The aeroplane, as crooked as a canoe
   It left this place

3. It crossed the top of Mt Hunabu
   Leaving this place

4. Over the crest of Mt Dagerabo
   It abandoned this place

5. It flew away to the land of the Wage River
   Abandoning this place

6.  Through the cloud covered mountains it went
    Leaving here

7.  Over the top of the dark blue mountain
    It left this place behind

8.  The aeroplane, as crooked as a canoe
    It left this place

9.  It pulled him inside and left
    Abandoning this place

10. The woman of the Sago Bark clan
    Her son, Terewaro

11. The *yerebi* bamboo clan boy
    *Dawabo*

# Women's Song 4

## Singers: Kunuhuaka and Wa'abiyu. Recorded 4 November 1984 at Hegeso village.

This song appeared in *The Empty Place* (Weiner 1991:144–46). It describes the indignation a woman feels when confronted with her husband's suspicions that she is trying to seduce another man. ♫ online example 16.

1. | *ĩ* | *huni* | *mabo* | *kabore* |
   |------|---------|--------|----------|
   | eye | beckons | steals | girl |

   | *na* | *wae* | | |
   |------|-------|--|--|
   | I | not | | |

2. | *ya* | *huni* | *mabo* | *kabore* |
   |------|---------|--------|----------|
   | hand | beckons | steals | girl |

   | *na* | *wae* | | |
   |------|-------|--|--|
   | I | not | | |

3.  *fufuruforabo*    *kabori*
    wander           girl

    *na*             *iyo'oyebe*
    I                is not me?

4.  *iri*   *irikaro*   *gõ*          *hagibu*    *kabore*
    tree    twigs       string bag    carrying    girl

    *na*    *wae*
    I       not

5.  *amena*      *oro*      *yerebi*    *dobo*
    men          bamboo     *yerebi*    clan

    *dawa-o*
    *dawabo*

6.  *amena*      *ira*      *ma'aru*    *dobo*
    men          tree       *ma'aru*    clan

    *dawa-o*
    *dawabo*

---

1.  The kind of girl who looks around furtively
    I'm not that type

2.  The kind of girl who beckons towards men with her hand
    That's not me

3.  The kind of girl that wanders around searching for men
    I'm not that kind

4.  The kind of girl who throws twigs at men's feet
    That's not me

5.  The men of the *yerebi* bamboo clan
    *Dawa*

6.  The men of the *ma'arua* tree clan
    *Dawa*

# Women's Song 5

## Singers: Kunuhuaka and Wa'abiyu. Recorded 4 November 1984 at Hegeso village.

A woman complains about her maltreatment by her husband: 'You beat me because I don't do all these tasks, but you have never told me to do them,' she sings. ♫ online example 17.

| | | | | | |
|---|---|---|---|---|---|
| 1. | *u'ubi*<br>child | *kama*<br>female | *ere*<br>mind | *dibure*<br>said | |
| | *nena*<br>no reason | *doma'ae*<br>say | | | |
| 2. | *wãsia*<br>pitpit | *neri*<br>neri | *hirima*<br>plant | *diburo*<br>talk | |
| | *nena*<br>nothing | *dee*<br>say | | | |
| 3. | *wãsia*<br>pitpit | *kamua*<br>kamua | *hirima*<br>plant | *diburo*<br>talk | |
| | *nena*<br>nothing | *dee*<br>say | | | |
| 4. | *nami*<br>pig | *buru*<br>black | *kirari*<br>rope | *ma*<br>take | *dibure*<br>said |
| | *nena*<br>nothing | *dee*<br>say | | | |
| 5. | *busu*<br>kin | *u'ubi*<br>children | *ere*<br>mind | *dibure*<br>said | |
| | *nena*<br>no reason | *do'abobi*<br>should say | | | |
| 6. | *ira*<br>tree | *do'a*<br>do'a | *ga*<br>base | *ke*<br>burn | *di'ame*<br>said perhaps |
| | *nena*<br>no reason | *dee*<br>say | | | |

| 7. | *kui* | *hu* | *tirarude* | *ma* | *diburo* |
|----|-------|------|------------|------|----------|
|    | sago  | pound | pith shredded | take | talk |

| | *nena* | *dee* |
|---|--------|-------|
| | no reason | say |

| 8. | *kare* | *kui* | *ini* | *diburo* |
|----|--------|-------|-------|----------|
|    | women's | sago | cook | talk |

| | *nena* | *dee* |
|---|--------|-------|
| | nothing | say |

| 9. | *amena* | *oro* | *yerebi* |
|----|---------|-------|----------|
|    | men | bamboo | *yerebi* |

| | *dawa-o* |
|---|----------|
| | dawabo |

| 10. | *amena* | *ira* | *ma'aru* |
|-----|---------|-------|----------|
|     | men | tree | *ma'aru* |

| | *dawa-o* |
|---|----------|
| | dawabo |

1. Look after our little girl, you say
   You tell me nothing

2. You want me to plant *neri* pitpit
   But you have said nothing to me

3. You want me to plant *kamua* pitpit
   But not a word have you said to me

4. Take the black pig rope, you say
   But did you say anything to me

5. Look after your maternal clan's children
   But shouldn't you tell me first

6. Burn down the *do'a* trees and make a garden
   But you have told me nothing

7. Prepare sago for washing
   I heard you say nothing

8.  Cook mid-day sago, you want
    But I have heard nothing

9.  The men of the *yerebi* bamboo clan
    *Dawa*

10. The men of the *ma'aru* tree clan
    *Dawa*

# Women's Song 6

## Singers: Yiakahua and Ama'a. Recorded 4 November 1984 at Hegeso village.

I discussed this song in *The Empty Place* (Weiner 1991:25). The subject is the hand of a man who planted vegetable crops in his garden, which has been stilled by death.

1.  | *sona* | *sa'ara* | *hirimaboya* |
    | sona | sa'ara | planted + taken |

    | *ya* | *derege* | |
    | hand | motionless | |

2.  | *kima* | *kamua* | *hirimaboya* |
    | pitpit | kamua | planted + taken |

    | *ya* | *kenage* | |
    | hand | stiff | |

3.  | *wãsia* | *wayane* | *hirimaboya* |
    | pitpit | wayane | planted + taken |

    | *ya* | *derege* | |
    | hand | stone-like | |

4.  | *wãsia* | *diame* | *hirimaboya* |
    | pitpit | diame | planted + taken |

    | *ya* | *kenage* | |
    | hand | stiff | |

| 5. | *ira* | *namani* | *dobo* | *yaroge* | *ma'ame* | | |
| | tree | *namani* | clan | Yaroge | thing | | |
| | *dawabo* | | | | | | |
| | *dawabo* | | | | | | |

| 6. | *wa'ari* | *dobo* | *hasobe* | *ma'ame* | | | |
| | palm | clan | Hasobe | thing | | | |
| | *dawabo* | | | | | | |
| | *dawabo* | | | | | | |

| 7. | *ira* | *namani* | *dobo* | *ma'ame* | | | |
| | tree | *namani* | clan | thing | | | |
| | *dawabo* | | | | | | |
| | *dawabo* | | | | | | |

| 8. | *wa'ari* | *dobo* | *ka* | *mege* | *ba* | *ma'ame* |
| | palm | clan | woman | only | that | thing |
| | *ba'a* | *sega* | | | | |
| | boy | Sega | | | | |

1. He who planted the *sa'ara sona*
   His hand is cold

2. He who planted the *kamua* pitpit
   His hand is stiff and lifeless

3. He who planted the *wayane* pitpit
   His hand is dead

4. He who planted the *diame* pitpit
   His hand is still and without life

5. He of the clan of the *namani* tree, Yaroge
   *Dawa*

6. She of the clan of the *wa'ari* tree, Hasobe
   *Dawa*

7.   The man of the *namani* tree clan
     Yaroge

8.   The child of the *wa'ari* tree woman only
     The boy Sega

# Women's Song 7

## Singers: Yiakahua and Ama'a. Recorded 4 November 1984 at Hegeso village.

In this song, the women make an equation between the covering over of a man's traces on his land and its reappropriation by another man, which among the Foi is usually a man from the same clan. This process of internal succession to a deceased man's habitual territory is a normative and collectively sanctioned process; nevertheless, in the context of this mourning song, in light of the feelings of loss caused by a death, it may be construed as theft of land by the deceased's relatives. ♫ online example 18.

1.   *ba'a*       *na'a*        *kone*              *ibu*
     boy          your          white               creek

     *memo*      *ga'ae*
     another     possesses

2.   *ba'a*       *na'a*        *da'arefai*        *ibu*
     boy          your          Da'arefai          creek

     *memo*      *ga'ae*
     another     possesses

3.   *ba'a*       *na'a*        *suanobo*          *ibu*
     boy          your          fish dammed        creek

     *aodoba'aye*
     let bush cover it

4. *ba'a*     *na'a*     *nafa*     *kobo*     *ibu*
   boy      your      nafa      taken     creek

   *kigiba'ae*
   bush covered

5. *ba'a*     *na'a*     *ibu*     *waya'arehabu*
   boy      your      creek    Waya'arehabu

   *ibu*      *aodoba'aye*
   creek     let bush cover it

6. *ba'a*     *na'a*     *dabahabo*     *ibu*
   boy      your      Dabahabo      creek

   *memo*     *ga'ae*
   another    possesses

7. *ba'a*     *na'a*     *baruagahabo*     *ibu*
   boy      your      Baruagahabo      creek

   *aodoba'aye*
   let bush cover it

8. *ba'a*     *na'a*     *orege*     *duma*
   boy      your      Orege      mountain

   *memo*     *ga'ae*
   another    possesses

9. *ba'a*     *na'a*     *domege*     *ibu*
   boy      your      Domege      creek

   *aodoba'aye*
   let bush cover it

10. *ba'a*    *na'a*    *igiri*    *ga*       *ibu*
    boy      your     Igiri     source    creek

    *memo*    *ga'ae*
    another   possesses

11. *ba'a*    *na'a*    *munusuhabo*    *ibu*
    boy      your     Munusuhabo     creek

    *kigiba'aye*
    let strong bush

12. *ba'a*      *na'a*      *faya'a*      *tonore*
    boy         your        Faya'a        island

    *memo*      *ga'ae*
    another     possesses

13. *ba'a*      *na'a*      *so'a*        *duma*
    boy         your        So'a          mountain

    *aginoboba'ae*
    let another steal it

14. *ba'a*      *na'a*      *yegi*        *kobo*        *ibu*
    boy         your        fish          taken         creek

    *kigiba'ae*
    bush covered

15. *ba'a*      *na'a*      *ira*         *sabe*        *hũga*
    boy         your        tree          sabe          larvae

    *gamage*    *aginoboba'ae*
    later       let another steal it

16. *ba'a*      *na'a*      *gibi*        *moge*
    boy         your        bush fowl     eggs

    *aodoboba'ae*
    bush covered

17. *ba'a*      *na'a*      *buduru*      *hũga*
    boy         your        *buduru*      larvae

    *viraba'aye*
    let them fly away

18. *orohuĩ*    *ibu*
    Orohuĩ      creek

    *aodoboba'ae*
    bush covered

19. *ba'a*      *na'a*      *ira*            *waria*       *bu'uni*
    boy         your        tree             waria         trap

    *aodoboba'ae*
    bush covered

20. *oro*       *masiba*    *ira*
    bamboo      masiba      tree

    *ira*       *waboba'ae*
    tree        let them come

21. *ba'a*      *na'a*      *metega*         *kui*
    boy         your        hidden           sago

    *aginoba'aye*
    let another steal it

22. *ba'a*      *na'a*      *oro*            *taru*        *ira*
    boy         your        bamboo           great         tree

    *aodoboba'ae*
    bush covered

23. *ba'a*      *na'a*      *dabi*           *bu'uni*
    boy         your        cave             trap

    *kigiboba'ae*
    tree covered

24. *ba'a*      *na'a*      *ibu*            *suanibibi*
    boy         your        creek            dammed-eaten

    *kigiboba'ae*
    tree covered

25. *ba'a*      *na'a*      *aiyebo'ao*      *ibu*
    boy         your        Aiyebo'ao        creek

    *ira*       *waba'ane*
    tree        let them come

26. *amena*     *oro*       *yerebi*
    men         bamboo      *yerebi*

    *ba'a*      *terewaro*
    boy         Terewaro

27. | *kane* | *baniyu* | *ka* | | *mege* | *ba* | *ma'ame* |
    |--------|----------|------|--|--------|------|---------|
    | vine   | *baniyu* | woman | | only  | that | thing   |

   | *na'abo* | *dibige* |
   |----------|----------|
   | to you   | stated   |

28. | *kui*  | *kenege*  | *dobo* | *ka* | *ba* | *ma'ame* |
    |--------|-----------|--------|------|------|---------|
    | sago   | mid-rib   | clan   | woman | that | thing  |

   | *ba'a* | *bebe* |
   |--------|--------|
   | boy    | Bebe   |

29. | *ira*  | *yaro*   | *dobo* | *ka*  | *mege* | *ba* | *ma'ame* |
    |--------|----------|--------|-------|--------|------|---------|
    | tree   | *ma'aru* | clan   | woman | only   | that | thing   |

   | *na'abo* | *dibige* |
   |----------|----------|
   | to you   | stated   |

1.  Boy, your swift white water
    Is another man's now

2.  Boy, your Da'arefai Creek
    Belongs to another

3.  Boy, your fish dammed creek
    Another has taken it

4.  Boy, your creek of the *nafa* fish
    Has been covered with bush

5.  Boy, your Waya'arehabu Creek
    The bush has hidden that creek

6.  Boy, your Dabahabo Creek
    It is another's now

7.  Boy, your Baruagahabo Creek
    Covered with jungle

8.  Boy, your Mt Orege
    It is another's

9.  Boy, your Domege Creek
    Bush reclaimed

10. Boy, your Igiri Creek
    It is someone else's now

11. Boy, your Munusuhabo Creek
    Let the jungle claim it

12. Boy, your Hegeso longhouse
    It is another's

13. Boy, your Mt So'a
    Stolen

14. Boy, your fish creeks
    Bush covered

15. Boy, your *sabe* tree grubs
    Another man will eat them

16. Boy, your bush fowl eggs
    Hidden by the bush

17. Boy, your *buduru* tree grubs
    Turned into butterflies

18. Orohuĩ Creek
    Bush covered

19. Your *waria* fruit traps
    Jungle hidden

20. Your *masiba* bamboo
    Tree hidden

21. Your secret sago palms
    Now another will eat them

22. Your *taru* bamboo
    Later will be eaten

23. Your cave deadfalls
    Bush covered

24. Your fish dam creeks
    Jungle taken

25. Your Aiyebo'ao Creek
    Let the trees come

26. The man of the *yerebi* bamboo clan
    Boy Terewaro

27. The woman of the *baniyu* fruit
    It is I who speak to you

28. The woman of the Sago Bark clan
    The Boy Bebe

29. The *ma'aru* tree clan woman
    I your mother am speaking to you

# Photographs

Photographs have been chosen to represent some of the images evoked in the song texts, to portray some of the singers who sang the songs transcribed here, and to show some features of the performance context. All photographs are by James Weiner, unless noted otherwise.

**Photo 1: Dafimi (Barutage) and her mother making sago, Hegeso village, c. 1980.**

**Photo 2: Kunuhuaka, her son Bebe, and James Weiner, at Hegeso, 1980.**

**Photo 3: Hegeso longhouse, near junction of Faya'a Creek and Mubi River, c. 1980.**

**Photo 4: Launching a new canoe in Faya'a Creek, Hegeso village, c. 1980.**

**Photo 5: View of Mubi River from low-flying aeroplane, c. 1980.**

**Photo 6: One of many small waterfalls along the creeks in the vicinity of Hegeso village.**

**Photo 7: Bush house near Hegeso village, c. 1980.**

**Photo 8: Rock ledge near Segemi Creek, place of the storage of bones of deceased Hegeso men, c. 1980.**

**Photo 9: Viya and his son Sese, eating sago grubs near Hegeso longhouse, c. 1980.**

**Photo 10: Large marsupial being butchered on a hunting trip to Ayamo, Hegeso village hunting area, c. 1980.**

**Photo 11: Kora of Hegeso searching for bush-fowl eggs, c. 1980.**

**Photo 12: Herebo longhouse, 1980.**

**Photo 13: Dancers outside of Herebo longhouse, 1980.**

Photo 14: Hegeso longhouse, c. 1980.

Photo 15: Decorated Foi men at Hegeso *Dawa* (pig-kill), c. 1980.

Photo 16: Contingent of decorated Fasu men, arriving at Hegeso *Dawa*, c. 1980.

Photo 17: Fasu man in Bosavi-style ceremonial dress, c. 1980.

**Photo 18: Hegeso men, *sorohabora* performance, 1980.**

**Photo 19: Abeabo of Hegeso, holding a *gasore* rattle during Hegeso *sorohabora*, c. 1980.**

**Photo 20: Men playing *gasore* rattles during the 3rd Kundu and Digaso Festival, Daga village, 20 September 2013. Photo by Don Niles.**

**Photo 21: A variety of *gasore* rattles played during the 3rd Kundu and Digaso Festival, Daga village, 20 September 2013. The instrument at left centre has a handle. Photo by Don Niles.**

# References

Aerts, Theo, and Karl Hesse. 1979. *Baining Dances*. Boroko: Institute of Papua New Guinea Studies.

Aikhenvald, Alexandra Y. 2014. '"Double Talk": Parallel Structures in Manambu Songs, and Their Origin.' *Language and Linguistics in Melanesia* 32/2: 86–109.

Austen, Leo. 1934. 'The Dance of the Gope in Kerewo.' *Man* 34: 4–8.

———. 1936. 'Head Dances of the Turama River.' *Oceania* 6: 342–49.

Baldwin, Bernard. 1945. 'Usituma! Song of Heaven.' *Oceania* 15 (March): 201–38.

———. 1950. 'Kadaguwai: Songs of the Trobriand Sunset Isles.' *Oceania* 20: 263–85.

Barton, F. R. 1910. 'The Annual Trading Expedition to the Papuan Gulf.' In *The Melanesians of British New Guinea*, by Charles G. Seligman, 96–120. Cambridge: Cambridge University Press.

Bateson, Gregory. 1932. 'Social Structure of the Iatmül People of the Sepik River.' *Oceania* 2: 245–91, 401–53.

Beaver, Wilfred N. 1920. *Unexplored New Guinea*. Philadelphia: Lippincott.

Bergmann, H. F. W. 1971. *The Kamanuku*. 4 vols. Harrisville, Australia.

Borchard, Terrance, and Philip Gibbs. 2011. 'Parallelism and Poetics in *Tindi* Narratives Sung in the Ipili Language.' In *Sung Tales from the Papua New Guinea Highlands: Studies in Form, Meaning, and Sociocultural Context*, edited by Alan Rumsey and Don Niles, 165–96. Canberra: ANU E Press.

Brash, Elton, and Nigel Krauth. 1973. Eds. *Traditional Poems, Chants and Songs of Papua New Guinea*. Papua Pocket Poets, 38. Port Moresby: [n.p.].

Brooksbank, John. 2012. 'Longhouse Communities: Coping with Change.' *Paradise* 5 (2012): 70–76.

Brown, D. J. J. 1979. 'The Structuring of Polopa Feasting and Warfare.' *Man* n.s. 14: 712–33.

Brown, Herbert A. 1968. *A Dictionary of Toaripi with English–Toaripi Index*. 2 vols. Oceania Linguistic Monographs, 11. Sydney: University of Sydney.

Brumbaugh, Robert. 1979. 'A Secret Cult in the West Sepik Highlands.' PhD dissertation, State University of New York, Stony Brook.

————. 1990. 'Afek Sang: The 'Old Woman' Myth of the Mountain-Ok.' In *Children of Afek: Tradition and Change among the Mountain-Ok of Central New Guinea*, edited by Barry Craig and David Hyndman, 54–87. Oceania Monograph, 40. Sydney: University of Sydney.

Bulmer, Ralph. 1967. 'Why Is the Cassowary Not a Bird? A Problem of Zoological Taxonomy among the Karam of the New Guinea Highlands.' *Man* 2: 5–25.

Busse, Mark, Susan Turner, and Nick Araho. 1993. *The People of Lake Kutubu and Kikori: Changing Meanings of Daily Life*. [Port Moresby]: Papua New Guinea National Museum and Art Gallery.

Chenoweth, Vida. 1979. *The Usarufas and Their Music*. SIL Museum of Anthropology Publication, 5. Dallas: SIL Museum of Anthropology.

————. 2000. *Sing-Sing: Communal Singing and Dancing in Papua New Guinea*. Christchurch: Macmillan Brown Centre for Pacfic Studies.

Chenoweth, Vida, and Bruce Hooley. 2010. 'Buang Music.' *Kulele* 4: 111–41.

Clay, Brenda Johnson. 1986. *Mandak Realities; Person and Power in Central New Ireland*. New Brunswick: Rutgers University Press.

Cooper, Russell E. 1975. 'Coastal Suau: A Preliminary Study of Internal Relationships.' In *Studies in Language of Central and South-East Papua*, edited by Tom E. Dutton, 227–78. Pacific Linguistics, C 29. Canberra: The Australian National University.

Coulter, Neil R. 2007. 'Music Shift: Evaluating the Vitality and Viability of Music Styles among the Alamblak of Papua New Guinea.' PhD dissertation, Kent State University.

Craig, Barry. 2010. Ed. *Living Spirits with Fixed Abodes: The Masterpieces Exhibition, Papua New Guinea National Museum and Art Gallery*. Adelaide: Crawford House Publishing Australia.

Crawford, Anthony L. 1981. *Aida: Life and Ceremony of the Gogodala*. Bathurst: National Cultural Council and Robert Brown & Associates.

Depew, Robert. 1983. 'Musical Traditions of the Upper Fly River Papua New Guinea.' 74 pp. Music Archive, Institute of Papua New Guinea Studies.

Donohoe, Patricia Mary. 1987. 'Breath of Dirima: A Research Project.' MA thesis, University of New South Wales.

Drüppel, Birgit. 2009. *Re-counting Knowledge in Song: Change Reflected in Kaulong Music*. Edited by Don Niles. With one compact disc. Apwitihire: Studies in Papua New Guinea Musics, 10. Boroko: Institute of Papua New Guinea Studies.

Fajans, Jane. 1985. 'They Make Themselves: Life Cycle, Domestic Cycle and Ritual among the Baining.' PhD dissertation, Stanford University.

Feld, Steven. 1978. 'To Make Men Cry: The Poetry of *Heyalo*.' *Gigibori* 4: 14–17.

———. 1981. *Music of the Kaluli*. Institute of Papua New Guinea Studies IPNGS 001. One 30 cm, 33 1/3 rpm disc.

———. 1982. *Sound and Sentiment: Birds, Weeping, Poetics, and Song in Kaluli Expression*. Publications of the American Folklore Society, New Series. Philadelphia: University of Pennsylvania Press.

———. 1985. *The Kaluli of Papua Niugini; Weeping and Song*. Bärenreiter-Musicaphon BM 30 SL 2702. One 30 cm, 33 1/3 rpm disc.

———. 1988. 'Aesthetics as Iconicity of Style, or, "Lift-Up-Over-Sounding": Getting into the Kaluli Groove.' *Yearbook for Traditional Music* 20: 74–113.

———. 1990. *Sound and Sentiment: Birds, Weeping, Poetics, and Song in Kaluli Expression*. 2nd ed. Publications of the American Folklore Society, New Series. Philadelphia: University of Pennsylvania Press.

———. 2001. *Bosavi: Rainforest Music from Papua New Guinea*. Smithsonian Folkways Recordings SFW CD 40487. Three CDs.

———. 2015. Email to Don Niles (28 January).

Flanagan, James. 1983. 'Wovan Social Organization.' PhD dissertation, University of Pennsylvannia.

Fortune, Reo F. 1932. *Sorcerers of Dobu*. New York: Dutton.

Fox, James J. 1977. 'Roman Jakobson and the Comparative Study of Parallelism.' In *Roman Jakobson: Echoes of His Scholarship*, edited by Daniel Armstrong and Cornelis H. van Schooneveld, 59–90. Lisse: Peter de Ridder Press.

Franklin, Karl J. 1970. 'Metaphorical Songs in Kewa.' In *Pacific Linguistic Studies in Honour of Arthur Capell*, edited by Stephan A. Wurm and Donald C. Laycock, 985–95. Pacific Linguistics, C 13. Canberra: The Australian National University.

————. 1978. 'Songs in Kewa.' In *A Kewa Dictionary*, edited by Karl J. Franklin and Joice Franklin, 389–97. Pacific Linguistics, C 53. Canberra: The Australian National University.

Gende, Edward. 1998. 'Highland Region of Papua New Guinea: Chimbu Province: Kuman.' In *Australia and the Pacific Islands*, edited by Adrienne L. Kaeppler and J. W. Love, 522–26. The Garland Encyclopedia of World Music, 9. New York: Garland Publishing.

Gibbs, Philip. 2001. 'Ol Singsing Enga.' *Kulele: Occasional Papers on Pacific Music and Dance* 3: 50–63.

————. 2011. 'Enga *Tindi Pii*: The Real World and Creative Imagination.' In *Sung Tales from the Papua New Guinea Highlands: Studies in Form, Meaning, and Sociocultural Context*, edited by Alan Rumsey and Don Niles, 151–65. Canberra: ANU E Press.

Gillespie, Kirsty. 2010. *Steep Slopes: Music and Change in the Highlands of Papua New Guinea*. Canberra: ANU E Press.

Gillespie, Kirsty, and Lila San Roque. 2011. 'Music and Language in Duna *Pikono*.' In *Sung Tales from the Papua New Guinea Highlands: Studies in Form, Meaning, and Sociocultural Context*, edited by Alan Rumsey and Don Niles, 49–64. Canberra: ANU E Press.

Goldman, Laurence R. 2007. 'Decorated Being in Huli: Parleying with Paint.' In *Body Arts and Modernity*, edited by Elizabeth Ewart and Michael O'Hanlon, 142–64. Wantage: Sean Kingston Publishing.

Goodale, Jane C. 1995. *To Sing with Pigs Is Human: The Concept of Person in Papua New Guinea*. Seattle: University of Washington Press.

Graf, Walter. 1950. *Die musikwissenschaftlichen Phonogramme Rudolf Pöchs von der Nordküste Neuguineas: Eine materialkritische Studie unter besonderer Berücksichtigung der völkerkundlichen Grundlagen*. Rudolf Pöchs Nachlass, B 2. Wien: Rudolf M. Rohrer.

Grove, Theodore Charles. 1978. 'Jaw's Harp Music of Papua New Guinea's Kalam People—the *Gwb*.' PhD dissertation, Univesity of California, San Diego.

Harrison, Simon. 1982. *Laments for Foiled Marriages: Love-songs from a Sepik River Village*. Boroko: Institute of Papua New Guinea Studies.

————. 1986. 'Laments for Foiled Marriages: Love-songs from a Sepik River Village.' *Oceania* 56 (June): 275–93.

Hays, Terence E. 1993. '"The New Guinea Highlands": Region, Culture Area, or Fuzzy Set?' *Current Anthropology* 34 (April): 141–64.

Heeschen, Volker. 1990. *Ninye bún: Mythen, Erzählungen, Lieder und Märchen der Eipo im zentralen Bergland von Irian Jaya (West-Neuguinea), Indonesien.* Beitrag zur Schriftenreihe 'Mensch, Kultur und Umwelt im zentralen Bergland von West-Neuguinea', 20. Berlin: Dietrich Reimer Verlag.

Helfert, Roy, and David Holdsworth. 1974. *Songs of Papua New Guinea.* Milton: Jacaranda Press. With one 18 cm, 33 1/3 rpm disc, Jacaranda OCW 1011. (IPNGS c80-141).

Hoenigman, Darja. in prep. 'Language Variation and Social Identity in Kanjimei, East Sepik Province, Papua New Guinea.' PhD dissertation, The Australian National University.

Hooley, Bruce A. 1987. 'Central Buang Poetry.' In *Perspectives on Language and Text: Essays and Poems in Honour of Francis I. Andersen's Sixtieth Birthday*, edited by Edgar W. Conrad and Edward G. Newing, 71–88. Winona Lake, Indiana: Eisenbrauns.

Huguet, Pierre. 1992. *Confluences: Papua New-Guinea: Sounds of Nature and Songs of Stone-Age Men.* Pithys 10102. CD.

Ingemann, Frances. 1968. 'The Linguistic Structure of an Ipili-Paiyala Song Type.' 6 pp. Paper presented at the 8th International Congress of Anthropological and Ethnological Sciences, Tokyo.

———. 2011. 'The Structure of Chanted Ipili Tindi.' In *Sung Tales from the Papua New Guinea Highlands: Studies in Form, Meaning, and Sociocultural Context*, edited by Alan Rumsey and Don Niles, 197–206. Canberra: ANU E Press.

Jakobson, Roman. 1960. 'Closing Statement: Linguistics and Poetics.' In *Style in Language*, edited by Thomas A. Sebeok, 350–77. Cambridge: Massachusetts Institute of Technology.

James, Graham G. 1978. 'An Introduction to the Music of the Cape Nelson Area, Northern Province, Papua New Guinea.' Thesis submitted as part of miscellaneous course, Queensland University.

Jenness, Diamond, and A. Ballantyne. 1926–29. 'Language, Mythology and Songs of Bwaidoga.' *Journal of the Polynesian Society* 35: 290–314 + map; 36: 48–71, 145–79, 207–238, 303–329; 37: 30–56, 139–64, 271–99, 377–402; 38: 29–47.

————. 1928. *Language, Mythology, and Songs of Bwaidoga, Goodenough Island, S.E. Papua*. Memoirs of the Polynesian Society, 8. New Plymouth: Thomas Avery & Sons. [Originally published in the *Journal of the Polynesian Society* 35–38 (1926–29).]

Jimben, Anna. 1984. 'Karim Lek Songs of the Mid-Wangi [sic] People.' *Bikmaus* 5 (September): 86–87. [Note: the author's name is incorrectly printed as 'Jinben'.]

Josephides, Lisette. 1982. 'Kewa Stories and Songs (Southern Highlands Province).' *Oral History* 10: 1–86.

Kasaipwalova, John. 1978. *Yaulabuta, Kolupa, deli Lekolekwa (Pilatolu Kilivila Wosimwaya)*. Port Moresby: Institute of Papua New Guinea Studies.

Kasaipwalova, John, and Ulli Beier. 1978a. Eds. *Lekolekwa: An Historical Song from the Trobriand Islands*. Port Moresby: Institute of Papua New Guinea Studies.

————. 1978b. Eds. *Yaulabuta: The Passion of Chief Kailaga; An Historical Poem from the Trobriand Islands*. Port Moresby: Institute of Papua New Guinea Studies.

————. 1979. 'Exile: An Historical Poem from the Trobriand Islands.' *Gigibori* 4 (August): 47–48.

Kelsey, John. 1993. 'The Music of the Irumu People, Morobe Province, Papua New Guinea.' PhD dissertation, Wesleyan University.

Kendoli, Kenny Yuwi. 2011. 'Yuna *Pikono*.' In *Sung Tales from the Papua New Guinea Highlands: Studies in Form, Meaning, and Sociocultural Context*, edited by Alan Rumsey and Don Niles, 39–48. Canberra: ANU E Press.

Kerema, Philip. 1976? 'Traditional Songs of Ialibu, S.H.P.' 14 pp. Music Archive, Institute of Papua New Guinea Studies.

Kirsch, Stuart. 1987. 'Preliminary Notes on the Musical Traditions of the Yongom.' 7 pp. Music Archive, Institute of Papua New Guinea Studies.

Knauft, Bruce M. 1985a. *Good Company and Violence: Sorcery and Social Action in a Lowland New Guinea Society*. Studies in Melanesian Anthropology, 3. Berkeley: University of California.

————. 1985b. 'Ritual Form and Permutation in New Guinea: Implications of Symbolic Process for Socio-Political Evolution.' *American Ethnologist* 12 (May): 321–40.

———. 2005. *The Gebusi: Lives Transformed in a Rainforest World*. Boston: McGraw-Hill.

———. 2012. 'Gebusi Music and Dance 1980–92.' http://www.anthropology. emory.edu/faculty/antbk/gebusiResearch/gebusi_music_dance.html (accessed 2 May 2012).

Koyati, Peandui. 1979. 'Traditional Songs of the Baiyer River.' *Oral History* 7: 42–106.

Laba, Billai, Thomas Lulungan, James Jesse Pongap, and Don Niles. 1980. 'Texts, Translations, and Additional Commentaries on IPNGS Recordings, Part I.' *Oral History* 8: 91–100.

Landtman, Gunnar. 1913. 'The Poetry of the Kiwai Papuans.' *Folklore* 24: 284–313.

———. 1927. *The Kiwai Papuans of British New Guinea*. London: Macmillan.

Laycock, Donald C. 1969a. *Akaru: Traditional Buin Songs*. Papua Pocket Poets, 12. Port Moresby: [n.p.].

———. 1969b. 'Buin Songs.' *Kovave* 1 (November): 5–8.

———. 1969c. 'Sublanguages in Buin: Play, Poetry, and Preservation.' In *Papers in New Guinea Linguistics, 10*, 1–23. Pacific Linguistics, A 22. Canberra: The Australian National University.

———. 1970. 'The Content of Buin Songs Today.' Paper read at Section 25, ANZAAS Conference, Port Moresby, August 1970.

———. 1972. 'Two Buin Songs.' *Kovave* 3 (June): 23–24.

LeRoy, John. 1978. 'Burning Our Trees: Metaphors in Kewa Songs.' *Yearbook of Symbolic Anthropology* 1: 51–72.

———. 1985. *Fabricated World: An Interpretation of Kewa Tales*. Vancouver: University of British Columbia Press.

Lewis, Gilbert. 1980. *Day of Shining Red: An Essay on Understanding Ritual*. Cambridge Studies in Social Anthropology, 27. Cambridge: Cambridge University Press.

Lewis, M. Paul, Gary F. Simons, and Charles D. Fennig. 2013. Eds. *Ethnologue: Languages of the World*. 17th ed. Dallas: SIL International. Online version: http://www.ethnologue.com/.

Lomas, Gabe C. J. 2011. 'Sung Tales in Héla Húli.' In *Sung Tales from the Papua New Guinea Highlands: Studies in Form, Meaning, and Sociocultural Context*, edited by Alan Rumsey and Don Niles, 75–108. Canberra: ANU E Press.

Luzbetak, Louis J. 1954. 'The Socio-Religious Significance of a New Guinea Pig Festival.' *Anthropological Quarterly* 2: 59–80, 102–28.

MacDonald, Mary N. 1991. *Mararoko: A Study in Melanesian Religion*. American University Studies, 9, 45. New York: Peter Lang.

May, Jean, and Eunice Loeweke. 1981. *Fasu (Námo Mē)–English Dictionary*. Ukarumpa: Summer Institute of Linguistics.

Mimica, Jadran. 1993. 'Review Article: The Foi and Heidegger: Western Philosophical Poetics and a New Guinea Life-World.' *Australian Journal of Anthropology* 4: 79–95.

Moyle, Richard M. 2007. *Songs from the Second Float: A Musical Ethnography of Takū Atoll, Papua New Guinea*. Pacific Islands Monograph Series, 21. Mānoa: Center for Pacific Islands Studies; Honolulu: University of Hawai'i Press.

National. 2012. 'Kutubu Culture Still Uncovered.' *The National* (25 September): 5.

National Arts School. [1986?]. *Igimi: The Biami Tribe*. [Boroko]: National Arts School.

Neuhauss, Richard. 1911. *Deutsch Neu-Guinea*. 3 vols. Berlin: Dietrich Reimer.

Niles, Don. 2000. *Papua New Guinea (1904–1909): The Collections of Rudolf Pöch, Wilhelm Schmidt, and Josef Winthuis*. Book (223 pp.), five compact discs (OEAW PHA CD 9/1–5), and one CD-ROM (OEAW PHA CD-ROM/9). Dietrich Schüller, series editor. Gerda Lechleitner, editor. Erna Mack, music transcriptions. Tondokumente aus dem Phonogrammarchiv der Österreichischen Akademie der Wissenschaften: Gesamtausgabe der Historischen Bestände 1899–1950 / Sound Documents from the Phonogrammarchiv of the Austrian Academy of Sciences: The Complete Historical Collections 1899–1950, series 3. Wien: Verlag der Österreichischen Akademie der Wissenschaften.

———. 2007. 'Sonic Structure in *Tom Yaya Kange*: Ku Waru Sung Narratives from Papua New Guinea.' In *Oceanic Music Encounters—the Print Resource and the Human Resource: Essays in Honour of Mervyn McLean*, edited by Richard Moyle, 109–22. Research in Anthropology and Linguistics Monograph, 7. Auckland: University of Auckland.

————. 2009. 'Editor's Introduction.' In *Re-counting Knowledge in Song: Change Reflected in Kaulong Music*, edited by Birgit Drüppel, xv–xl. Apwitihire: Studies in Papua New Guinea Musics, 10. With one compact disc (IPNGS 013). Boroko: Institute of Papua New Guinea Studies.

————. 2011a. 'Metric Melodies and the Performance of Sung Tales in the Hagen Area.' In *Sung Tales from the Papua New Guinea Highlands: Studies in Form, Meaning, and Sociocultural Context*, edited by Alan Rumsey and Don Niles, 275–302. Canberra: ANU E Press.

————. 2011b. 'Structuring Sound and Movement: Music and Dance in the Mount Hagen Area.' PhD dissertation, Anthropology and Sociology, University of Papua New Guinea.

Niles, Don, and Edward Gende. 2013. '[Notes accompanying recordings and photos from the 3rd Kundu and Digaso Festival].' Institute of Papua New Guinea Studies Music Archive IPNGS 13-056, 13-057, and 13-059.

Niles, Don, and Alan Rumsey. 2011. 'Introducing Highlands Sung Tales.' In *Sung Tales from the Papua New Guinea Highlands: Studies in Form, Meaning, and Sociocultural Context*, edited by Alan Rumsey and Don Niles, 1–38. Canberra: ANU E Press.

Niles, Don, and Michael Webb. 1987. *Papua New Guinea Music Collection*. Boroko: Institute of Papua New Guinea Studies. IPNGS 008. Eleven cassettes and book.

O'Brien, Denise. 1969a. 'The Economics of Dani Marriage: An Analysis of Marriage Payments in a Highland New Guinea Society.' PhD dissertation, Yale University.

————. 1969b. 'Marriage among the Konda Valley Dani.' In *Pigs, Pearlshells, and Women: Marriage in the New Guinea Highlands*, edited by Robert M. Glasse and Mervyn J. Meggitt, 198–234. Englewood Cliffs: Prentice Hall.

Oil Search Limited. 2012. 'Kutubu.' http://www.oilsearch.com/Our-Activities/PNG/Kutubu.html (accessed 11 May 2012).

Oliver-Berg, Marie H. 1979. 'Music and Meaning of Buin Songs.' BA Honours thesis, University of Queensland.

Oméga Studio. 1981? *P.N.G*. Oméga Studio OM 67.026. One 30 cm, 33 1/3 rpm disc. (IPNGS c86-110).

Paia, Robert, and Andrew Strathern. 1977. *Beneath the Andaiya Tree: Wiru Songs*. Boroko: Institute of Papua New Guinea Studies.

Pawley, Andrew, and Ralph Bulmer. 2011. *A Dictionary of Kalam with Ethnographic Notes*. With the assistance of John Kias, Simon Peter Gi, and Ian Saem Majnep. Pacific Linguistics, 630. Canberra: The Australian National University.

Petterson, Robert. 1999. *Rumu–English–Hiri Motu Dictionary; Rumuhei– Hohei–Mutuheu Hei Ke Tei Kopatë*. Occasional Paper, 6. [Palmerston North]: International Pacific College.

Pöch, Rudolf. 1905. 'Beobachtungen über Sprache, Gesänge und Tänze der Monumbo anläßlich phonographischer Aufnahmen in Deutsch-Neu-Guinea.' *Mitteilungen der Anthropologischen Gesellschaft in Wien* 35 (5): 230–37, Tafel 1.

Pospisil, Leopold. 1963. *The Kapauku Papuans of West New Guinea*. Case Studies in Cultural Anthropology. New York: Holt, Rinehart & Winston.

Pugh-Kitingan, Jacqueline. 1981. 'An Ethnomusicological Study of the Huli of the Southern Highlands, Papua New Guinea.' PhD dissertation, University of Queensland.

Rappaport, Roy A. 1968. *Pigs for the Ancestors: Ritual in the Ecology of a New Guinea People*. New Haven: Yale University Press.

Reesink, Ger P. 1992. Review of *The Empty Place: Poetry, Space, and Being among the Foi of Papua New Guinea*, by James F. Weiner. *Oceanic Linguistics* 31(2) (Winter): 310–12.

Reigle, Robert. 1995. 'Sound of the Spirits, Song of the Myna.' In *New Guinea Ethnomusicology Conference: Proceedings*, edited by Robert Reigle, 121–28. Occasional Papers in Pacific Ethnomusicology, 4. Auckland: University of Auckland.

———. 2001. 'Sacred Music of Serieng Village, Papua New Guinea.' PhD dissertation, University of California, Los Angeles. With 2 CDs.

Reithofer, Hans. 2011. 'Skywalkers and Cannibals: Chanted Tales among the Angal.' In *Sung Tales from the Papua New Guinea Highlands: Studies in Form, Meaning, and Sociocultural Context*, edited by Alan Rumsey and Don Niles, 207–46. Canberra: ANU E Press.

Riley, E. Baxter. 1925. *Among Papuan Headhunters*. London: Seeley Service.

Roberts, Christopher. 1996. *Xingchen Shan li de gong ming: Xin Jineiya zhong bu ge yao* 星辰山裡的共鳴：新幾內亞中部歌謠 [Music of the Star Mountains: Traditional singing in Central New Guinea]. Translated by Wang Ling-kang 王靈康. Illustrations by Patricia Hills. In Chinese. Taipei: Yuan-Liou.

———. 2014. *Music of the Star Mountains: A Naturalist's Guide to the Composition of Songs in Central New Guinea*. Edited by Don Niles. With one compact disc. Apwitihire: Studies in Papua New Guinea Musics, 11. Boroko: Institute of Papua New Guinea Studies.

Rule, W. Murray. 1993. *The Culture and Language of the Foe: The People of Lake Kutubu, Southern Highlands Province, Papua New Guinea*. Commissioned by Chevron Niugini Pty., Ltd., for Kutubu Joint Venture. Merewether, Australia: Murray Rule.

Rumsey, Alan. 1995. 'Pairing and Parallelism in the New Guinea Highlands.' In *SALSA II: Proceedings of the Second Annual Symposium about Language and Society, Austin*, edited by Pamela Silberman and Jonathan Loftin, 108–18. Texas Linguistic Forum, 34. Austin: University of Texas.

———. 2001. '*Tom Yaya Kange*: A Metrical Narrative Genre from the New Guinea Highlands.' Journal of Linguistic Anthropology 11: 193–239.

———. 2005. 'Chanted Tales in the New Guinea Highlands of Today: A Comparative Study.' In *Expressive Genres and Historical Change: Indonesia, Papua New Guinea and Taiwan*, edited by Pamela J. Stewart and Andrew Strathern, 41–81. Anthropology and Cultural History in Asia and the Indo-Pacific. Hants: Ashgate Publishing.

———. 2007. 'Musical, Poetic, and Linguistic Form in *Tom Yaya* Sung Narratives from Papua New Guinea.' *Anthropological Linguistics* 49: 235–82.

———. 2010. 'A Metrical System That Defies Description by Ordinary Means.' In *A Journey through Austronesian and Papuan Linguistic and Cultural Space: Papers in Honour of Andrew K. Pawley*, edited by John Bowden, Nikolaus P. Himmelmann, Malcolm Ross, and Edgar Suter, 39–56. Pacific Linguistics, 615. Canberra: Pacific Linguistics.

———. 2011. 'Style, Plot, and Character in *Tom Yaya Kange* Tales from Ku Waru.' In *Sung Tales from the Papua New Guinea Highlands: Studies in Form, Meaning, and Sociocultural Context*, edited by Alan Rumsey and Don Niles, 247–74. Canberra: ANU E Press.

Sankoff, Gillian. 1977. 'Le parallélisme dans la poésie Buang.' *Anthropologica* 19: 27–48.

Schieffelin, Bambi B., and Steven Feld. 1998. *Bosavi–English–Tok Pisin Dictionary (Papua New Guinea) / Bosabi towo:liya: Ingilis towo:liya: Pisin towo:liya: bugo: / Tok ples Bosavi, Tok Inglis, na Tok Pisin diksineli*. Pacific Linguistics, C 153. Canberra: The Australian National University.

Schieffelin, Edward L. 1968. 'The Sorrow of the Lonely and the Burning of the Dancers.' Paper read at [Eighth] International Congress of Anthropological and Ethnological Sciences, at Tokyo.

———. 1976. *The Sorrow of the Lonely and the Burning of the Dancers*. New York: St. Martin's Press.

Schmidt-Ernsthausen, Victor. 1890. 'Über die Musik der Eingebornen von Deutsch Neu-Guinea.' *Vierteljahrsshrift für Musikwissenschaft* (Leipzig) 6: 268–74.

Schmidt, Wilhelm. 1909. 'Über Musik und Gesänge der Karesau-Papuas, Deutsch Neu-Guinea.' In *3. Kongress der Internationalen Musikgesellschaft, Wien, 25. bis 29. Mai 1909, Bericht*, 297–98. Wien: Artaria; Leipzig: Breitkopf & Härtel.

Seligman, Charles G. 1910. *The Melanesians of British New Guinea*. Cambridge: Cambridge University Press.

Senft, Gunter. 1999. 'The Presentation of Self in Touristic Encounters: A Case Study from the Trobriand Islands.' *Anthropos* 94/1–3: 21–33.

———. 2011. *The Tuma Underworld of Love: Erotic and Other Narrative Songs of the Trobriand Islanders and Their Spirits of the Dead*. Culture and Language Use: Studies in Anthropological Linguistics, 5. Amsterdam: John Benjamins Publishing Company.

Shaw, R. Daniel. 1975. 'Samo Social Structure: A Socio-Linguistic Approach to Understanding Interpersonal Relationships.' PhD dissertation, University of Papua New Guinea.

———. 1982. 'Samo Initiation: Its Context and Its Meaning.' *Journal of the Polynesian Society* 91 (September): 417–34.

Simon, Artur. 1978. 'Types and Functions of Music in the Eastern Highlands of West Irian.' *Ethnomusicology* 22: 441–55.

———. 1993. *Musik aus dem Bergland West-Neuguineas Irian Jaya: Eine Klangdokumentation untergehender Musikkulturen der Eipo und ihrer Nachbarn*. Museum für Völkerkunde Collection Berlin CD 20. Six compact discs. (IPNGS c93-200).

Sollis, Michael. 2010. 'Tune–Tone Relationships in Sung Duna *Pikono*.' *Australian Journal of Linguistics* 30 (January): 67–80 (special issue, 'The Language of Song').

———. 2011. 'Parallelism in Duna *Pikono*.' In *Sung Tales from the Papua New Guinea Highlands: Studies in Form, Meaning, and Sociocultural Context*, edited by Alan Rumsey and Don Niles, 65–74. Canberra: ANU E Press.

Sørum, Arve. 1980. 'In Search of the Lost Soul: Bedamini Spirit Seances and Curing Rites.' *Oceania* 50 (June): 273–96.

———. 1982. 'The Seeds of Power: Patterns of Bedamini Male Initiation.' *Social Analysis* 10 (March): 42–62.

Spearritt, Gordon D., and Jürg Wassmann. 1996. 'Myth and Music in a Middle Sepik Village.' *Kulele: Occasional Papers on Pacific Music and Dance* 2: 59–84.

Steadman, Lyle B. 1971. 'Neighbours and Killers: Residence and Dominance among the Hewa of New Guinea.' PhD dissertation, The Australian National University.

Stella, Regis N. 1990. *Forms and Styles of Traditional Banoni Music*. Edited by Don Niles. Apwitihire: Studies in Papua New Guinea Musics, 1. Boroko: National Research Institute.

Stewart, Pamela J., and Andrew Strathern. 2002. *Gender, Song, and Sensibility: Folktales and Folksongs in the Highlands of New Guinea*. Westport: Praeger.

Strathern, Andrew. 1974. *Melpa Amb Kenan: Courting Songs of the Melpa People*. Boroko: Institute of Papua New Guinea Studies.

———. 1988. 'Conclusions: Looking at the Edge of the New Guinea Highlands from the Center.' In *Mountain Papuans; Historical and Comparative Perspectives from New Guinea Fringe Highlands Societies*, edited by James F. Weiner, 187–212. Ann Arbor: University of Michigan Press.

Strathern, Andrew, and Pamela J. Stewart. 2005. 'Melpa Songs and Ballads: Junctures of Sympathy and Desire in Mount Hagen, Papua New Guinea.' In *Expressive Genres and Historical Change: Indonesia, Papua New Guinea and Taiwan*, edited by Pamela J. Stewart and Andrew Strathern, 201–33. Anthropology and Cultural History in Asia and the Indo-Pacific. Hants: Ashgate Publishing.

———. 2011. 'Bamboo Knives, Bows, and Waterfalls: The Presentation of "Traditional Knowledge" in Melpa *Kang Rom*, Duna *Pikono*, and the Works of Hesiod and Virgil.' In *Sung Tales from the Papua New Guinea Highlands: Studies in Form, Meaning, and Sociocultural Context*, edited by Alan Rumsey and Don Niles, 303–16. Canberra: ANU E Press.

Strathern, Gomb, and Andrew Strathern. 1985. *Kintu Songs*. Boroko: Institute of Papua New Guinea Studies.

Talyaga, Kundapen. 1973. *Enga Eda Nemago: Meri Singsing Poetry of the Yandapo Engas*. Papua Pocket Poets, 40. Port Moresby: [n.p.].

————. 1974. 'Five Enga Songs about Missions.' *Gigibori* 1 (December): 40.

————. 1975. *Modern Enga Songs*. Boroko: Institute of Papua New Guinea Studies.

Telban, Borut. 1998. *Dancing through Time: A Sepik Cosmology*. Oxford Studies in Social and Cultural Anthropology. Oxford: Clarendon Press.

————. 2008. 'The Poetics of the Crocodile: Changing Clutlural Perspectives in Ambonwari.' *Oceania* 78/2 (July): 217–35.

Thurnwald, Richard. 1912. *Forschungen auf den Salomo-Inseln und dem Bismarck-Archipel; vol. 1: Lieder und Sagen aus Buin*. Berlin: Reimer.

————. 1936. *Profane Literature of Buin, Solomon Islands*. Yale University Publications in Anthropology, 8. New Haven: Yale University.

————. 1941. 'Alte und neue Volkslieder aus Buin.' *Zeitschrift für Ethnologie* 73: 12–28.

Turner, James West. 1993. Review of *The Empty Place: Poetry, Space, and Being among the Foi of Papua New Guinea*, by James F. Weiner. *Anthropos* 88 (1–3): 288–89.

Voorhoeve, C. L. 1977. 'Ta-Poman: Metaphorical Use of Words and Poetic Vocabulary in Asmat Songs.' In *New Guinea Area Languages and Language Study, Vol. 3: Language, Culture, Society and the Modern World*, edited by Stephen A. Wurm, 19–38. Pacific Linguistics, C 40. Canberra: The Australian National University.

Vormann, Franz. 1911. 'Tänze und Tanzfestlichkeiten der Monumbo-Papua (Deutsch-Neuguinea).' *Anthropos* 6: 411–27.

Wagner, Roy. 1967. *The Curse of Souw*. Chicago: University of Chicago Press.

————. 1972. *Habu: The Innovation of Meaning in Daribi Religion*. Chicago: University of Chicago Press.

Waiko, John D. 1982. '*Be Jijimo*: A History according to the Tradition of the Binandere People of Papua New Guinea.' PhD dissertation, The Australian National University.

————. 1984. 'Binandere Songs.' *Bikmaus* 5 (September): 87.

———. 1991. 'Literary Art Forms among the Binandere.' In *Man and a Half: Essays in Pacific Anthropology and Ethnobiology in Honour of Ralph Bulmer*, edited by Andrew Pawley, 369–75. Polynesian Society Memoir, 48. Auckland: Polynesian Society.

———. 1995. 'Binandere *Ario* Dance and Music.' In *New Guinea Ethnomusicology Conference: Proceedings*, edited by Robert Reigle, 171–82. Occasional Papers in Pacific Ethnomusicology, 4. Auckland: University of Auckland.

Wassmann, Jürg. 1982. *Der Gesang an den fliegenden Hund: Untersuchungen zu den totemistischen Gesängen und geheimen Namen des Dorfes Kandingei am Mittelsepik (Papua New Guinea) anhand der kirugu-Knotenschnüre*. Basler Beiträge zur Ethnologie, 22. Basel: Ethnologisches Seminar der Universität und Museum für Völkerkunde.

———. 1988. *Der Gesang an das Krokodil: Die rituellen Gesänge des Dorfes Kandingei an Land und Meer, Pflanzen und Tiere (Mittelsepik, Papua New Guinea)*. Basler Beiträge zur Ethnologie, 28. Basel: Ethnologisches Seminar der Universität und Museum für Völkerkunde.

———. 1991. *The Song to the Flying Fox: The Public and Esoteric Knowledge of the Important Men of Kandingei about Totemic Songs, Names and Knotted Cords (Middle Sepik, Papua New Guinea)*. Translated by Dennis Q. Stephenson. Edited by Don Niles. Apwitihire: Studies in Papua New Guinea Musics, 2. Boroko: National Research Institute.

Webb, Michael, and Don Niles. 1986. *Riwain! Papua New Guinea Pop Songs*. Institute of Papua New Guinea Studies IPNGS 007. Two cassettes and book.

———. 1990. *Ol Singsing bilong Ples*. Boroko: Institute of Papua New Guinea Studies IPNGS 010. Two cassettes and book.

Weiner, James F. 1988a. *The Heart of the Pearl Shell: The Mythological Dimension of Foi Sociality*. Studies in Melanesian Anthropology, 5. Berkeley: University of California Press.

———. 1988b. 'Introduction: Looking at the New Guinea Highlands from Its Edge.' In *Mountain Papuans; Historical and Comparative Perspectives from New Guinea Fringe Highlands Societies*, edited by James F. Weiner, 1–38. Ann Arbor: University of Michigan Press.

———. 1991. *The Empty Place: Poetry, Space, and Being among the Foi of Papua New Guinea*. Bloomington: Indiana University Press.

———. 1993. 'To Be at Home with Others in an Empty Place: A Reply to Mimica.' *Australian Journal of Anthropology* 4: 233–44.

———. 1995. *The Lost Drum: The Myth of Sexuality in Papua New Guinea and Beyond*. Madison: University of Wisconsin Press.

———. 1998a. 'Foi Memorial Songs.' In *Australia and the Pacific Islands*, edited by Adrienne L. Kaeppler and J. W. Love, 339–40. The Garland Encyclopedia of World Music, 9. New York: Garland Publishing.

———. 1998b. 'Gender, Embodiment, and Movement in Foi Song.' In *Australia and the Pacific Islands*, edited by Adrienne L. Kaeppler and J. W. Love, 246–47. The Garland Encyclopedia of World Music, 9. New York: Garland Publishing.

———. 2001. *Tree Leaf Talk: A Heideggerian Anthropology*. Oxford: Berg.

Welsch, Robert L. 2006. 'Coaxing the Spirits to Dance.' In *Coaxing the Spirits to Dance: Art and Society in the Papuan Gulf of New Guinea*, edited by Robert L. Welsch, 4–45. Hanover, NH: Hood Museum of Art.

Whiteman, Josephine. 1965. 'Girls' Puberty Ceremonies amongst the Chimbu.' *Anthropos* 60/1–6: 410–22.

Williams, Francis E. 1924. *The Natives of the Purari Delta*. Territory of Papua, Anthropology Report, 5. Port Moresby: Government Printer.

———. 1936. *Papuans of the Trans-Fly*. Territory of Papua, Anthropology Report, 15. Oxford: Clarendon Press.

———. 1939. 'A Cycle of Ceremonies in Orokolo Bay.' *Mankind* 2/6 (May): 145–55.

———. 1940. *Drama of Orokolo: The Social and Ceremonial Life of the Elema*. Territory of Papua, Anthropology Report, 18. Oxford: Clarendon Press.

———. 1940–42. 'Natives of Lake Kutubu, Papua.' *Oceania* 11: 121–57, 259–94, 374–401; 12: 49–74, 134–54. [also appears in *Francis Edgar Williams: 'The Vailala Madness' and Other Essays*, edited by Erik Schwimmer (Honolulu: University Press of Hawaii, 1977)].

———. 1977. 'Natives of Lake Kutubu, Papua.' In *Francis Edgar Williams: 'The Vailala Madness' and Other Essays*, edited by Erik Schwimmer, 161–330. Honolulu: University Press of Hawaii. (originally published in *Oceania* 11 (1940): 121–57, 259–94, 374–401; 12:49–74, 134–54).

Wolffram, Paul. 2007. '*Langoron*: Music and Dance Performance Realities among the Lak People of Southern New Ireland, Papua New Guinea.' PhD dissertation, Victoria University, Wellington.

Wood, Michael. 1982. 'Kamula Social Structure and Ritual.' PhD dissertation, Macquarie University.

Yamada, Yōichi. 1997. *Songs of Spirits: An Ethnography of Sounds in a Papua New Guinea Society*. Translated by Jun'ichi Ohno. Edited by Don Niles. With one compact disc. Apwitihire: Studies in Papua New Guinea Musics, 5. Boroko: Institute of Papua New Guinea Studies.

Young, Rosemary. 1968. 'Words under a Bushel.' *Practical Anthropology* 15 (September–October): 213–16.

Zahn, Heinrich. 1996. *Mission and Music: Jabêm Traditional Music and the Development of Lutheran Hymnody*. Translated by Philip W. Holzknecht. Edited by Don Niles. Apwitihire: Studies in Papua New Guinea Musics, 4. Boroko: Institute of Papua New Guinea Studies.

# Index of Performers

The names of the performers of the songs included in this volume are listed below.

**Abeabo**   men's songs 1–5, 27, 33, 37–39, 43; ♫ online examples 8–9

**Abuyu**   men's songs 26, 35

**Agiri**   men's songs 19, 21–22; ♫ online examples 10–12

**Ama'a**   women's songs 6–7; ♫ online example 18

**Ayadobo**   men's song 34

**Bogo**   men's songs 13–15; ♫ online example 10

**Damu**   men's song 34

**Dunubu**   men's song 26

**Fahaisabo**   men's songs 16–18, 20, 42; ♫ online examples 10–12

**Garibi**   men's songs 9–10; ♫ online examples 8–9

**Gebo**   women's sago songs 3, 5; ♫ online examples 3, 5

**Gesa**   men's songs 11–12; ♫ online example 10

**Gobero**   men's song 43

**Gofe**   men's song 25

**Habeyu**   men's song 23

**Hasuabo**   men's songs 28–29

**Hira**   men's song 23

**Hobe**   men's song 25

**Komo'o**   men's songs 30–32

**Kora**   men's songs 9–10, 27, 39–41, 44; ♫ online examples 8–9

**Kunuhuaka**   women's sago songs 2, 4, 6–7; women's songs 1–5; ♫ online examples 2, 4, 6–7, 13–17

**Kuri**   men's songs 28–29

**Kusabuyu**   men's song 36

**Maniname**   men's song 24

**Mare**   men's song 24

**Memene**   men's songs 1–5, 38; ♫ online examples 8–9

**Midibaru**   men's songs 6–8; ♫ online examples 8–9

**Mu'ubiaka**   women's sago song 1; ♫ online example 1

**Muya**   men's songs 19, 21–22; ♫ online examples 10–12

**Nabu**   men's songs 13–15; ♫ online example 10

**Oromene**   men's songs 16–18, 20, 42; ♫ online examples 10–12

**Sariaba**   men's songs 11–12; ♫ online example 10

**Sega**   men's songs 33, 37, 40

**Siyame**   women's sago songs 6–7; ♫ online examples 6–7

**Tari**   men's song 35

**Viya**   men's songs 30–32

**Wa'abiyu**   women's songs 1–5; ♫ online examples 13–17

**Wa'o**   men's songs 6–8; ♫ online examples 8–9

**Webirabo**   men's songs 36, 41, 44

**Yiakahua**   women's songs 6–7; ♫ online example 18

# List of Online Examples

Although the main focus of this publication has been on the texts of Foi songs, the poetry is only part of the total performance. To better convey some other aspects, photographs and verbal descriptions are also included; the sound of these songs is illustrated by the online examples (http://press.anu.edu.au/titles/ monographs-in-anthropology/songs-of-the-empty-place/).

Note that in compiling this collection, occasional discrepancies may be found between the performances and the transcribed texts. There may appear to be different, missing, or too many words; lines may be absent; words may seem to be mispronounced, etc. Such variations may result from differences in sung and elicited language, varying interpretations of what is sung by different assistants, lines or words being inadvertently skipped, unnoticed errors, or a variety of other reasons. The beginning words of some songs are also clipped—a familiar problem to anyone who has tried to record music in context. It is likely that the missing words were supplied during transcription by someone at the performance and who was familiar with the performer's textual style and use of language, perhaps even the singer involved. Ideally we would like to have corrected such discrepancies, but any such attempts would have further delayed the already long-overdue publication of these materials. It was felt best to make the material available in its present form, where it can inspire and guide future research efforts.

The original recordings of the songs in this volume were all made between 1980 and 1988 by James F. Weiner on a Sony Walkman Professional audio-cassette recorder. These 79 audio cassettes plus his field notebooks have been deposited in The Australian National University Archives (series 432: http://archivescollection.anu.edu.au/index.php/james-f-weiners-cassettes). Specifically for this project, the audio recordings were digitised by the Pacific and Regional Archive for Digital Sources in Endangered Cultures (PARADISEC). (http://catalog.paradisec.org.au/repository/JW1). For permission to access these digitised recordings, please contact James Weiner. For each online example below, reference is given to the original PARADISEC digitisation, noting in minutes and seconds where example begins in that recording.

The examples listed below have been selected in order to provide audio examples of the songs considered in this book.

# Women's Sago Songs (*Obedobora*)

**Online example 1** (JW1-053-A.mp3, from 20:15)
Sago Song 1, performed by Mu'ubiaka
**Online example 2** (JW1-053-B.mp3, from 06:09)
Sago Song 2, performed by Kunuhuaka
**Online example 3** (JW1-053-A.mp3, from 16:02)
Sago Song 3, performed by Gebo
**Online example 4** (JW1-053-B.mp3, from 10:35)
Sago Song 4, performed by Kunuhuaka
**Online example 5** (JW1-053-A.mp3, from 18:02)
Sago Song 5, performed by Gebo
**Online example 6** (JW1-072-B.mp3, from 09:36)
Sago Song 6, performed by Kunuhuaka (with Siyame)
**Online example 7** (JW1-072-B.mp3, from 14:16)
Sago Song 7, performed by Kunuhuaka (with Siyame)

# Men's Songs (*Sorohabora*)

**Online example 8** *Sorohabora* A (JW1-067-A.mp3, from 20:39)
Men's Song 2, performed by Memene and Abeabo
Men's Song 7, performed by Wa'o and Midibaru
Men's Song 9, performed by Kora and Garibi
**Online example 9** *Sorohabora* B (JW1-067-A.mp3, from 26:00)
Men's Song 3, performed by Memene and Abeabo
Men's Song 8, performed by Wa'o and Midibaru
Men's Song 10, performed by Kora and Garibi
**Online example 10** *Sorohabora* C (JW1-067-A.mp3, from 31:32)
Men's Song 11, performed by Gesa and Sariaba
Men's Song 13, performed by Nabu and Bogo
Men's Song 17, performed by Oromene and Fahaisabo
Men's Song 19, performed by Muya and Agiri
**Online example 11** *Sorohabora* D (first line slightly cut)
(JW1-068-A.mp3, from 05:42)
Men's Song 20, performed by Oromene and Fahaisabo
Men's Song 21, performed by Muya and Agiri
**Online example 12** *Sorohabora* E (JW1-068-A.mp3, from 17:00)
Men's Song 42, performed by Fahaisabo and Oromene
Men's Song 22, performed by Muya and Agiri

# Women's Songs (*Sorohabora*)

**Online example 13** (JW1-073-A.mp3, from 05:37)
> Women's Song 1, performed by Kunuhuaka and Wa'abiyu

**Online example 14** (JW1-073-A.mp3, from 09:07)
> Women's Song 2, performed by Kunuhuaka and Wa'abiyu

**Online example 15** (JW1-073-A.mp3, from 14:02)
> Women's Song 3, performed by Kunuhuaka and Wa'abiyu

**Online example 16** (JW1-073-A.mp3, from 19:35)
> Women's Song 4, performed by Kunuhuaka and Wa'abiyu

**Online example 17** (JW1-073-A.mp3, from 22:29)
> Women's Song 5, performed by Kunuhuaka and Wa'abiyu

**Online example 18** (JW1-073-A.mp3, from 32:50)
> Women's Song 7, performed by Yiakahua and Ama'a

www.ingramcontent.com/pod-product-compliance
Lightning Source LLC
Chambersburg PA
CBHW061245270326
41928CB00041B/3421